Gerard Sullivan
Peter A. Jackson
Editors

MW01481978

Gay and Lesbian Asia: Culture, Identity, Community

Gay and Lesbian Asia: Culture, Identity, Community has been co-published simultaneously as *Journal of Homosexuality,* Volume 40, Numbers 3/4 2001.

Pre-publication
REVIEWS,
COMMENTARIES,
EVALUATIONS . . .

"Sullivan and Jackson are to be congratulated on this unprecedented compilation. For the first time, voices from gay, lesbian and transgender Asia come through with an unfiltered directness and clarity.

From Manila to Mumbai, Beijing to Bangkok, layers of political, religious and cultural oppression are vividly described, and in the words of those living under it.

This is a landmark study that will inform, disturb and encourage."

Phillip W. Jones, PhD
Head, School of Social Policy
and Curriculum Studies
The University of Sydney, Australia

Gay and Lesbian Asia: Culture, Identity, Community

Gay and Lesbian Asia: Culture, Identity, Community has been co-published simultaneously as *Journal of Homosexuality,* Volume 40, Numbers 3/4 2001.

The *Journal of Homosexuality* Monographic "Separates"

Below is a list of "separates," which in serials librarianship means a special issue simultaneously published as a special journal issue or double-issue *and* as a "separate" hardbound monograph. (This is a format which we also call a "DocuSerial.")

"Separates" are published because specialized libraries or professionals may wish to purchase a specific thematic issue by itself in a format which can be separately cataloged and shelved, as opposed to purchasing the journal on an on-going basis. Faculty members may also more easily consider a "separate" for classroom adoption.

"Separates" are carefully classified separately with the major book jobbers so that the journal tie-in can be noted on new book order slips to avoid duplicate purchasing.

You may wish to visit Haworth's website at . . .

http://www.HaworthPress.com

. . . to search our online catalog for complete tables of contents of these separates and related publications.

You may also call 1-800-HAWORTH (outside US/Canada: 607-722-5857), or Fax 1-800-895-0582 (outside US/Canada: 607-771-0012), or e-mail at:

getinfo@haworthpressinc.com

Gay and Lesbian Asia: Culture, Identity, Community, edited by Gerard Sullivan, PhD, and Peter A. Jackson, PhD (Vol. 40, No. 3/4, 2001). *"Superb. . . . Covers a happily wide range of styles . . . will appeal to both students and educated fans." Gary Morris, Editor/Publisher,* Bright Lights Film Journal

Queer Asian Cinema: Shadows in the Shade, edited by Andrew Grossman, MA (Vol. 39, No. 3/4, 2000). *"An extremely rich tapestry of detailed ethnographies and state-of-the-art theorizing. . . . Not only is this a landmark record of queer Asia, but it will certainly also be a seminal, contributive challenge to gender and sexuality studies in general." Dédé Oetomo, PhD, Coordinator of the Indonesian organization GAYa NUSANTRA: Adjunct Reader in Linguistics and Anthropology, School of Social Sciences, Universitas Airlangga*

Gay Community Survival in the New Millennium, edited by Michael R. Botnick, PhD (cand.) (Vol. 38, No. 4, 2000). *Examines the notion of community from several different perspectives focusing on the imagined, the structural, and the emotive. You will explore a theoretical overview and you will peek into the moral discourses that frame "gay community," the rift between HIV-positive and HIV-negative gay men, and how Israeli gays seek their place in the public sphere.*

The Ideal Gay Man: The Story of Der Kreis, by Hubert Kennedy, PhD (Vol. 38, No. 1/2, 1999). *"Very Profound. . . . Excellent insight into the problems of the early fight for homosexual emancipation in Europe and in the USA. . . . The ideal gay man (high-mindedness, purity, cleanness), as he was imagined by the editor of 'Der Kreis,' is delineated by the fascinating quotations out of the published erotic stories." (Wolfgang Breidert, PhD, Academic Director, Institute of Philosophy, University Karlsruhe, Germany)*

Multicultural Queer: Australian Narratives, edited by Peter A. Jackson, PhD, and Gerard Sullivan, PhD (Vol. 36, No. 3/4, 1999). *Shares the way that people from ethnic minorities in Australia (those who are not of Anglo-Celtic background) view homosexuality, their experiences as homosexual men and women, and their feelings about the lesbian and gay community.*

Scandinavian Homosexualities: Essays on Gay and Lesbian Studies, edited by Jan Löfström, PhD (Vol. 35, No. 3/4, 1998). *"Everybody interested in the formation of lesbian and gay identities and their interaction with the sociopolitical can find something to suit their taste in this volume." (Judith Schuyf, PhD, Assistant Professor of Lesbian and Gay Studies, Center for Gay and Lesbian Studies, Utrecht University, The Netherlands)*

Gay and Lesbian Literature Since World War II: History and Memory, edited by Sonya L. Jones, PhD (Vol. 34, No. 3/4, 1998). *"The authors of these essays manage to gracefully incorporate the latest insights of feminist, postmodernist, and queer theory into solidly grounded readings . . . challenging and moving, informed by the passion that prompts both readers and critics into deeper inquiry." (Diane Griffin Growder, PhD, Professor of French and Women's Studies, Cornell College, Mt. Vernon, Iowa)*

Reclaiming the Sacred: The Bible in Gay and Lesbian Culture, edited by Raymond-Jean Frontain, PhD (Vol. 33, No. 3/4, 1997). *"Finely wrought, sharply focused, daring, and always dignified . . . In chapter after chapter, the Bible is shown to be a more sympathetic and humane book in its attitudes toward homosexuality than usually thought and a challenge equally to the straight and gay moral imagination." (Joseph Wittreich, PhD, Distinguished Professor of English, The Graduate School, The City University of New York)*

Activism and Marginalization in the AIDS Crisis, edited by Michael A. Hallett, PhD (Vol. 32, No. 3/4, 1997). *Shows readers how the advent of HIV-disease has brought into question the utility of certain forms of "activism" as they relate to understanding and fighting the social impacts of disease.*

Gays, Lesbians, and Consumer Behavior: Theory, Practice, and Research Issues in Marketing, edited by Daniel L. Wardlow, PhD (Vol. 31, No. 1/2, 1996). *"For those scholars, market researchers, and marketing managers who are considering marketing to the gay and lesbian community, this book should be on required reading list." (Mississippi Voice)*

Gay Men and the Sexual History of the Political Left, edited by Gert Hekma, PhD, Harry Oosterhuis, PhD, and James Steakley, PhD (Vol. 29, No. 2/3/4, 1995). *"Contributors delve into the contours of a long-forgotten history, bringing to light new historical data and fresh insight . . . An excellent account of the tense historical relationship between the political left and gay liberation." (People's Voice)*

Sex, Cells, and Same-Sex Desire: The Biology of Sexual Preference, edited by John P. De Cecco, PhD, and David Allen Parker, MA (Vol. 28, No. 1/2/3/4, 1995). *"A stellar compilation of chapters examining the most important evidence underlying theories on the biological basis of human sexual orientation." (MGW)*

Gay Ethics: Controversies in Outing, Civil Rights, and Sexual Science, edited by Timothy F. Murphy, PhD (Vol. 27, No. 3/4, 1994). *"The contributors bring the traditional tools of ethics and political philosophy to bear in a clear and forceful way on issues surrounding the rights of homosexuals." (David L. Hull, Dressler Professor in the Humanities, Department of Philosophy, Northwestern University)*

Gay and Lesbian Studies in Art History, edited by Whitney Davis, PhD (Vol. 27, No. 1/2, 1994). *"Informed, challenging . . . never dull. . . . Contributors take risks and, within the restrictions of scholarly publishing, find new ways to use materials already available or examine topics never previously explored." (Lambda Book Report)*

Critical Essays: Gay and Lesbian Writers of Color, edited by Emmanuel S. Nelson, PhD (Vol. 26, No. 2/3, 1993). *"A much-needed book, sparkling with stirring perceptions and resonating with depth . . . The anthology not only breaks new ground, it also attempts to heal wounds inflicted by our oppressed pasts." (Lambda)*

Gay Studies from the French Cultures: Voices from France, Belgium, Brazil, Canada, and The Netherlands, edited by Rommel Mendès-Leite, PhD, and Pierre-Olivier de Busscher, PhD (Vol. 25, No. 1/2/3, 1993). *"The first book that allows an English-speaking world to have a comprehensive look at the principal trends in gay studies in France and French-speaking countries." (André Bèjin, PhD, Directeur, de Recherche au Centre National de la Recherche Scientifique (CNRS), Paris)*

If You Seduce a Straight Person, Can You Make Them Gay? Issues in Biological Essentialism versus Social Constructionism in Gay and Lesbian Identities, edited by John P. De Cecco, PhD, and John P. Elia, PhD (cand.) (Vol. 24, No. 3/4, 1993). *"You'll find this alternative view of the* *age old question to be one that will become the subject of many conversations to come. Thought-provoking to say the least!" (Prime Timers)*

Gay and Lesbian Studies: The Emergence of a Discipline, edited by Henry L. Minton, PhD (Vol. 24, No. 1/2, 1993). *"The volume's essays provide insight into the field's remarkable accomplishments and future goals." (Lambda Book Report)*

Homosexuality in Renaissance and Enlightenment England: Literary Representations in Historical Context, edited by Claude J. Summers, PhD (Vol. 23, No. 1/2, 1992). *"It is remarkable among studies in this field in its depth of scholarship and variety of approaches and is accessible." (Chronique)*

Coming Out of the Classroom Closet: Gay and Lesbian Students, Teachers, and Curricula, edited by Karen M. Harbeck, PhD, JD, Recipient of Lesbian and Gay Educators Award by the American Educational Research Association's Lesbian and Gay Studies Special Interest Group (AREA) (Vol. 22, No. 3/4, 1992). *"Presents recent research about gay and lesbian students and teachers and the school system in which they function." (Contemporary Psychology)*

Homosexuality and Male Bonding in Pre-Nazi Germany: The Youth Movement, the Gay Movement, and Male Bonding Before Hitler's Rise: Original Transcripts from Der Eigene, the First Gay Journal in the World, edited by Harry Oosterhuis, PhD, and Hubert Kennedy, PhD (Vol. 22, No. 1/2, 1992). *"Provide[s] insight into the early gay movement, particularly in its relation to the various political currents in pre-World War II Germany." (Lambda Book Report)*

Gay People, Sex, and the Media, edited by Michelle A. Wolf, PhD, and Alfred P. Kielwasser, MA (Vol. 21, No. 1/2, 1991). *"Altogether, the kind of research anthology which is useful to many disciplines in gay studies. Good stuff!" (Communique)*

Gay Midlife and Maturity: Crises, Opportunities, and Fulfillment, edited by John Alan Lee, PhD (Vol. 20, No. 3/4, 1991). *"The insight into gay aging is amazing, accurate, and much-needed. . . . A real contribution to the older gay community." (Prime Timers)*

Male Intergenerational Intimacy: Historical, Socio-Psychological, and Legal Perspectives, edited by Theo G. M. Sandfort, PhD, Edward Brongersma, JD, and A. X. van Naerssen, PhD (Vol. 20, No. 1/2, 1991). *"The most important book on the subject since Tom O'Carroll's 1980 Paedophilia: The Radical Case." (The North America Man/Boy Love Association Bulletin, May 1991)*

Love Letters Between a Certain Late Nobleman and the Famous Mr. Wilson, edited by Michael S. Kimmel, PhD (Vol. 19, No. 2, 1990). *"An intriguing book about homosexuality in 18th Century England. Many details of the period, such as meeting places, coded language, and 'camping' are all covered in the book. If you're a history buff, you'll enjoy this one." (Prime Timers)*

Homosexuality and Religion, edited by Richard Hasbany, PhD (Vol. 18, No. 3/4, 1990). *"A welcome resource that provides historical and contemporary views on many issues involving religious life and homosexuality." (Journal of Sex education and Therapy)*

Homosexuality and the Family, edited by Frederick W. Bozett, PhD (Vol. 18, No. 1/2, 1989). *"Enlightening and answers a host of questions about the effects of homosexuality upon family members and the family as a unit." (Ambush Magazine)*

Gay and Lesbian Youth, edited by Gilbert Herdt, PhD (Vol. 17, No. 1/2/3/4, 1989). *"Provides a much-needed compilation of research dealing with homosexuality and adolescents." (GLTF Newsletter)*

Lesbians Over 60 Speak for Themselves, edited by Monika Kehoe, PhD (Vol. 16, No. 3/4, 1989). *"A pioneering book examining the social, economical, physical, sexual, and emotional lives of aging lesbians." (Feminist Bookstore News)*

Monographs "Separates" list continued at the back

Gay and Lesbian Asia:
Culture, Identity, Community

Gerard Sullivan, PhD
Peter A. Jackson, PhD
Editors

Gay and Lesbian Asia: Culture, Identity, Community has been co-published simultaneously as *Journal of Homosexuality,* Volume 40, Numbers 3/4 2001.

Harrington Park Press
An Imprint of
The Haworth Press, Inc.
New York • London • Oxford

Published by

Harrington Park Press®, 10 Alice Street, Binghamton, NY 13904-1580 USA

Harrington Park Press® is an imprint of The Haworth Press, Inc., 10 Alice Street, Binghamton, NY 13904-1580 USA.

Gay and Lesbian Asia: Culture, Identity, Community has been co-published simultaneously as *Journal of Homosexuality,* Volume 40, Numbers 3/4 2001.

The Haworth Press, Inc., 10 Alice Street, Binghamton, NY 13904-1580, USA

Cover by Marylouise E. Doyle

Library of Congress Cataloging-in-Publication Data

Gay and lesbian Asia : culture, identity, community / Gerard Sullivan, Peter A. Jackson, editors.
      p. cm.
    "Has been co-published simultaneously as Journal of homosexuality, volume 40, numbers 3/4 2001."
    Includes bibliographical references and index.
    ISBN 1-56023-145-9 (hard : alk. paper)–ISBN 1-56023-146-7 (pbk : alk. paper)
    1. Gay men–Asia–Social conditions. 2. Gay men–Asia–Identity. 3. Lesbians–Asia–Social conditions. 4. Lesbians–Asia–Identity. 5. Gay communities–Asia. 6. Lesbian communities–Asia. I. Sullivan, Gerard. II. Jackson, Peter A. III. Journal of homosexuality.
HQ76.3.A78 G37 2001
306.76′6′095–dc21
                                                  00-140108

Indexing, Abstracting & Website/Internet Coverage

This section provides you with a list of major indexing & abstracting services. That is to say, each service began covering this periodical during the year noted in the right column. Most Websites which are listed below have indicated that they will either post, disseminate, compile, archive, cite or alert their own Website users with research-based content from this work. (This list is as current as the copyright date of this publication.)

Abstracting, Website/Indexing Coverage .... Year When Coverage Began

- *Abstracts in Anthropology* **1982**
- *Academia ASAP <www.ga/egroup.com>* **1989**
- *Academic Abstracts/CD-ROM* **1993**
- *Academic Search: database of 2,000 selected academic serials, updated monthly* **1995**
- *Academic Search Elite (EBSCO)* **1993**
- *Alternative Press Index <www.nisc.com>* **1996**
- *Applied Social Sciences Index & Abstracts (ASSIA) (Online: ASSI via Data-Star) (CD-Rom: ASSIA Plus)* ... **1987**
- *This periodical is indexed in ATLA Religion Database, published by the American Theological Library Association <www.atla.com>* **1986**
- *Book Review Index* **1994**
- *BUBL Information Service, an Internet-based Information Service for the UK higher education community* **1995**

(continued)

(continued)

(continued)

Special Bibliographic Notes related to special journal issues (separates) and indexing/abstracting:

- indexing/abstracting services in this list will also cover material in any "separate" that is co-published simultaneously with Haworth's special thematic journal issue or DocuSerial. Indexing/abstracting usually covers material at the article/chapter level.
- monographic co-editions are intended for either non-subscribers or libraries which intend to purchase a second copy for their circulating collections.
- monographic co-editions are reported to all jobbers/wholesalers/approval plans. The source journal is listed as the "series" to assist the prevention of duplicate purchasing in the same manner utilized for books-in-series.
- to facilitate user/access services all indexing/abstracting services are encouraged to utilize the co-indexing entry note indicated at the bottom of the first page of each article/chapter/contribution.
- this is intended to assist a library user of any reference tool (whether print, electronic, online, or CD-ROM) to locate the monographic version if the library has purchased this version but not a subscription to the source journal.
- individual articles/chapters in any Haworth publication are also available through the Haworth Document Delivery Service (HDDS).

Gay and Lesbian Asia:
Culture, Identity, Community

CONTENTS

ABOUT THE EDITORS

Peter A. Jackson, PhD, is a Fellow in Thai History in the Research School of Pacific and Asian Studies at Australian National University in Canberra. Fluent in spoken and written Thai, Dr. Jackson has conducted extensive research on gay and lesbian communities in Bangkok and nearby provinces. Dr. Jackson was a founding member of the Australian Gay and Lesbian Immigration Task Force and helped develop a Thai language curriculum in Australian high schools. His book, *Dear Uncle Go: Male Homosexuality in Thailand* (1995), was the first major study of male homoeroticism in Thailand. His other books include *Buddhism, Legitimation, and Conflict: The Political Functions of Urban Thai Buddhism* (1989), *The Intrinsic Quality of Skin* (1994), *Multicultural Queer: Australian Narratives* (The Haworth Press, Inc., 1999), and *Lady Boys, Tom Boys, Rent Boys: Male and Female Homosexuality in Contemporary Thailand* (The Haworth Press, Inc., 1999).

Gerard Sullivan, PhD, teaches in the Faculty of Education at the University of Sydney in Australia. His research interests in gay and lesbian studies include civil rights, health issues, and the social construction of homosexuality in different cultural contexts. A board member of the Australian Centre for Lesbian and Gay Research, Dr. Sullivan is also co-editor of *Gays and Lesbians in Asia and the Pacific: Social and Human Services* (The Haworth Press, Inc., 1995), *Multicultural Queer: Australian Narratives* (The Haworth Press, Inc., 1999) and *Lady Boys, Tom Boys, Rent Boys: Male and Female Homosexuality in Contemporary Thailand* (The Haworth Press, Inc., 1999).

Acknowledgments

A former director of the Australian Centre for Lesbian and Gay Research at the University of Sydney, Robert Aldrich, persuaded us to collaborate and organize a conference in 1995 on homosexuality and cultural differences, which led to the idea for this book and two others: *Multicultural Queer: Australian Narratives* (New York: Haworth, 1999), and *Lady Boys, Tom Boys, Rent Boys: Male and Female Homosexualities in Contemporary Thailand* (New York: Haworth, 1999). The project was supported in part by the University of Sydney *AusAID* (the Australian Agency for International Development), the Sydney Gay and Lesbian Mardi Gras, and the HIV/AIDS branches of the Australian Commonwealth Department of Human Services and Health and New South Wales Department of Health. Inthira Padmindra and Warren Losberg provided administrative support for the project.

Gerard Sullivan and Peter Jackson

———

Pre-Gay, Post-Queer:
Thai Perspectives on Proliferating Gender/Sex Diversity in Asia

Peter A. Jackson

INTRODUCTION

In recent years, a number of authors have observed that the proliferation of gay, lesbian, and transgender/transsexual (g/l/t)[1] identities is
increasingly a global phenomenon.[2] In Asia, new gender/sex[3] categories and erotic cultures have emerged at the intersection of multiple
influences. These influences include: economic, social, and technological transformations in the context of globalizing market capitalism;
intensifying hybridization of local and Western cultures/discourses;
increasing rates of human movement through tourism and migration;
and expanding international cooperation on issues such as HIV/AIDS
prevention and the human rights of gender/sex minorities.

To date, discussion of what Dennis Altman (1996a) has called
"global queering" has largely been based on anecdotal observations
of the emergence of new gendered and eroticised identities in Asian
and other non-Western societies. While there is no doubting the accu-
racy of these observations, we, nevertheless, lack detailed historical
studies of the transformations in Asian discourses which have incited
the proliferation of new modes of eroticised subjectivity. We also lack
studies of the changes in economies, social organization, and political
systems which have created the spaces for the emergence of Asian gay

[Haworth co-indexing entry note]: "Pre-Gay, Post-Queer: Thai Perspectives on Proliferating Gender/
Sex Diversity in Asia." Jackson, Peter A. Co-published simultaneously in *Journal of Homosexuality*
(Harrington Park Press, an imprint of The Haworth Press, Inc.) Vol. 40, No. 3/4, 2001, pp. 1-25; and: *Gay
and Lesbian Asia: Culture, Identity, Community* (ed: Gerard Sullivan, and Peter A. Jackson) Harrington
Park Press, an imprint of The Haworth Press, Inc., 2001, pp. 1-25. Single or multiple copies of this article are
available for a fee from The Haworth Document Delivery Service [1-800-342-9678, 9:00 a.m. - 5:00 p.m.
(EST). E-mail address: getinfo@haworthpressinc.com].

and lesbian scenes. Current histories, ethnographies, and sociologies of gay and lesbian identities are overwhelmingly from the West, and we need studies of gay Bangkok, gay Seoul, gay Mumbai, gay Taipei, and other major Asian cities that are as detailed and comprehensive as those we have of gay Sydney, gay New York, gay London, and gay Amsterdam.

The study of cultural intersection is a relatively new field, and analytical approaches are still poorly developed. It is often the case that we simply do not know enough to be able to make definitive statements about what is happening globally in the gender/sex domain. This ignorance is compounded by the fact that the "objects" of study are not only the categories and identities constituted within discrete discursive domains, but also the "interference effects" and "diffraction patterns" formed when cultures intersect. Key notions in cross-cultural inquiries are hybridity, complexity, and syncretism, but these terms remain empty without detailed accounts of the precise articulation of discourses and practices at actual sites of cultural intersection. The following analyses of gay and lesbian Asia provide some of the details that are needed in order to begin answering important questions on what is universal in human erotic cultures and what are local and variable forms.

In this volume, a diverse range of perspectives from South, East and Southeast Asia are presented, providing rich insights on gay and lesbian identities and communities across the region during the final decade of the twentieth century. This has been a period of such dramatic and rapid transformations, from Beijing to Manila and from Jakarta to Seoul, that it will undoubtedly be seen as one of the century's major turning points. Sexual and gender minorities have been prominent in Asia's "roaring 1990s." Industrialization, urbanization, increasing wealth, and new communications technologies provided opportunities for gender/sex difference to be expressed more openly in many Asian societies. The anonymity of the region's burgeoning cities provided spaces for gay men and lesbians to socialise and build local communities and commercial scenes of bars, restaurants, discos, and other venues away from the heteronormative pressures of families and tight-knit village communities. New-found affluence gave many the opportunity to travel and experience gay/lesbian cultures in Australia, North America, Europe, and neighbouring Asian countries. And in the second half of the 1990s, the Internet provided a means to establish virtual networks in countries where authoritarian and often homophobic governments limited opportunities for public expression.

It is important to note at the outset that Asian g/l/t identities are not so new. Some recent discussion of global queering, such as in the Australian journals *Critical InQueeries* (see Donald Morton 1997; Fran Martin & Chris Berry 1998) and the *Australian Humanities Review* (see Dennis Altman 1996b) has at times given the impression that gay and lesbian identities have emerged in Asia only in the past decade as responses to post-Cold War capitalist globalization and the spread of the Internet. However, gay and lesbian Asia is not merely a phenomenon of the 1990s. Rather, the East and Southeast Asian economic boom of the first half of the decade, which seemed to portend these regions becoming new global centres rather than a subsidiary postcolonial periphery, meant that in the 1990s many Western academics who previously had not taken an interest in the people or societies of Asia began to investigate the dramatic changes in the region. When, in the 1990s, increasing numbers of Western scholars began looking at Asian gay and lesbian cultures, they found many things that looked familiar. It was at times assumed that Western-styled gay and lesbian identities and lifestyles were products of the boom years, being sexual/cultural expressions of the changing economies and technologies of the 1990s. As Chris Berry (1994: 11) stated:

> Behind the adoption and adaptation of lesbian and gay sexual identities into Asian metropolitan cultures lies the global spread of postmodern consumer capitalism and the construction of identity not around national production but multiple niche markets.

While the 1990s forms of Asian gay and lesbian cultures and identities may indeed follow postmodern patterns, such an account implies that gay and lesbian Asians could not be found before this decade. However, visible gay, lesbian, and transgender cultures emerged in Bangkok several decades before the Internet era, and the word "gay" was being used as a self-identificatory label by homosexually active men in that city some years before the June 1969 Stonewall riots in New York City saw the establishment of the modern gay liberation movement (see Jackson 1999b). Neil Garcia (1996) also dates the origins of the Philippine gay scene to the 1960s. Bangkok's and Manila's commercial gay scenes are largely contemporaneous with similar gay scenes in non-metropolitan Western countries, such as Australia and New Zealand, and in studying Asian societies such as Thailand and the Philippines the issue is not so much to consider how these cultures appeared after they did in the West, but rather how they emerged at much the same time as they did in many parts of the West. It may be necessary to revise current accounts which imagine the West, in particular the United States, as the original site of contemporary gay and other identities and instead see these identities emerging by processes of parallel development in diverse locales.

BACKGROUND TO THIS VOLUME

This volume records part of an Australia-Asian gay and lesbian dialogue. All the authors, as well as the editors, are either from the Asian region or are Australia-based academics writing on Asia. In the 1990s, economic, political, cultural, and intellectual links between Australia and Asia multiplied as the predominantly White European settler society (located next door to Indonesia) attempted to reimagine its position in global networks. While there has been much rhetoric about globalization in recent years, the growth of geographical regionalism has perhaps been a more concrete phenomenon of the 1990s. Indeed, one can see parallels between Australia's intensified engagement with Asia, Britain's attempt to reimagine itself as a European country, and the intensification of the United States' links with Latin America.

In the 1990s, Australian and Asian gay and lesbian scenes also became more closely interconnected. This happened through increasing two-way tourism and migration, regional collaboration on HIV/AIDS issues, and the impact of widespread media coverage in Asia of Australia's highly visible gay and lesbian cultures. For example, international marketing to Asian tourists of Sydney's annual Gay and Lesbian Mardi Gras has seen this festival become a major focus for gay and lesbian pride celebrations in the Asia-Pacific. While Australia is not the focus of the following studies, this volume can, nevertheless, be seen as reflecting the many cultural and attitudinal changes that have taken place in that country in recent years. The article in this volume by Offord and Cantrell on notions of human rights reflects on some of the issues that Australian gay/lesbian researchers have had to address in conducting their dialogues with Asian colleagues.

This collection has grown out of a conference convened by the

Australian Centre for Lesbian and Gay Research and held at the University of Sydney in September 1995 called "Emerging Lesbian and Gay Identities and Communities in Asia." The conference attracted participants from around East and Southeast Asia. In order to cater to the interests of many who were unable to attend, the conference convenors, who are the editors of this volume, invited those who had presented papers as well as others to submit papers for a book on the same subject. The response to the call for papers was overwhelming and enough material was gathered for three separate volumes.[4]

THE CHALLENGE OF UNDERSTANDING GAY AND LESBIAN ASIA

Asia is a considerably more diverse continent than Europe or North America. There is as much linguistic and cultural difference between societies located within the geographically contiguous domain now called "Asia" as there is between this complex set of Asian societies and those of Europe, the Americas, or Oceania. Despite this diversity, it is possible to make some generally valid observations. Every contemporary Asian society marginalizes gender and sexual difference in the sense that heterosexuality is valorised by cultural norms and sometimes by legal regimes that seek to enforce heteronormativity. However, the forms of marginalization differ, both in character and intensity, from one society to the next. In the face of historical and contemporary marginalization, homoeroticism and transgenderism have, nevertheless, claimed spaces for expression, whether, as in Korea and Singapore, in the semi-visible gaps in hegemonic forms of hetero- normativity (see Seo and Heng, this volume), or, as in the Philippines or Thailand, in the form of a publicly tolerated but still derided transgender role (see Tan, this volume; Jackson & Sullivan 1999b). Large numbers of Asian men and women continue to live within the "traditional" spaces for gender/sex difference and to understand themselves and their lives in "pre-gay" terms that often relate more to the pre-industrial rural pasts of their societies than to the postmodernizing urban present. However, there are also large numbers of men and women who are reacting against what they see as the historical constraints on homoeroticism in their respective societies and who are actively engaging in relocating homoeroticism from the shadows and the periphery to the centre stage of their lives. The chapters in this volume describe both traditional forms of gender/sex difference (e.g., Khan) as well as recent gay and lesbian activisms (e.g., Tan, Chou, Heng, Seo).

Because the forms of marginalization are so different among Asian societies and because the historical spaces for homoerotic and transgender expression have also varied, the contemporary forms of gender/sex resistance that contribute to moulding new g/l/t identities also differ from one society to another. No general analysis can be provided for all new Asian identities. To understand 1990s Asian g/l/t identities in different societies, we need to know the local homoerotic and transgender pasts that they emerged from and against which they often counterposed themselves. The influence of Western ideas and cultures on these new imaginings of Asian homoeroticism is complex. Western gay/lesbian styles and terminology have often been appropriated as strategies to resist local heteronormative strictures and carve out new local spaces. However, these appropriations have not reflected a wholesale recreation of Western sexual cultures in Asian contexts, but instead suggest a selective and strategic use of foreign forms to create new ways of being Asian *and* homosexual.

The work of Mark Johnson (1997) has shown the complexity of this Western-Asian interaction in his study of a contemporary Filipino transgender culture. Johnson documents the culture of transgender males, variously called by the local term *bantut* or the borrowed term "gay," in the predominantly Muslim Tausug culture on the Southern Philippine island of Sulu. Central to Johnson's study is the argument that contemporary Tausug *bantut/gay* identity is in part configured in relation to a local imagining of America, a society which none of Johnson's informants had in fact experienced first hand. Johnson found that the Tausug notion of *gay* is inscribed within local discourses of transgenderism/femininity, and the borrowing of this lexical item has not been accompanied by a related borrowing of the discourses of homosexuality/masculinity within which gayness is understood in the West. Rather, the word "gay" has been appropriated to bolster the Tausug transgender understanding of homoeroticism and does not represent an intrusion of foreign discourses. This is because the "America" against which Tausug *bantut/gay* define themselves is not a "real" America but rather an exoticized other imagined from afar whose content is constituted upon an idealised projection of the local. That is, the *bantut/gay* imagining of "America" does not represent an actual Americanization of local gender/sex formations.

Instead, the symbol of a prestigious American other is used in order to enhance the status of the Filipino transgender formation. "Gay" then becomes a label for an idealised image of how these men would like to live their lives as Tausug transgender persons, not as American-style masculine identified gay men.

Understanding gay and lesbian Asia requires us to appreciate the relations between three phenomena: (1) the local historical forms of transgenderism and homoeroticism that have emerged in the context of different Asian regimes of heteronormativity; (2) contemporary gay/lesbian resistances to these heteronormative systems, which at times involve self-conscious separation from and even critique of the historical forms of gender/sex difference; and (3) the different ways that Western gay/lesbian discourses and styles have been appropriated as aspects of the local resistances.

Analyses of gay and lesbian Asia present fundamental challenges to Western-centred theories of sexuality. A key challenge is to incorporate an awareness of the specificity of historical Asian forms of gender/sex difference–those that existed before the identities now labelled "gay" and "lesbian"–with an appreciation that, despite being labelled with borrowed English terms, contemporary Asian identities often represent quite different forms of gendered eroticisms and eroticised genders from those that exist in the West. Some Asian erotic identities are "pre-gay," while others are "post-queer" in the sense that they exist outside Eurocentric understandings of sexual and gender difference. The expansion of Western-based knowledge to incorporate historical and contemporary forms of Asian erotic diversity will decentre many aspects of Eurocentric theory, forcing us to see Western eroticisms not as *the* model but as one set of historically specific forms beside many others.

In working through the limitations of current theoretical approaches, a number of related forms of analysis are required in order to arrive at non-Eurocentric understandings of g/l/t Asia. First, Western analysts engaged in this enterprise need to reflect critically on their motivations for engaging in cross-cultural research. Second, we need to develop detailed and nuanced understandings of the histories and societies of g/l/t Asia. And finally, priority needs to be given to avoiding seeing g/l/t Asians as reflections of Western gay men, lesbians, or transgender people. In summary, attempts at understanding g/l/t Asia must be underpinned by a systematic deprivileging of Western-centred perspectives.

THE POLITICS OF WRITING
ABOUT GLOBAL QUEERING IN ASIA

It is easy to see parallels in the lives of gay-identified men and lesbian-identified women in many Asian countries who have constructed social networks, lifestyles, and gay-oriented businesses similar to those found in many large Western cities. However, we need to be aware of the gender/sex political implications of placing an explanatory emphasis upon either "global/Western influences" or "local history" in developing accounts of the proliferation of Asian g/l/t identities. It may be argued that the idea of "gay" or "lesbian" as global identities can promote international collaboration between homosexually active men and women from diverse societies in their respective struggles for human rights or appropriate HIV/AIDS interventions. The label "gay" is indeed extremely popular amongst male gender/sex minorities around the planet although, at least in Thailand, the English word "lesbian" is strenuously avoided by "women who love women" (*ying rak ying*).[5]

However, there can also be a political downside to a globally uniform view of gay identity, which in some situations has been used as a weapon against Asian g/l/t people when it has been seen as being too closely associated with foreign models. The idea that gay is a Western phenomenon has been used by some conservative Asian governments to deny the significant histories of homoeroticism and transgenderism within their own societies. In Singapore and Malaysia in the 1990s, gayness was labelled as a Western phenomenon that at best was considered irrelevant and at worst was represented as a polluting foreign influence to be actively opposed. In a study of the politics of homosexual rights in non-Western societies, Chris Berry (1994: 73) observes that at the 1993 United Nations World Human Rights Conference in Vienna, then-Singaporean Foreign Minister Wong Kan Seng stated bluntly, "Homosexual rights are a Western issue, and are not relevant to this conference." This response was made after an Australian delegation had sought to have the UN include homosexuals within the ambit of its human rights charter. The political complexities of taking either a "global/Western influences" or "local history" explanatory line in the global queering discussion alert us to the need to avoid over-hasty generalizations in specifying what unites and what distinguishes different national or regional forms of g/l/t identity and culture. Indeed, in order to promote g/l/t issues in some Asian countries, it may be politically strategic to argue for a local rather than a global/Western view of homoeroticism.

THE WESTERN QUEER WILL TO KNOW G/L/T ASIA

The history of Western imperialism and the West's continuing domination of global economic, informational, and cultural flows influence the productin of knowledge of g/l/t Asia, and, also, often the wishes of Western g/l/t activists to aid local resistances against Asian heteronormative regimes of power/knowledge. Only by critically reflecting on the motivations underpinning their intellectual and political interests in g/l/t Asia can Westerners imagine forms of collaborative activity that do not reproduce Western hegemony.

Western academics' explorations of non-Western gender/sex systems often reflect their culture-specific subjectivities and expectations. For example, in numerous conversations with Australian, North American, and British colleagues, I have noticed that when a gender/sex category in an Asian society happens to be labelled with an indigenous term, such as *kathoey* in Thailand, then Western analysts are often prepared to grant that category a local history. However, if a Thai man self-identifies with the label "gay," then Western observers commonly overlook the possibility of a local history for this identity, and talk instead of "globalizing influences" and the "borrowing" of Western models. Despite queer studies' emphasis on multiplicity and diversity, there is still a tendency to be enchanted by the three letters "gay" and to see in them a reflection of sameness where we should be open to the possibility of finding difference. As American queer historian Scott Bravman (1997: 26) has stated, "[Western] gay and lesbian history can be criticized for reiterating culturally specific identity categories as universal." The articles in this volume challenge, to cite Chris Berry (1996: 14), "the often presumed universality of the post-Stonewall Anglo-American models of gay identity which are now beginning to appear as more culturally and historically specific."

Research by Western gay men and lesbians on homoeroticism in the rest of the world often seems to be motivated by concerns similar to those which lie behind the search for extraterrestrial life. A dominant but unspoken question guiding such research is: "Is there someone else out there like me?" This Western quest for global self-affirmation is a successor to the naive gay and lesbian historiography of earlier decades which was often dominated by a concern to find eminent "gays" or "homosexuals" in past eras when these categories did not yet exist. This research was motivated more by a concern to legitimate contemporary homosexualities than to inquire into historical or social difference. A form of narcissism at times appears to underpin the academic interest in looking to the Asian horizon for signs of identities and cultures similar to those that exist in the West. The global queering discussion, in part, appears to have been based on a wish to find "clones" of Western-type identities in the rest of the world. Fran Martin (1996) has commented on this phenomenon:

> Are we dealing with transparent "description" of the global scene or a veiled desire for sameness on the part of the "Western" critic? . . . [the] Western subject seems able to see in another cultural context only that which he already knows, missing complex and potentially productive interactions and hybridizations both within and between cultures.

Academic narcissism can distort perceptions, with understanding remaining stuck within the internally reflecting mirrors of one's own culture-delimited subjectivity. Western analysts need to abandon the expectation, or hope, that Asian g/l/t people are becoming like "us" before it will be possible to begin seeing "them" for who "they" are. An account of homoerotic desire in cross-cultural imaginings and relations is, therefore, epistemologically important in arriving at an understanding of the forms taken by knowledge of gender/sex others, the issues that are explored and those which are overlooked.

"THAT'S WHAT RICE QUEENS STUDY!"

In this context, it is important to consider the way that research on g/l/t Asia has at times been minoritized within the Western queer academy by the same race-based exclusions that operate within Western gay cultures. The desires underpinning the gay Caucasian will to know Asian genders and sexualities are often marked by competing but ultimately related discourses of racism and fetishization. Dominant discourses within contemporary Western gay male cultures stereotype Caucasian-Asian erotic relations in terms of two opposed models. These two models–of erotic denial and erotic fetishization–are, firstly, the exclusion of Asian men as erotically attractive and, secondly, the fetishization of Asian men as the only possible objects of erotic interest. Tony Ayres (1999), Kent Chuang (1999), and other writers document and critique these racist/fetishizing discourses in their contributions to a recent collection, of essays, *Multicultural Queer: Australian Narratives* (Jackson & Sullivan 1999a). As Audrey Yue (1999) indicates in the same collection, a similar account can be constructed for Western lesbian cultures. These two models are established by binaries that set up rigid race-based exclusions, not only within discourse but also in desire and social interaction within Western queer communities. Gays and lesbians in Asia (as well one might add gays and lesbians from Asian backgrounds living in Western countries) are often excluded both from their indigenous culture and from the Western queer cultures that supposedly hold out the promise of the full acceptance of sexual diversity. As Chris Berry observes, "there's plenty of evidence that neither heterosexist Asian patriarchies of that region nor established Eurocentric lesbian and gay cultures want to include them in" (1994, p. 12).

A dominant narrative in popular discourses within Western gay scenes involves the de-eroticization and effeminization of Asian men and a related privileging of a model of masculinity based on a fetishization of the attributes of an idealized Caucasian male body. The effeminization of Asian males has a long history in Western imperialist imaginings of the "exotic Orient" and has been explored in a number of recent studies (see Lane 1995, Sinha 1995) which relate this phenomenon to nineteenth century colonialist rationalizations of the European domination of Asia. A subordinate narrative within contemporary Western gay scenes related to the dominant exclusion of Asian men is that of the marginalized "rice queen," a Caucasian gay man whose desire is based on a fetishization of Asian men as the sole or preferred object of erotic interest and a denial of the attractiveness of race-same Caucasian men. Within expatriate gay Asian circles in Australia, the "rice queen" is mirrored by the "potato queen," an Asian man who fetishizes Caucasian men as the preferred or only object of erotic interest and who rejects other Asian men as sexual partners. The Caucasian rice queen occupies a stigmatized position within popular gay discourses, being stereotyped as a sexually unattractive man who is unable to find a Caucasian partner. The rice queen is mocked as a man who "only Asians find attractive."

These competing discourses of race-based exclusion and fetishization at times speak unconsciously through the subjectivities of queer academics. Studies of g/l/t Asia have been marginalized within "mainstream" Western gay/queer research because of an implicit attitude that "that is what rice queens study." In other words, the dominant stereotyping of Asian men as sexually unattractive has contributed to the minoritizing of studies of Asian homosexualities within the White queer academy. However, both Caucasian anti-Asian racism and fetishization of Asian men involve the privileging of certain racialized bodies as erotically more desirable and hence intellectually more "interesting" than others. In order to write without privileging one particular position of knowing, whether Western or Asian, it is necessary to deconstruct the race-based exclusions that underpin the Western will to know, or to ignore, g/l/t Asians. I have explored this issue in a novel, *The Intrinsic Quality of Skin* (Jackson 1994), in which the gay Caucasian protagonist negotiates the contradictions of living and loving across both Western and Thai discourses of homoeroticism (see also Jackson 2000).

GLOBALIZATION THEORY VERSUS FOUCAULDIAN HISTORY OF SEXUALITY

In the light of the above reflexive critiques, how then are we to proceed in understanding the proliferation of gender and sexual diversity in Asia and, more particularly, the apparent similarities of many new categories and identities to Western-styled gay and lesbian forms? Two ultimately related explanatory models have been put forward. One, the "global queering" model propounded by Dennis Altman (1996a), argues that globalizing economic and technological forces have facilitated cross-cultural borrowing from the West. For Altman (1996a: 78), the emergence of "the global gay" is best understood as "the expansion of an existing Western category" and as being "part of the rapid globalization of lifestyle and identity politics." The other model argued by Rosalind Morris (1994) in the case of Thailand, draws on Michel Foucault's (1980) analysis in *The History of Sexuality Volume 1* and maintains that gay and lesbian identities have emerged as a consequence of the institution of a new discursive regime based on sexuality. According to Morris, this contrasts with an older not yet fully superseded Thai discursive regime based on gender. Morris's model, in fact, assumes processes of cross-cultural borrowing in the context of globalization when she describes Thailand as "a society that is deeply influenced but not fully determined by transnational forces and ideologies" (1994: 17).

Although both globalization theory and the Foucauldian history of sexuality have been invoked to explain global queering, there is an analytical tension between these two approaches. In studies of globalization the historical boundaries of nation states, ethnic regions and linguistic and cultural domains are often downplayed with an emphasis on phenomena such as the electronic media, migration, mass tourism, and transnational capital flows which cross the planet's increasingly permeable political and cultural boundaries. This stands in contrast to the Foucauldian emphasis on discourses as highly bounded domains marked by sudden discontinuities and sharp breaks. Foucauldian studies concentrate on the internal specificities of discourses, analysing the concepts, categories, and identities which exist only within a given discursive domain.

If one's analytical focus is on those commercial spaces in major cities commonly called "gay scenes," then the many transnational fashion, style, musical, and other connections among these localities will undoubtedly be a dominant concern. The commercial gay scenes of bars, saunas, discos, fashion boutiques, and restaurants in Bangkok's Silom Road, Sydney's Oxford Street, Paris's Marai quarter, London's Soho, New York's Greenwich Village, San Francisco's Castro, and so on are just as intimately related with each other as an interlocking global set of spaces as they are with the national cultures within which they are located. However, if one focuses on the indigenous discourses within each of these widely separated spaces, then instead of global homogeneity, one is impressed by local specificity and difference. In a discourse-centered analysis, materially and economically similar spaces are revealed as sites of remarkably diverse understandings of same-sex eroticism and equally diverse imaginings of possible gendered futures.

I suspect that it is no coincidence that advocates of the globalization theory approach have conducted their research in English, while those who follow a more Foucauldian model of gender/sex differentiation have worked within the local languages of Asian g/l/t cultures. Many cross-cultural differences are only brought into sharp focus when one attains fluency in more than one language and experiences first hand the problems of representation and meaning that arise when one attempts to move between radically different linguistic and discursive systems. All the contributors to this volume have had to struggle with issues of translation and the specificity of Asian cultural forms.

We can also understand the analytical tension between globalization theory and Foucauldian historiography as emerging from the fact that each focuses on one of the interrelated dual processes that are at work in the creation of globalized cultural forms. Globalization theory is often invoked in attempts to appreciate transnational processes of homogenization while Foucauldian theory is more likely to be called into play in attempts to understand processes of indigenization or localization within the frame of globalization. Arjun Appadurai has identified the tension between cultural homogenization and cultural heterogenization as "the central problem of today's global interactions." As he states:

> A vast array of empirical facts could be brought to bear on the side of the homogenization argument, and much of it has come from the left end of the spectrum of media studies. . . . Most often, the homogenization argument subspeciates into either an argument about Americanization or an argument about commoditization. What these arguments fail to consider is that at least as rapidly as forces from various metropolises are brought into new societies they tend to become indigenised in one or another way. . . . The dynamics of such indigenisation have just begun to be explored systematically. . . . (Appadurai 1996, p. 32)

I agree with Appadurai that we need to critique the universalist assumptions of some accounts of globalization. Globalization is not merely a one-way process transferring ideas, aesthetics and sex-cultural patterns from the West to "the rest." Globalization also needs to be understood as the operation of common processes in diverse locales, inciting semi-independent and parallel developments in these different places. In other words, gay and other new identities may have multiple origins in a globalizing world. We need to problematize the assumption that the correct answer to questions about cross-cultural connection can be provided by one model and only one model. It is clear that no current formulation of the history of eroticism–whether based on Foucauldian or globalization analyses–is adequate to the task of explaining the global proliferation of gender/sex diversity in the twentieth century and that the challenge of understanding this phenomenon requires a refinement of our analytical tools in addition to detailed empirical studies.

EROTICISM AFTER FOUCAULT

Both the descriptive and theoretical issues in this discussion are much more complex than many authors have acknowledged. For example, how should we describe the proliferation of new Asian identities? In the global queering debates, the question of what is being "seen" or "described" in Asia and elsewhere has tended to be assumed as part of the explanatory theories that have been adduced. For example, to adduce Foucault's study on the history of sexuality in explaining recent shifts in Asian discourses is to assume that the new identities are sexualities. However, if identity is constituted within discourse, and if Asian gender/sex discourses are revealed to be qualitatively distinct from Western discourses, then Asian subjectivities will need to be seen as distinctive constructs that are not reducible to the Western notion of sexual identity. I have argued that in Thailand the "objects" of this inquiry are not sexual identities, but rather varieties of what in Thai discourses are called *phet* or eroticized genders (Jackson 1999a). I summarize this research below.

The analyses in Foucault's text *The History of Sexuality Volume 1* may not be immediately relevant for research on Asian discourses. Foucault, in fact, explicitly defined his study as excluding the non-West, noting that his object was "to define the regime of power-knowledge-pleasure that sustains the discourse on human sexuality *in our part of the world*" (Foucault 1980: 11, emphasis added). Foucault's "part of the world" was, after all, Paris (and to some extent San Francisco), not Beijing, Delhi, or Singapore. To mark my divergence from Foucault's analysis, in my own research I prefer to talk of eroticism and discourses of the erotic in Thailand in order to avoid the Eurocentric connotations that, since Foucault, now attach to the term "sexuality" and the notion of "discourses of sexuality." However, I am also aware that some Asian researchers (see Chao, Seo in this volume) have found Foucault useful, and the significant differences between Asian societies may mean that Western analytical accounts provide better descriptions of some societies than others. However, this cannot be determined in any *a priori* manner and the relevance or otherwise of different theoretical models can only emerge in the process of undertaking empirically grounded studies.

GAY IDENTITY WITHOUT "SEXUALITY"?

Here I reflect on my research on Thai gender/sex cultures in order to consider some of the complexities of researching global queering in Asia. Before the 1960s, male homoerotic relations in Thailand were structured within discourses that ascribed masculine (*phu-chai*) and feminine/effeminate (*kathoey*) gender positions to same-sex partners. Historically, the *kathoey* category had included all forms of gender/sex variance from normative forms of maleness/masculinity and female-ness/femininity. However, in the 1960s this formerly undifferentiated category fractured into an array of *kathoey* varieties which labelled specific forms of difference in the domains of sex (hermaphroditism), gender (cross-dressing), and sexuality (homosexuality). In succession, gay men, lesbians, and hermaphrodites were relabelled and differentiated from *kathoey*. The extent and rapidity of the linguistic and conceptual shift has been so great that younger Thais are no longer aware that only three decades ago a woman was called a *kathoey* if she acted like a man. By the 1970s, *kathoey* had come to mean only a person who is born male but subsequently enacts a feminine role (male transvestite) or undergoes a sex change operation (male-to-female transsexual).

While borrowed English-derived terms came to mark some new identities (*gay* for men, *tom* [from "tom boy"] for butch lesbians, *dee* [from "lady"] for femme lesbians), in some cases these words merely replaced preexisting Thai expressions, and their introduction did not mark the emergence of a new phenomenon but rather a relabelling. For example, recognition of masculine men who are attracted to other masculine men predated use of the label *gay,* with expressions such as "second type of *kathoey*" being used for these men in the early 1960s. A "second type of *kathoey*" was a homosexually active male who did not fit the prevalent stereotype of effeminacy. Those categories which are still labelled *kathoey* today are those which tend to be conceived in terms of the mythicized equal blending of maleness/masculinity and femaleness/femininity which lay at the core of the earlier meaning of the term. The linguistic persistence of *kathoey* means that popular English terms for transsexuality and transgenderism, such as "drag queen" or "tranny," have not been borrowed and are all but unknown in Thailand, except amongst those who have traveled to the West.[6]

The Thai borrowing of English terms for gender/sex difference has been highly selective and has involved a high degree of playful innovation. Male erotic cultures have enthusiastically appropriated the now dominant English label for male homoeroticism, *gay*. However, they have also felt a need to reflect persistent notions of the gendering of male homoeroticism through the uniquely Thai usage of *gay king* and *gay queen*. In contrast, female erotic cultures have trenchantly resisted the dominant English label for female homoeroticism, *lesbian*, instead appropriating and adapting the terms *tom boy* to *tom*, and *lady* to *dee*, to reflect the gendering of female same-sex relations. From a linguistic standpoint, Thailand's transgender cultures are largely uninfluenced by English borrowings and continue to use the long-established term *kathoey*. The complexity of this linguistic history–involving a combination of enthusiastic appropriation, resistance, playful adaptation to local patterns, and disinterest–alerts us to the fact that it is highly improbable that a simple unmediated process of "borrowing" from the West is the sole source of the explosion of Thai homosexual and transgender identities.

Thai discourses continue to be framed in terms of the indigenous category of *phet*, a notion that incorporates sexual difference (male vs. female), gender difference (masculine vs. feminine), and sexuality (heterosexual vs. homosexual). Within these discourses, *gay* and *kathoey* are not distinguished as a sexuality and a gender, respectively. Rather, *gay* and *kathoey*, together with "man," "woman," *tom* and *dee*, are collectively labeled as different varieties of *phet*. The new categories have not been constituted as a consequence of the emergence of a new type of discourse *a la* Foucault, but rather by a process of multiplication within the preexisting domain of *phet*.

The historical system of *phet*, with the *kathoey* imagined as blending genders within one body and psyche, has proved capable of capturing all the new categories by a refinement of the gender continuum to incorporate increasingly diverse and refined mixings of masculinity and femininity. This means that categories such as *gay queen* and *gay king* are imagined first in terms of their mixing of masculinity and femininity and only secondarily in terms of the types of erotic partner-ing engaged in. Indeed, it is a person's location on the multipositional scale or gender continuum of *phet*–from one hundred percent "man" at one end to one hundred percent "woman" at the other and any proportional combination in between–that is imagined as determining his or her erotic preference. This means that within the *phet* hierarchy, it is more important to know how masculine or feminine one is than to know the types of sexed bodies and gendered performances one finds erotically interesting. In other words, gender remains the core of all Thai identities, with eroticism being imagined as a secondary or deriv-ative component.

In Thailand, the words *gay, tom, dee* or *kathoey* primarily evoke images of gender-blending and only secondarily notions of same-sex eroticism. In contrast, in the West, the words "gay" or "lesbian" are more likely to be linked first to homosexuality, with thoughts of gen-der being secondary. It is not that eroticism is absent from Thai con-ceptions of *phet* categories or that gender is not a part of popular understandings of "gay" and "lesbian" in the West. Rather, eroticism and gender are articulated differently in the discourses and identities that are prevalent in the two cultures. Because eroticism continues to be seen as a byproduct or consequence of gender status, and because the *phet* system has proved so capable of expanding to incorporate new imagined blendings of the masculine and the feminine, an inde-pendent discourse of sexuality has not taken root in Thailand. Mascu-line gay identity is increasingly common in urban Thailand, but it is understood in a quite different way from gay identities in the West.

THE HISTORY OF EROTICISM AFTER QUEER

Current Western gay and queer research takes the gender/sexuality distinction as its starting point, and the history of sexuality can be conceived of as that discipline which inquires into the origins and consequences of this discursive break. As Donald Morton (1997: 14) states:

> The separation of "sexuality" from "gender" . . . marks the birth of queer theory. In *Epistemology of the Closet* . . . Eve Sedgwick (1990) declares the separation of sexuality from gender to be "axiomatic" for investigating sexual alterity: endorsing the hy-

pothesis of Gayle Rubin, Sedgwick says, "the question of gender and the question of sexuality . . . are . . . not the same question."

However, the proliferation of Thai categories cannot be interpreted in these terms. The impact of Western sexual and gender knowledges upon Thai discourses cannot be denied. However, this influence has not led to the emergence of a discourse of sexuality such as Foucault proposes occurred in Western societies in the nineteenth century. The interaction of Western discourses with other cultures/discourses does not necessarily reproduce the gender/sexuality split that is widely represented as now being hegemonic in the West. We need to understand the proliferation of Thai categories and identities as the consequence of an initial destabilization within the local discourses of *phet* followed by the institution of a new, more complex and re-stabilized discursive formation, not in terms of the "borrowing" or unmediated reproduction of a Western-modeled discursive regime.

Strictly speaking, sexuality as conceived in Foucauldian terms has no history in Thailand, remaining discursively bound to gender and so conceptually inchoate. Yet it would be Eurocentric to ascribe to the West a "true" history of sexuality and to Thai discourses only a "prehistory," with the implication that Thailand's "prehistoric" or inchoate sexuality may one day emerge into the light of global discursive history. The lack of a categorical separation between gender and sexuality should not be seen as an "underdeveloped" discursive state. What we have here is a demarcation between different histories of the erotic, not of history *versus* a lack of history. Thai discourses of *phet* need to be understood as autonomous from Western understandings, which means that, in tracing their recent transformations, it is necessary to conceive of new gay identities in that country as being new genders (alongside man and woman) as much as new sexualities. The categories used in writing the history of gender/sex transformations in the West have emerged from internal studies of Western texts and critical reflection upon Western discourses. A similar approach needs to be adopted in writing the history of the erotic in Asian societies, developing analytical categories from studies of local texts and reflections upon indigenous discourses and practices rather than imposing Eurocentric notions in an *a priori* manner.

The culture-specific analyses of *History of Sexuality Volume 1,* or any other text of Western gay and lesbian historiography, cannot be used as a universal template for understanding the proliferation of gender/sex diversity in Asia–simply remove the French or American examples and plug in "parallel" instances from Asia. A much more fundamental and laborious undertaking needs to be engaged in. Foucault provides a model for this task, not in his theoretical conclusions but in his careful attention to the details of transformation within a given society. In the case of Thailand, China, India, or other Asian society, the most important insights will emerge from a similar attention to the subtleties of discourses of eroticism in each of those localities.

REIMAGINING INTERNATIONAL G/L/T COLLABORATION

This brief survey has considered some of the multiple levels at which an inquiry into the global proliferation of gender/sex diversity needs to be conducted. In seeking to understand the specificity of Asian g/l/t identities, the foundations of current Western gay/queer knowledges may need to be rethought. While the above critiques have emphasized the importance of acknowledging the difference of Asian g/l/t gender/sex formations, it should also be emphasized that this inquiry emerges from a practical interest in imagining international and cross-cultural collaboration. The investigation of Asian specificities should be conducted with the objective of facilitating cooperation, not in order to argue for the impossibility of working together across cultural and linguistic divides. It is the vital question of imagining the practice of international g/l/t collaboration that motivates Dennis Altman's inquiry into global queering such and which imbues his project with such relevance and immediacy. In the light of the above critiques, how is this collaboration to be imagined? A formulation is possible, but it should be emphasized that it is as tentative and subject to critical revision as all of the preceding analyses.

G/L/T peoples across the globe do not necessarily share a common genesis. However, what often is shared is a dynamic of resistance. G/L/T-identified people often see themselves–whether by choice or fate–as being in conflict with their own society's gender/sex ideology. This is as true in Bangkok or Mumbai as it is in Sydney or San Francisco. "Gay" may not always be associated with a Western-styled political movement, but it is almost always linked with resistance to local heteronormative discourses and institutions. Perhaps it is in the rhetoric, style, and practice of resistance, rather than in any common origin, that "gay" assumes its global commonalities. Rather than inquiring into the past in order to search for historical sources of cross-cultural commonality, we should perhaps investigate how different g/l/t peoples imagine their respective futures. Historical critiques remain relevant, for they provide an essential corrective to the Eurocentric presumptions and imaginings which hinder Western subjects from appreciating Asian worlds in their own terms. However, instead of looking in the rear vision mirror to see from where different g/l/t people have all come, it is perhaps more productive to look at how the road ahead is envisioned.

In a recent conference paper, Australian historian of Japan Tessa Morris-Suzuki (1999) remarked on the similarities between minority indigenous communities in diverse contemporary societies. Despite the cultural differences between indigenous people in Australia, Japan, Taiwan, or the Americas, the common experience of marginalization, and at times cultural if not biological genocide, means that these diverse people are often engaged in very similar struggles for cultural or political autonomy. Morris-Suzuki remarked that at international conferences on indigenous rights these people often find that the common experience of marginalization provides them with a frame of reference, a common language of expression and a common political agenda. One can see parallels here with the situation of g/l/t people from diverse societies who are not united in any essential way, but whose common yet always different experience of being marginalized because of their perceived gender or erotic difference provides a basis of communication and a sense of common purpose.

However, to be effective in changing local conditions, g/l/t resistance must always be locally modulated. In one place, the dominant form of resistance may be street marches and agitation for law reform. In another place, the most important form of resistance may be avoiding arranged marriage. In yet other places, the most urgent form of gay activism may be articulated primarily through style as masculine resistance to effeminization, while lesbian activism may focus on public declarations and expressions which challenge the historical silencing of female desire. The local inflections of male, female, and transgender identities will differ as local forms of heteronormative power incite different modalities of resistance.

What emerges from the following studies is that there is no global gay, lesbian, or queer subject, only locally constituted g/l/t subjects, who at times appropriate elements of a global idiom and style as strategies in their locally determined and locally directed resistances. Labels such as "gay" do not denote a common origin or even prefigure a single destiny. What gay does label is the possibility of resisting local gender/sex norms. It gives a name to the idea that things might be different, that people marginalized within dominant gender/sex regimes can talk back and carve out spaces by strategic acts of subversion. It is in the imagining of how things can be different at the local level that we find the source of the infectious excitement that surrounds the label "gay" in many Asian cultures. However, appropriation of the language of "gay," "lesbian," or "queer" does not mean that Asian g/l/t people have become who they are from hearing these words spoken. When Asian g/l/t people call themselves "gay," they are not necessarily expressing a wish to become American, Australian, or European. Rather, they are articulating a desire to become who they imagine they can be as Thai, Singaporean, Filipino, Indian, Taiwanese, Korean, and so on. To be able to aid rather than hinder the realization of these imagined Asian futures, Western g/l/t peoples must be able to participate in recovering histories that are not their own and to share in lives within which their own aspirations may be irrelevant. As Chris Berry says, "it is only by recognising the ways in which Asian lesbians and gays change what it means to be lesbian or gay, and what it means to be Asian, that Western gays and lesbians can participate in the global rights decisions so vital their lives . . . " (1994: 19).

NOTES

1. I follow Fran Martin and Chris Berry (1998) in the use of the shorthand expression "g/l/t" to refer to all homoerotic and transgender identities considered "different" from heteronormative masculinity and femininity.

2. See, for example, Neil Miller (1992), Dennis Altman (1995), Gerard Sullivan and Laurence Wai-Teng Leong (1995).

3. The expression "gender/sex" used here inverts the word order of Gayle Rubin's (1975, 1984) influential notion of "sex/gender system" in order to mark what I believe to be the continuing priority of gender over sexuality in Thai and other Southeast Asian identities. The inversion of Rubin's sequence of terms also signals my disagreement with the contention that gender and sexuality can be considered independent constructs that require distinctive theories and modes of inquiry (see Jackson 1999a).

4. The two other volumes related to the conference themes have already been

published. One deals with the intersection of ethnicity and homosexuality in Australia (Jackson & Sullivan 1999a) while the other deals with male and female homosexuality in contemporary Thailand (Jackson & Sullivan 1999b).

5. Thai "women who love women" avoid calling themselves "lesbian" because this term entered the language to describe female homosexual visual pornography produced for a heterosexual male audience. It is also understood as representing woman-centred relationships in overly sexualised terms, with many Thai women who love women preferring to imagine their relationships in emotional rather than explicitly erotic terms. (Source: private communication with Anjana Suvarnananda).

6. A similar process appears to have taken place in the Philippines and Indonesia, where established local terms such as *bakla* (northern Philippines), *bantut* (southern Philippines), *banci* (Java), and *waria* (Indonesia) continue to be used to denote transgender and transsexual identities while "gay" denotes masculine homoeroticism. However, the reception of "gay" has not been uniform across all Thai, or Filipino, g/l/t cultures. "Gay" is commonly identified with the transgender *kathoey* and *bakla/bantut*, respectively, in non-metropolitan and rural areas of both countries. Mark Johnson (1997), in writing of the southern Philippines, and Jan Willem de Lind van Wijngaarden (1999) and Prue Borthwick (1999), in writing of northern Thailand, describe local g/l/t cultures within which "gay" is appropriated to rather than being distinguished from established transgender categories.

REFERENCES

Altman, Dennis. (1995). The new world of 'gay' Asia. In Suvendrini Perera (Ed.), *Asian and Pacific Inscriptions* (pp. 121-38), Melbourne: Meridien Books.

Altman, Dennis. (1996a). Rupture or continuity? The internationalisation of gay identities, *Social Text*, 14 (3), 77-94.

Altman, Dennis. (1996b). On global queering. *Australian Humanities Review,* Internet Edition (www.lib.latrobe.edu.au/AHR/archive/Issue-July-1996/altman.html).

Appadurai, Arjun. (1996). *Modernity at Large: Cultural Dimensions of Globalisation,* Minneapolis: University of Minnesota Press.

Ayres, Tony. (1999). China doll: The experience of being a gay Chinese Australian. In Peter A. Jackson & Gerard Sullivan (Eds.), *Multicultural Queer: Australian Narratives* (pp. 87-98), New York: The Haworth Press, Inc.

Berry, Chris. (1994). *A Bit on the Side: East-West Topographies of Desire,* Sydney, EMPress.

Chris, Berry. (1996). Kiss 'n kin: Queer Asian cinema. *Sydney Gay and Lesbian Mardi Gras Film Festival Program Notes.* Sydney: Queer Screen.

Borthwick, Prue. (1999). HIV/AIDS Projects with and for Gay Men in Northern Thailand. In Jackson, Peter A. & Sullivan, Gerard (Eds.) *Lady Boys, Tom Boys, Rent Boys: Male and Female Homosexualities in Contemporary Thailand* (pp. 61-80), New York: The Haworth Press, Inc.

Bravman, Scott. (1997). *Queer Fictions of the Past: History, Culture and Difference,* Cambridge, New York & Melbourne: Cambridge University Press.

Chauncey, George. (1994). *Gay New York: Gender, Urban Culture and the Making of the Gay Male World 1890-1940,* New York: Basic Books.

Chuang, Kent. (1999). Using chopsticks to eat steak. In Peter A. Jackson & Gerard Sullivan (Eds.), *Multicultural Queer: Australian Narratives* (pp. 29-42), New York: The Haworth Press, Inc.

Foucault, Michel. (1980). *The History of Sexuality Volume 1: An Introduction,* trans. Robert Hurley, New York: Vintage Books.

Garcia, Neil. (1996). *Philippine Gay Culture: The Last 30 Years, Binabae to Bakla, Silahis to MSM,* Manila: University of the Philippines Press.

Jackson, Peter A. (1994). *The Intrinsic Quality of Skin,* Bangkok: Floating Lotus Books.

Jackson, Peter A. (2000a in press). An explosion of Thai identities: peripheral genders and the limits of queer theory, *Culture, Health & Sexuality.*

Jackson, Peter A. (1999b). An American death in Bangkok: the murder of Darrell Berrigan and the hybrid origins of gay identity in 1960s Bangkok. *GLQ: A Journal of Gay and Lesbian Studies,* 5(3) 361-411

Jackson, Peter A. & Sullivan, Gerard (Eds.) (1999a). *Multicultural Queer: Australian Narratives,* New York: The Haworth Press, Inc.

Jackson, Peter A. & Sullivan, Gerard (Eds). (1999b). *Lady Boys, Tom Boys, Rent Boys: Male and Female Homosexualities in Contemporary Thailand,* New York: The Haworth Press, Inc.

Johnson, Mark. (1997). *Beauty and Power: Transgendering and Cultural Transformation in the Southern Philippines,* Oxford: Berg.

Lane, Christopher. (1995). *The Ruling Passion: British Colonial Allegory and the Paradox of Homosexual Desire,* Durham and London: Duke University Press.

Martin, Fran. (1996). Fran Martin responds to Dennis Altman. *Australian Humanities Review,* Internet Edition (www.latrobe.edu.au/AHR/emuse/Globalqueering/Martin.html).

Martin, Fran & Berry, Chris. (1998). Queer'n'Asian on the Net: Syncretic Sexualities in Taiwan and Korean Cyberspaces. *Critical InQueeries,* 2(1), 67-94.

Miller, Neil. (1992). *Out in the World: Gay and Lesbian Life from Buenos Aires to Bangkok,* London: Penguin Books.

Morris, Rosalind C. (1994). Three sexes and four sexualities: redressing the discourses on gender and sexuality in contemporary Thailand. *Positions* 2(1), 15-43.

Morris-Suzuki, Tessa. (1999). Anti-Area Studies: Alternatives to Imagining Asia as Social and Historical Space. Paper presented to the conference, *Alter/Asians: Exploring Asian/Australian Identities, Cultures and Politics in an Age of Crisis,* 18-21 February 1999, Sydney.

Morton, Donald. (1997). Global (Sexual) Politics, Class Struggle, and the Queer Left. *Critical InQueeries,* 1(3), 1-30.

Rubin, Gayle. (1975). The Traffic of Women: Notes on the Political Economy of Sex. In R. Reiter (Ed.), *Toward an Anthropology of Women* (pp. 157-210), New York: Monthly Review Press.

Rubin, Gayle. (1984). Thinking Sex: Notes for a Radical Theory of the Politics of Sexuality. In C. Vance (Ed.), *Pleasure and Danger: Exploring Female Sexuality,* (pp. 267-319), London: Routledge and Kegan Paul.

Sedgwick, Eve Kosofsky. (1990). *Epistemology of the Closet,* Berkeley: University of California Press.

Sinha, Mrinalini. (1995). *Colonial Masculinity: The 'Manly Englishman' and the 'Effeminate Bengali' in the Late Nineteenth Century,* Manchester and New York: Manchester University Press.

Sullivan, Gerard & Laurence Wai-Teng Leong (Eds). (1995). *Gays and Lesbians in Asia and the Pacific: Social and Human Services,* New York: Harrington Park Press.

van Wijngaarden, Jan Willem de Lind. (1999). Between Money, Morality and Masculinity: The Dynamics of Bar-based Male Sex Work in Chiang Mai, Northern Thailand. In Peter A. Jackson & Gerard Sullivan (Eds.), *Lady Boys, Tom Boys, Rent Boys: Male and Female Homosexualities in Contemporary Thailand* (pp. 193-218), New York: The Haworth Press, Inc.

Homosexuality
and the Cultural Politics of *Tongzhi*
in Chinese Societies

Chou Wah-Shan

INTRODUCTION

This paper examines the cultural specificity of same-sex eroticism in Chinese societies where the family-kinship system, rather than an erotic object choice, is taken as the basis of the identity of a person. I will argue for the need to build up indigenous *tongzhi* politics that need not reproduce Anglo-American experiences and strategies of lesbigay liberation. I will use "lesbigay" when referring to lesbians, bisexuals, and gay people in the West, "PEPS" when referring to **People** who are **Erotically** attracted to **People** of the **Same** sex in traditional (defined as pre-twentieth century) Chinese societies, and *tongzhi* when referring to contemporary Chinese lesbigay people.

Tongzhi is the most popular contemporary Chinese word for lesbians, bisexuals, and gay people. The word is a Chinese translation from a Soviet communist term "comrade," which refers to the revolutionaries that shared a comradeship. The term was first adopted by Chinese in Republican China, and then taken both by the Communist and Nationalist Party to refer to comrades struggling for the communist/nationalist revolution. *Tong* literally means "same/homo," the same Chinese word for "homo (sexual)," and the word *zhi* means "goal," "spirit," or "orientation."

It is a telling point that as Hong Kong approached reintegration with

[Haworth co-indexing entry note]: "Homosexuality and the Cultural Politics of *Tongzhi* in Chinese Societies." Wah-Shan, Chou. Co-published simultaneously in *Journal of Homosexuality* (Harrington Park Press, an imprint of The Haworth Press, Inc.) Vol. 40, No. 3/4, 2001, pp. 27-46; and: *Gay and Lesbian Asia: Culture, Identity, Community* (ed: Gerard Sullivan, and Peter A. Jackson) Harrington Park Press, an imprint of The Haworth Press, Inc., 2001, pp. 27-46. Single or multiple copies of this article are available for a fee from The Haworth Document Delivery Service [1-800-342-9678, 9:00 a.m. - 5:00 p.m. (EST). E-mail address: getinfo@haworthpressinc.com].

27

China in 1997, *tongzhi* adopted the most sacred term in Communist China as their identity, signifying both a desire to indigenize sexual politics and to reclaim their cultural identity. The reappropriation struck the community for its positive cultural references, gender-neutrality, de-sexualizing of the stigma of homosexuality, its politics beyond the homo-hetero binarism, and its indigenous cultural identity for integrating the sexual into the social. Within several years, it has become the most common usage in Hong Kong and Taiwan, though the English term "gay" is also still commonly used, sometimes interchangeably with *tongzhi*.

The emergence of the discourses of *tongzhi* signifies an endeavor to integrate the sexual into the social and cultural. In a cultural tradition which has never felt the need to divide people by the gender of their erotic object choice, PEPS may find the identity of gay or homosexual alienating, not because of homophobia, but because they do not feel the need to segregate themselves from those who love the opposite sex. Chinese culture has a cosmology in which sexuality is not a separable category of behavior and existence, but an integral force of life. Chinese *tongzhi* who have resisted adopting the categories "lesbian" or "gay" and the idea of coming out, have often been criticized as being closeted, dishonest, and self-denying. This may not be untrue, but it may also be seen as an attempt to resist the imposition of the homo-hetero binarism upon the relational and fluid Chinese conception of sexuality.

Tongzhi achieves a similar political contribution as "queer politics" does, but whereas queer politics confronts the mainstream by appropriating a formerly derogatory label, *tongzhi* harmonizes social relationships by taking the most sacred title from the mainstream culture. It is an indigenous strategy of proclaiming one's sexual identity by appropriating rather than denying one's familial-cultural identity.

For White, Anglo-Saxon, middle-class gay men and lesbians living in Western societies, sexuality may be the site of greatest oppression. But for people from third world, working-class, Black or Asian backgrounds, who love people of the same sex, it may be race, ethnicity, culture, class, or family that is far more important than sexuality. A motto such as "We are here, we are queer, get used to it!" is predicated upon individualism and confrontational politics where the right to one's body is of central cultural importance. Asking all PEPS to come out and identify themselves as lesbian or gay because they love people of the same sex is to prioritize and absolutize sexuality at the expense of all other identities and differences. It can be an act of racism, classism, sexism, or cultural imperialism.

This by no means minimizes the immense achievement and contribution of the confrontational strategies. Given the acute extent of homophobia and gay-bashing which has lasted for centuries in the West, coupled with the state hypocrisy and hostility during the AIDS epidemic, confrontational politics is needed to fight for the basic rights of lesbigay people. My only reservation is in the universalizing of the Anglo-American experience and its imposition upon other cultures.

THE HOMO-HETERO BINARY
AND CULTURAL TOLERANCE OF SAME-SEX EROTICISM

Strictly speaking, there were no heterosexuals, bisexuals, or homosexuals in Chinese history. The concept of sexual orientation, i.e., dividing people by the gender of their erotic object choice, did not exist. Chinese culture recognizes the differences between same-sex and opposite-sex eroticism, but sex is not a ground on which to classify people. The traditional Chinese world did not dichotomize sexual desire into a gender binarism of same-sex desire and opposite-sex desire.

In traditional China, same-sex activities are portrayed in predominantly social, rather than sexual terms, with homosocial roles being used in expressions such as *xiang gong* (male prostitute), *pi* (favourite), *duan xiu* (cut sleeve), *lung yang, fen tao* (shared peach), *hanlu* (the dry canal), and *tuzi* (little rabbit); homosocial relations are described in terms such as *jinlan zimei* (golden orchid sisters), *qidi* and *qixiong* (adopted brothers), and *hanlu yingxiong* (stranded heroes), or a style, such as *nanfeng* (male wind, male custom, male practice, male style), *nanse* (male eroticism, beauty, and seductiveness), or as specific behaviourial practices, *such as mo jing* (polishing mirrors), *mou dou fu* (grinding bean-curd), *hou ting hwa* (the backyard flower), *dui shi* (paired eating), or *chui xiao* (to play a vertical bamboo flute). All the terms describing the same-sex sexual acts are rather poetic, with no sense of social or moral condemnation. The first derogatory term for a homosexual act, *jijian* (chicken lewdness, with reference to the belief that domesticated fowls commonly engage in same-sex acts), appears as late as the Tang dynasty, and it implies disparagement rather than hostility. Most importantly, all these terms referring to same-sex activities do not denote a generic personality.

Contrary to modern Western culture, which divides human beings into a homo-hetero binarism, the Chinese sexual world is constructed predominantly along hierarchical class lines. The one with power, stereotypically the upper-class adult male, could sexually dominate social inferiors like his wife, second wife, or concubines. He could also dominate and penetrate younger male servants who were socially inferior to him without carrying severe social stigma of being a homo/bisexual. From the viewpoint of an emperor or a wealthy lord, there was only a minimal differentiation between his desire for a female and for a young male–the sexual activities of both would equally confirm and exhibit his social power.

It is, therefore, dangerous to romanticize Chinese traditions of same-sex eroticism. The cultural tolerance of same-sex eroticism was neither unconditional nor wholehearted, but was tolerated with a vital qualifier–it occured only when the social hierarchy was not challenged. Ironically, the most distinctive features of the Chinese history of homosexuality are neither homophobia nor homoeroticism but rather classism, sexism, and ageism, which permeate and construct both homosexual relationships and mainstream culture.

Chinese culture has not supported or accepted homosexuality. The family-kinship system and the pressure upon both women and men to get married pose a limiting boundary to and pressure on same-sex erotic practices. People may have gossiped, but they rarely took action against it. Homosexuality was not treated as intrinsically evil and sinful. Gay-bashing, as seen in America and Britain, does not exist in traditional Chinese societies. "Homophobia," if used in an indiscriminate manner, either explains too much–as if Chinese culture rejects homosexuality as sinful or perverse–or too little–as if Chinese understand homosexuality as a generic or essentialized category. Both senses of homophobia fail to capture the unique specificity of the Chinese cultural attitude which understands the sexual in terms of the social.

It is only since the Republican period that the Chinese people's long historical cultural tolerance of same-sex eroticism began to fade. In the process of Westernization, what Chinese intellectuals accepted was not homophobia per se but rather a scientific discourse of biological determinism that marginalized and pathologized all non-reproductive sexuality (Dikotter, 1995). Chinese scholars, "enlightened" by Western scientific discourses, began to see homosexuality as a temporary aberration and mental disease. Cheng Hao, a famous sex educator, in his *The Sexual Life of Mankind* (1934:133-134), adopted the Western sexology notion of "homosexuality as gender perversity," seeing homosexuals as having the gender traits of the opposite sex. He also criticized homosexuality as a bad habit which is abnormal, dirty, and inhuman. The notion that one person is both *yin* and *yang* was overwhelmed by a biologically-determined gender polarity, thus making homosexuality appear to be unnatural and anti-biological.

In an ironic reversal, since the 1950s and 60s, the contemporary Western world has gradually departed from the mental illness model towards greater respect for differences and individuality. Yet China abandoned its traditional tolerance of PEPS for the now out-dated Western mental illness model at the turn of the century. Since 1949, PEPS could be arrested and sent to labor reform camps, prisons, or clinics for electric therapy, or even executed in extreme cases.

Compared to PEPS throughout Chinese history, contemporary Chinese *tongzhi* are having a much harder time. The major reason is, ironically, the popularization of courtship culture and the romanticization of marital relations. In traditional China, marriage had nothing to do with romantic love or sexual orientation. One was married not to one's husband or wife, but also one's parents-in-law and the entire kinship household. Same-sex eroticism could co-exist with marriage without conflict.

However, with the advocacy and popularization of romantic love in the twentieth century, marriage became a personal pursuit of (sexual) happiness. Instead of pleasing one's parents and parents-in-law, one also had to please one's partner, emotionally and sexually. And during courtship, one had to be intimate, passionate, seductive, flirtatious, sexual, touching, even jealous. The invention of courtship culture has, therefore, inflicted much pain upon PEPS, who now have to pretend to be turned on by a person of the opposite sex. Therefore, marriage in contempory China has become a most oppressive and torturous institution for PEPS, in a way it never was before.

A cause of yet more pain for *tongzhi* is their romanticization of the Western lesbigay world, which is perceived as non-homophobic, carefree, and liberating. Most Chinese residents can not obtain a visa to the Western world, so the only knowledge they have about the Western lesbigay world are the images of lesbigay marriages and parades where thousands of lesbigay people march in a most relaxed and proud manner. They tend to romanticize the Western world as a lesbigay haven and are shocked to be informed of the prevalence of gay-bashing and the extent of homophobia in the USA and UK. Some simply find this unbelievable. What is new in post-war China, and also in Taiwan and Hong Kong, is the intervention of state apparatus, especially the police, court, and legal systems, to prosecute (male) PEPS for their sexual activities. This state intervention, together with its scientific grounding in the medicalization and pathologization of same-sex eroticism, is another crucial reason accounting for the pain felt by contemporary PEPS in China, Taiwan, and Hong Kong, especially in the 1970s and 1980s.

FROM COMING OUT TO COMING HOME

There are many different ways through which a person's sexual desire can be classified. Only in the contemporary Western world do we use the gender of one's erotic object-choice to classify people, thus producing the binary categories homosexual and heterosexual. The labelling practices of the sexologist created the possibility for what Foucault called "reverse affirmation" by which the stigmatized could begin to organize around the label and assert the legitimacy of their identity. Identity politics–we share an identity, and, therefore, we form a political alliance–became the ground of the lesbigay movement.

The Western notion of "coming out" is not only a political project of the lesbigay movement, but is often a cultural project of affirming the Western value of individualism, discourse of rights, talking culture, high level of anonymity in metropolitan cities, and the prioritization of sex as the core of selfhood. The model of coming out is hinged upon notions of the individual as an independent, discrete unit segregated economically, socially, and geographically from the familial-kinship network. In America, individual frankness, the willingness to verbalize one's feelings, and the determination to defend one's right to speak up are treated as major salient features of the individual's life (Carbaugh, 1988). Honesty to one's parents through verbal communication is seen as vital to a genuine self. USA also has a political institution marked by parliamentary politics governed by one person one vote. Therefore, turning one's sexual rights into political rights through coming out is commonly agreed upon by lesbigays as a major way to defend their interests.

This by no means minimizes the pain of coming out for Americans nor the diversities of lesbigay strategies in the USA. Many of the White American lesbigay anthologies of coming out include enormous discussions of their bitter negotiations with their parents and the emotional disturbances in verbalizing their sexual identities. There are also immense debates and controversies among the USA lesbigay population concerning the strategies of liberation and coming out. The notion of "the USA lesbigay movement" is perhaps a misnomer. It is only certain political activists in New York, Los Angeles, and San Francisco who opt for a more confrontational strategy. The vast majority of lesbigay people living in the South and Mid-west believe and behave otherwise. They are generally more quiet, subtle, and even closeted. Yet the confrontational images of drag queens in parades and the attention-getting tactics of ACT UP, Queer Nation, and Outrage make news. This is the image of Western lesbigay people as presented in the mainstream media, especially in Asian societies.

Zhan chu lai (coming out) has very different cultural and political connotations in Chinese communities. In 1992, a *tongzhi* group in Hong Kong decided to launch a pride parade, planning to walk from Queen's Pier to Lan Kwai Fong on 21st August. Yet only about 10 expatriates and two Chinese (both overseas Chinese) intended to go. Fearing the event might reinforce the mainstream stereotype of "homosexuality as a Western import," the organizers cancelled the parade. Meanwhile, local *tongzhi* were being criticized by local Caucasian gay, Hong Kong based activists for not being sufficiently courageous and liberated (*Eastern Express*, 22 Aug 1992).

This event reflects the issue of whether a confrontational model of lesbigay politics is applicable in a different cultural context where the family-kinship system rather than personal sexual desire is counted as the basis of what a person is. The confrontational model is more appropriate in a society where individuality and self-affirmation are the basis of personal and cultural identity.

What constitutes a person is culturally specific. In traditional Chinese societies, nobody is a discrete, isolated being; rather everyone becomes a full person only in the context of family and social relationships. Everyone is, first, a daughter or son of her/his parents (that is, a certain role in the social-familial system) before s/he can be anything else (Hsu, 1953). In this construct, the family is perceived to be the most basic and profound social institution, and *xiao* (filial piety) is given central value. The Chinese conception of self has generated a very different scenario for *tongzhi* issues than that of their Western counterparts:

1. While the basic tenet of Western lesbigay discourses is to regard the lesbigay subject as an individual with unalienable rights, the traditional Chinese culture simply refuses to classify people into homo or hetero because individuals (both women and men, homo or heterosexually inclined ones) are first and foremost members of the family and wider society.
2. It is inappropriate to treat a *tongzhi* merely as an isolated self seeking personal liberation. Instead a *tongzhi* should be located within her/his context of *guanxi*, especially the family.
3. The major problem for most *tongzhi* is not state oppression, religious fundamentalism, or job discrimination, but the ones they love most–their parents.
4. The problem for parents is not only accepting that their child is a *tongzhi,* but the shame of losing face for having a deviant child who does not get married.
5. In a society where filial piety is given the utmost importance in defining a person, hurting one's parents can be the most terrible thing for a *tongzhi* to experience.
6. The focus of the *tongzhi* movement is not an isolated self called gay, lesbian, or bisexual, but the family and social relations that both constitute and oppress *tongzhi*.

The problem for parents is not just the acceptance of their child as a *tongzhi,* but how to "face" their relatives, neighbours, and ancestors. Parents would feel wronged and shamed through the loss of face if a *tongzhi* child came out. Traditional Chinese parents like to compare their children with the daughters and sons of other people, in terms of social status, achievement, and extent of filial piety. The closer the family ties and the bigger the extended family network, the more pressure and shame would be felt by parents for having a *tongzhi* child.

The lexicon of "coming out" and to "be out and proud" can be culturally problematic for Chinese, as "out" implies leaving the family, parents, and the culture to become lesbian or gay, and "proud" is culturally derogatory, especially for a "deviant" form of sexuality. It seems necessary to articulate indigenous categories and strategies that can reclaim *tongzhi* voices not by denying one's family-cultural identity but by integrating *tongzhi* into the family and cultural context.

"Coming home" can be proposed as an indigenous lexicon of *tongzhi* self-confirmation. *Jia* (home/family) is a culturally unique category that does not have an equivalent parallel in Western language. While *jia* condenses the meaning of family and home in the English speaking world, it is also a mental space which refers to the ultimate home and roots to which a person belongs. *Hui-jia* (coming home) means not only going back home but also, more fundamentally, searching the ultimate place/space to which one belongs. Home refers not only to the biological family with whom a *tongzhi* has struggled her/his whole life, but could also signify the chosen family of *tongzhi* friends that is her/his second home of comfort and support. In that sense, *tongzhi* is a process of home-coming and be-coming–integrating the sexual with the socio-cultural. *Tongzhi* come out not by segregating the sexual from the social and confronting the public, but by coming home. *Come home* articulates the visibility of *tongzhi* not as an isolated sexual self abstracted from social relations, but as a means of exactly locating the *tongzhi* in the mainstream social relations.

Local *tongzhi's* reservations about coming out can be clearly detected in the linguistic discourses they use. *Tongzhi* rarely use the term "come out" in Chinese. In the first anthology of coming out stories in Hong Kong, Samshasha (a pioneering activist in Hong Kong), has written an article "Coming out *Ershinian*" (Twenty Years of Coming Out). In his short article of less than 2000 Chinese characters, the English term "coming out" appears around 20 times. The second most frequent English words are *"gay"* and *"gay lib,"* as if these terms cannot be translated into Chinese. In another coming out story written by Almond, the only English phrase she uses is "coming out," which appears more than 10 times, as if "coming out" is a Western concept and cannot be expressed in Chinese. Indeed, most authors in that book automatically switch to English when they write the words "coming out" (Chou, Mak & Kwong, 1995). While such mixed-code bilingualism is common in Cantonese, it is not coincidental that it is only Western concepts like "coming out," "gay," and "gay liberation" that are spoken and written by Chinese *tongzhi* in English in an otherwise wholly Chinese context.

TONGZHI'S *EXPERIENCES OF COMING HOME*

Despite the immense pressures *tongzhi* face, smooth integration of a positive *tongzhi* identity into the familial context is not unheard of. Coming home can be explicated as a negotiative process of bringing one's sexuality into the family-kin network, not by singling out same-sex eroticism as a site for conceptual discussion but by constructing a same-sex relationship in terms of family-kin categories. The *tongzhi* would establish such a relationship with his/her parents by mundane practices like shopping or playing mahjong together. Dinner has often been quoted as a crucial cultural marker for breaking the insider-outsider distinction. The *tongzhi* may then use quasi-kin categories like half sisters/brothers to integrate her/his partner into the family.

Breaking the Insider (zi-ji ren)–Outsider (wei ren) Distinction

In all the successful cases, the insider-outsider distinction between the parents and *tongzhi"s* partner has been broken down, and the partner is accepted as a member of the in-group. The boundaries of the Chinese familial group are fluid and elastic, including not just parents, siblings, and close relatives, but certain close friends who can be accepted as familial members. It is not uncommon for Chinese to take an adopted friend of the same sex and integrate her/him as one's own family member. Indeed, the practices of *qi xiong-di* in the province of Fujian last century was the most famous institutional practice of same-sex "marriage." And the "Five Relations" relationship among friends is one of these practices. Chinese proverbs such as "relying on parents at home, and on friends outside home" show the importance of friend-ship. Proverbs such as "within the four seas, all people are brothers" also signify a unique cultural comprehension of friendship through kin categories like sisters and brothers. Given the particular ethics of Confucian culture, all strangers need a third party to locate themselves in the *ren-lun* (family-kin human relationship) in order to be accepted into the social network. Once located properly in the *ren-lun,* this stranger has immense room to manoeuvre within this family-kin net-work. Here lies a strategy through which contemporary *tongzhi* inte-grate their partners into the family context.

Twenty-five-year-old Ching told me a fascinating story. She has a steady relationship with her partner, Yee, who comes to her place every weekend, sometimes staying overnight in the same bed. They have dinner together with Ching's family in the same house. Ching's mother treats Yee almost like her daughter. Does she understand her daughter's *tongzhi* relationship with Yee? Ching replied:

> It is so obvious, she understands, of course. But does she accept it? Never! How can a Chinese mother accept her daughter or son being *tongxinglian* (homosexual). It is suicidal to tell them. You do not confront your parents. You build up a harmonious relationship in order to let things go. My parents are doing their best in the Chinese way–tacit recognition without mentioning it. I want to be their daughter, not a different person called lesbian. And my parents simply do not have the cultural space to support lesbian politics. Why should they?
>
> I did try to tell her. Once, my mum was watching television with me. There was an advertisement on AIDS. Mum said something weird: "You should take good care of yourself. Don't give me trouble. I am too old now, I can't afford too much excitement." I was stunned, thinking that it may be the right time. After all, I have struggled for many years. So I said, "Mum, I have something very serious to tell you." Dead silence. Mum stared at me. Strangely enough, my mother interrupted me and said, "Don't tell me. I don't want to know. You are old enough to decide your road." Nowadays, Mum has no right to say anything: "You do what you want. I don't even force you to get married." Well, she denies the subject, but it is ironically her way of accepting it. I don't think she wants to know clearly that I am *tongxinglian*. She will have difficulty handling her extended family and friends. I never give up educating her. Last month was mother's birthday and she invited Yee to come for the dinner. You know, my parents, two brothers, Yee and me as a couple. She passes completely, isn't that beautiful!

It is not easy. For the last two years, Yee always came to visit Ching's mother, going shopping and playing mahjong with her. Only recently was Yee accepted as "a special friend." After that dinner, Ching's mother told her, "If you live with Yee and don't get married, you will have a hard time. People will gossip about you. Marriage is not necessarily happy, but it is what everyone has done for thousands of years."

Ching once had a serious fight with Yee, and they almost split up. One afternoon, Ching was very sad and stayed in her room. Ching's mother opened the door and asked her something. Just before her mother closed the door, she said in a caring but ironic tone, "Quarrel?" Ching was stunned: "Did my mother know it?" Then Ching overheard her mother tell her father in the living room: "Oh dear, the sweet couple split up." Ching's mother said this in a tone as if they should stay together.

It is perhaps crucial that Ching uses food and dinner as cultural markers to break the insider-outsider distinction. Yee's active involvement in activities such as shopping and playing mahjong with Ching's mother has significantly enhanced the relationship between them. That is why Yee gradually came to be seen by Ching's parents as their quasi-daughter. Indeed, Ching uses kin categories to express their relationship in three stages: "I think at first my mother treated Yee as my younger sister, then later as her second daughter, and now Yee and me are treated as a couple, like wife and husband." In all the successful cases of coming home, the partner of a *tongzhi* is perceived by her/his parents through quasi-kin categories, which is a crucial indication of breaking the insider-outsider distinction.

Coming Out by Bypassing Tongxinglian

Most *tongzhi* have said that the implicit and subtle way of coming out is more suitable to a Chinese family. *Tongzhi* would introduce their partners as good friends and let the parents understand their *tongzhi* relationship through actual practices in everyday lives. They come out by avoiding the discussion of homosexuality. Tat-ming (aged 36) is a typical case, who says:

> My parents should know it but I never tell them directly. I have never dated women, and only men phone me. It is so obvious! Once, when my mother and I were watching a TV programme on AIDS, she was so attentive, listening to every word. After the programme, she said to me: "Tat-ming, you must be careful, AIDS is a fatal disease. You are a doctor and know better than anyone. I never control your private life, but I am too old, don't let me worry." And last month when the TV broadcast Xu You-sheng's marriage, my father said, "I really don't know what is in your mind, but we are Chinese, I think you should marry. It is a

social obligation that obliges everyone." But the most fascinating experience was last year when I split up with Travis who had been with me for four years. My mother knows Travis as my best friend. One night, my mother suddenly asked me whether I was very unhappy. I was really depressed at that time, so I didn't say a word. She then asked me, "Is it because of Travis?" I was shocked and didn't know how to respond. She knew that she caught me and said, "Don't think that I am dumb and blind, just because I didn't say anything. You two are a good couple, a good relationship needs lots of effort." I was speechless. Two days later, my mother called Travis for playing mahjong and now they still meet once or twice a month. I have separated with my boyfriend, but he maintains a smooth relationship with my mother. Isn't it amazing?

Tat-ming says that his mother accepts him because she does not see him as a gay man, but as a whole person in a concrete relationship. Tat-ming stresses that a parent would not reject her/his *tongzhi* child like they reject the concept *tongxinglian*. What his mother accepts is not *tongxinglian* per se but her son's specific relationship with Travis. It is crucial that Travis is someone she knows, likes, and relates to closely. For her, Travis is neither an outsider nor an abstract person called "gay"; Travis is a special friend of her son.

Rachel (aged 29) grew up in a working class background. She got a scholarship when she was 18 and went to Britain for three years. When she moved out to live with her partner Wu, her mother asked her: "What if you get old?" Then Rachel replied: "Wu and I will take care of each other, like ordinary people." After the long chat, her mother said, "You are who you are, but you don't have to tell other people. I would not tell my relatives, friends or your father. He cannot take it. He is so stubborn. I worry that you will be hurt." Her mother even reminded her that "You should find a Chinese friend, not a *gweilo!* (foreigner, especially Caucasian)." When Rachel met her present partner (Mandy), Rachel's mother asked: "Is she also this kind of person? I don't want you to waste time with those who are not. And don't make normal people go wrong."

Rachel has three siblings who have married or emigrated, only she lives with her parents and plays a very filial role. She said:

My parents always worry that no one will take care of them in their old age. My mother actually invited Mandy to live with us. Mandy is very good at pleasing the elderly, she is now part of my family. For example, she changed her schedule from going to the gym four times a week to having a morning walk with my parents. And she would drive my parents to see the fire-works at Ching-Ma Bridge, and sometimes give my Daddy a lift to work as they are in the same direction. My father is very proud of me. We don't directly talk about it, but I think they understand.

Tat-ming and Rachel's experiences illustrate a distinctive feature about these integrative strategies–*tongzhi* identity is integrated into the family, but it will not be spoken as such around the family table. The Chinese family, given its hegemonic cultural status, has an immense capacity to absorb certain troublesome and undesirable issues by making them invisible in words but, nevertheless, clearly understood by every family member. Rachel, who had an American girlfriend during her three-year study in UK, made an interesting remark:

It seems to be very high-tech in being Chinese when one should or should not say certain things which will be emotionally disturbing, especially to one's parents. It is not just about *tongzhi*, but all the sensitive issues. My mother clearly understands my situation, as she said: "Is she also this kind of person? I don't want you to waste time with those who are not. And don't make normal people go wrong." But we never say the word [*tongxing-lian*]. It is too visible and Western. It is ironic that she accepts my relationship with my girlfriend by making it disappear in words but it actually permeates in my actual relationship. I think it is both good and bad: I don't need to emphasize my sexual orientation, but neither can I mention it directly.

ESTABLISH GUANXI RATHER
THAN CONCEPTUAL ARGUMENT

James (aged 27) has lived with his boyfriend Xiao-liu (aged 29) in Beijing for three years. They live together with James' parents, brother, and his brother's wife. James experienced his first same-sex love with his school mate when they were both 17. After graduation, James went to university, and his lover went to work in a factory. Their relationship started to turn sour, and they finally split up. James was very hurt and thought that there was no prospect in loving a man. Four months later, James received a letter from Xiao-liu saying that he now had a girlfriend and was planning to get married. Towards the end of the letter he said: "Our previous relation is *biantai* (perverted). I am now converted to normality by the real love of my girlfriend. You should try to enjoy the love of women. Or maybe, you should see a doctor."

Obviously, the letter was devastating to James, especially at a time when he was still fantasizing about getting together again with this former classmate. That night, James drank two bottles of dish-washing liquid, together with 50 pills. He was unconscious for two days. James's best friend thought that James might pass away, and decided to tell James's parents the full story after being pressed by them desperately. James survives, but has serious stomach aches and kidney problems as a result.

Since then, James's parents have been very kind to him. They do not mention a word about *tongxinglian*. Even in recent years, rarely have they encouraged James to get married, which by Chinese standards is incredible as most Chinese in their 20s would be pressured to get married. James said:

> My parents seriously worry and care for my health. They prefer our family members to stay together so that we can take care of each other. I think my previous suicide attempt really scared them, and they would do everything to avoid it happening again. So when they feel that I really love Xiao-liu who is such a nice guy, they are quite happy. From their point of view, Xiao-liu is mature enough to take care of me, which is more preferable than me getting married and having to take care of my wife and the household. Another thing is, Xiao-liu works as a professional, he is very mature, and he is rich. . . . At first I only introduced Xiao-liu as a good friend of mine. Then he often came to visit me and have dinner together with my parents. He gets along very well with my parents. They would invite him to stay overnight if it is too late, I mean in the same bed with me. He gradually came to attend all our family dinners and became part of my family. Until two years ago when he changed to a new job where there is

no housing allocation for him, my mother simply invited him to move in! Isn't that cool! My parents treat him as their son, and never say a word about sex. I think it is better to come out by action than by words or arguments. I can't expect my parents to understand the concepts of *tongxinglian*. The terms "gay" and *tongxinglian* would be very scary for my parents as they would be associated with perversity and Western corruption. But they understand intimate *ganging* and *guanxi*, they accept Xiao-liu full not as a man but as an intimate friend."

James has thus manipulated "food" as a cultural marker to bring Xiao-liu into his family. As James said, "He gradually attends all our family dinners and becomes part of my family." James integrates sexuality into family life, not by confronting his parents, but by integrating Xiao-liu into his family's life. James manipulated the kin category in drawing Xiao-liu into becoming a quasi kin-member in his family. He also retains and develops his parents' cultural innocence and tolerance towards same-sex eroticism. Instead of provoking a debate on the status of *tongxinglian*, Xiao-liu establishes an intimate relationship with James's parents and literally lives with them.

The above mentioned strategies and cases are neither exhaustive, nor necessarily Chinese. Many lesbigays in other societies are using similar strategies to negotiate acceptance from and integration with the family. The above elucidation of *tongzhi* strategies should also not be mistaken as essentialist arguments for the so-called "Chinese culture." Indeed, the differences among various Chinese societies make any monolithic articulations of "Chinese culture" highly contestable. Different *tongzhi* have different needs and use different strategies to tackle their problems. *Tongzhi* is not a monolithic discourse. It is the complexity and diversity of their strategies of resistances that enrich the scenario of *tongzhi* resistance.

TONGZHI IDENTITY POLITICS AS QUEERING THE MAINSTREAM

While the situations in Taiwan, mainland China, and Hong Kong are each unique and different, I will use the case of the "Ten Great *Tongzhi* Dreamy Lovers Election" in Taiwan (1996) to exemplify the possibility of developing different strategies of coming out at the public and political level. The event was organized by a Taiwan *tongzhi* group, *TF (Tongzhi Front for Space Rights)*, which set up polling boxes in different *tongzhi* venues, listing twenty male and twenty female celebrities, politicians, and social figures for *tongzhi* to select as their dreamy lovers.

By incorporating mainstream celebrities into the *tongzhi* scene, *TF* no longer speaks from the outside as a marginalized group. Instead, it penetrates into the mainstream and challenges the apparent straightness of the straight world by *queering* mainstream celebrities. It is a deliberate move to queer the mainstream and challenge the rigid homo-hetero binarism of mainstream culture by selecting the most popular mainstream celebrities and politicians. Indeed, the mainstream media turned it into an interesting social event by interviewing the listed celebrities and reporting their responses, ranging from very homophobic to very positive reactions. Leslie Cheung, the famous movie star and singer, said that he was glad to know that he is welcomed by everyone irrespective of age, gender, and sexuality. Huang Lu Er, a famous Taiwan singer, who got the highest votes in the election, said *"Tongzhi* are no longer silent or trembling in the dark street corner. *Tongzhi* have come out courageously to say hello to anyone." The most homophobic response among the celebrity candidates was the male singer Zhong Han-Liang from Hong Kong. He said: "I am very angry, how can I be picked by *tongzhi*. I think I have to be more macho and masculine."

It is culturally significant that the most homophobic response among the celebrity candidates in this event comes from a person from Hong Kong, a place of 150 years of colonialism where Western homophobic hostility has become deep rooted. The Taiwan *tongzhi* were quick to tease Zhong by retorting: "If you were more macho and masculine, we would love you more!" *TF* also asked Taiwanese *tongzhi* to dress up in the rainbow colours from the 8th to the 14th of February: 8th in red (enlightenment), 9th in orange (reconciliation), 10th in yellow (sunlight), 11th in green (peace), 12th in blue (artistic), 13th in purple (spiritual), and 14th in rainbow colours (lesbigay liberation). The purpose was not to count the exact numbers of *tongzhi* but to exhibit visibility and collective power. Since thousands of citizens would coincidentally dress in red on the 8th, orange on the 9th, and so on, such an event problematized the stability of the straight identity by posing and simultaneously challenging the impossible question of who is and who is not *(tongzhi)*. At that time, it was not the *tongzhi* being put under the spotlight of the mainstream media's voyeurism. Instead, it was the general public dressing in the "rainbow colour" who have to engage with their own sexualities in an unprecedented way. The events of "Dreamy Lover Election" and "Rainbow Dressing" successfully created a social aura where discourses of homoerotic desire flowed everywhere and flirted with everyone. *TF* broke the rigid boundary between private and public by penetrating into each family through the newspaper, TV and other public media discussion about the celebrities' responses concerning homo-eroticism.

In recent years, the Taiwan *tongzhi* community has proposed the notion of *Ji ti xian xiang* (exposing collective identity), which is a kind of coming out as a collective rather than by showing individual faces. It is a strategy used in the specific context of Taiwan where the severe pressure to get married and the dominance of traditional Chinese values have made the model of coming out simply inappropriate for most Taiwan *tongzhi*.

The "Ten Great *Tongzhi* Dreamy Lovers Election" was just one small example of pursuing a more indigenous strategy of coming out and exhibiting visibility, not by confronting one's parents, but by coming out as an event. In such cases, it is really homoerotic desires, not any single person, that comes out and seduces the public. Homoeroticism is stirred up, and it becomes difficult to answer discreetly "who is and who is not." It is because of a focus on homoerotic desire, rather than a fixation on some minority persons, that it becomes a potential and a fantasy from which no one is immune. Homoeroticism goes beyond boundaries, not being the private property of a definite sexual minority. This event of "coming out" further exposes the absurdity of the rigid homo-hetero binarism that is always used by the straight world to "protect" themselves from homoeroticism. In the press conference for the "Dreamy Lovers Election," a non-*tongzhi* opened the polling boxes with more than 11,000 voting papers literally throwing them out in front of the reporters. He said, "People always said that they cannot see the existence of *tongzhi*. Now you see it, we are out and visible, by thousands of votes." In this event of collective coming out without personal exposure, Taiwan *tongzhi* indigenized and redefined the notion of visibility. They managed to go mainstream and seduce the public to engage with their own erotic desire: "Are you really as 100% straight as you may think you are?"

Instead of demanding that the sexual minority comes out and faces more severe oppression, the "Ten Great *Tongzhi* Dreamy Lovers Election" shifted the focus literally to every citizen to face his or her own sexuality. It implies a very different strategy of the *tongzhi* movement; it is no longer minority rights but majority's rights to reclaim the space to love beyond gender binarism. Instead of homo/bisexuals criticizing mainstream heterosexuals, which would then create and antagonize a heterosexually conscious majority, now *tongzhi* invite everyone–irrespective of their sexual orientation–to join them in exploring their own sexual desires. It implies a strategy going beyond the binarism between minority vs majority, gay vs straight, homo vs hetero, in order to envision and attain social harmony for everyone without losing the specificity of the *tongzhi's* identitiy and struggle.

Oppositional identity like homosexual, gay, or lesbian, despite its empowering impact, is produced and implicated in the very homo-hetero binary structure it claims to go beyond. Confrontational politics often reenact the homo-hetero binarism which produces the lesbigay's stigmatized position in the first place. Chu Wei-cheng, in his Ph.D thesis on Taiwan *tongzhi* discourse, concludes that:

> A metropolitan-style (gay) movement may after all require a metropolitan-styled homophobic oppression to provoke it. In other words, if the (gay) activism in question could achieve postcolonial autonomy by devoting meticulous attention to the specificity of local oppression and then devising effective interventionary strategies accordingly, it may well flourish without the local reproduction of an oppression as fierce as that in the metropolitan world (Chu, 1977: 259).

Indeed, the rigid homo-hetero binarism has historically been a strategy used by the straight world to "protect" itself from homoerotic flirtation by externalizing and projecting their own homoerotic anxiety onto the stigmatized minority. Perhaps we should remember the striking statement by Kate Millet twenty years ago: "Homosexuality was invented by a straight world dealing with it's own bisexuality" (Millet, 1975: 50).

If same-sex eroticism is not a private property of a stigmatized minority but a performance, an act, a social role, a possibility, and a potential that anyone can experience, then the imagined us-them dichotomy between gay-straight or homo-hetero and the concomitant homophobic enterprise immediately loses its solid foundation. It would imply a different strategy for liberation, not just the sexual liberation of homosexuals and bisexuals, but a *tongzhi* movement that invites everyone to explore their own eroticism beyond the homo-hetero binarism. The goal it is striving for ultimately is not a contractual and individualistic society where *tongzhi's* rights are observed by the heterosexual world only because of legal restrictions, but a society where it is simply unnecessary to stress one's sexuality, whatever it is. In this case, same-sex eroticism is no longer a minority issue but a basic human issue that concerns everyone and permeates every aspect of social life.

REFERENCES

Carbaugh, D. (1988). *Talking American*. Norwood, NJ: Ablex.

Cheng, Hao. (1934). *Renlai de Shenghuo (The Sexual Life of Human Beings)*. Shanghai: Yadong Shuju.

Chou Wah-shan, Anson Mak, and Daniel Kwong (Eds.). (1995). *Xianggang Tonqzhi Zhanchulai*. (Coming Out Stories of Hong Kong Tongzhi). Hong Kong: Hong Kong Queer Studies Forum.

Chu, Wei-cheng. (1997). *Homo and Other: Articulates Postcolonial Queer Subjectivity*. PhD Thesis, University of Sussex.

Dikotter, F. (1995). *Sex, Culture and Modernity in China*. Hong Kong: Hong Kong University Press. 145.

Hsu, F. (Ed.). (1953). *Americans and Chinese: Two Ways of Life*. New York: Abelard-Schuman.

Millett, Kate. (1975). *Flying*. Quoted in Wolff Charlottee, 1977. *Bisexuality*. London: Quartet Books.

Becoming a Gay Activist in Contemporary China

Wan Yanhai

LI JIANQUAN'S STORY

In 1994, events happened that stirred up a controversy among gay men in Beijing. Li Jianquan's story illustrates in a nutshell how far lesbian and gay life in China has come and how far it still has to go. On one hand, there is the rapid transformation under which many Chinese women and men who engage in homosexual behavior have also developed lesbian or gay identities and a knowledge of global lesbian and gay cultures. However, on the other, there are the contradictory and uncertain conditions particular to China under which we still live today and the difficulty of becoming visible and active. In the rest of this essay, I try to give a fuller background to Li Jianquan's story. I consider the entry of homosexuality into public debate in China, the legal circumstances concerning homosexuality in China, and the impact of AIDS on the development of gay culture. In the final part of the essay, I turn to my own story to give an account that illustrates in more detail and precision the effects of these Chinese circumstances on both my professional development into a gay activist and my psychological development.

In June of 1994, Li Jianquan, a Beijing delegate at the World Lesbian and Gay Conference in New York, made a widely reported speech (see for example, *Newsweek*). "In China, homosexuality is treated as illegal and as an illness," he told his audience. He added that homosexuality is also frequently the object of social discrimination,

This article was edited and translated by Chris Berry.

[Haworth co-indexing entry note]: "Becoming a Gay Activist in Contemporary China." Yanhai, Wan. Co-published simultaneously in *Journal of Homosexuality* (Harrington Park Press, an imprint of The Haworth Press, Inc.) Vol. 40, No. 3/4, 2001, pp. 47-64; and: *Gay and Lesbian Asia: Culture, Identity, Community* (ed: Gerard Sullivan, and Peter A. Jackson) Harrington Park Press, an imprint of The Haworth Press, Inc., 2001, pp. 47-64. Single or multiple copies of this article are available for a fee from The Haworth Document Delivery Service [1-800-342-9678, 9:00 a.m. - 5:00 p.m. (EST). E-mail address: getinfo@haworthpressinc.com].

and he called upon the international community to pay attention to the human rights of lesbians and gays in mainland China. Following this, Li applied for political asylum in the USA and announced that he was setting up "The Great Stonewall Society" to protect and promote the human rights of lesbians and gays in China.

In 1990, just before the Asian Games were held in Beijing, the police had taken in Li and some of his friends. According to his speech, no reason was given. After this, Li lost his job. In 1991, Li and some of his friends began to collect materials about attacks on lesbians and gays in China and the difficulties they faced. In 1993, they began to think about setting up what is now "The Great Stonewall Society."

The very reference to the New York riots of 1968 in the name of the group indicates clear knowledge of Western ideas and achievements. Indeed, it was with the help of Western human rights activists that Li contacted international lesbian and gay organizations, members of the Chinese democracy movement overseas, and international human rights organizations. This also led to the invitation to speak in New York in June of 1994. At the same time, the police began to investigate Li and his friends. Li left China quickly, and began a new life as an exile. He managed to escape, but his friends were followed, beaten, taken into custody, and driven out of their wits.

At the time, many members of the emergent gay community in Beijing were very critical of Li's speech in New York. Some said he was exaggerating, making China out to be much worse than it is. As has been noted in articles published outside China (Berry, 1996; Richardson, 1995), the last few years have seen the development of a considerable semi-public culture of cruising zones, unadvertised gay bars and restaurants, gay corners in discos, and so forth, as well as the efforts of social movement activists discussed in further detail below. Some said Li had tied the lesbian and gay cause too closely to political liberation. Others said that his public work was too mixed up with his personal aims and that maybe he was only doing this so that he could represent himself as a persecuted political activist and could thus stay in the U.S.

However, not long after, Li's pronouncements were proved correct when the Beijing police carried out a thorough crackdown on gay meeting places, arresting many gay men between August and December 1994. This made it impossible to tell whether Li had been forced to flee by the police's actions or whether Li's speech had angered our government. However, it was hard for anyone to criticize Li Jianquan again after this, and he became a hero to the local Beijing gay community.

FROM TABOO TO OPEN DISCUSSION

Li Jianquan's story indicates that the situation in China is complex and that many people there are still uncertain of their status. Perhaps this is not surprising when one remembers that until recently the entire topic of homosexuality was totally taboo. China's laws, mass media, and scientific reports never even mentioned homosexuality. Chinese people had very few opportunities to read foreign or ancient Chinese documents. If anyone was reported for homosexual behavior, they faced lengthy jail terms. During those times when the ordinary people of China were completely ignorant of homosexuality, we have no way of knowing how many misunderstandings and personal tragedies occurred. All lesbians and gays were effectively forced to lead double lives, and the great bulk of the rest of the population were unaware of their very existence.

This situation began to change when Deng Xiaoping and his followers ascended to power in the late 1970s. They introduced two main policy directions. One is known by the umbrella title of "reform" (*gaige*). It consists of a roll back of state control through the command economy in an effort to stimulate production through the development of a parallel market economy. Some people used the opportunities created by this loosening of central control to break away from their old lives, leaving family and friends and moving to new cities or even overseas in an effort to find a space of their own. As time went by, it also made it much easier to publish articles, organize public seminars, and so forth.

The second main policy direction consists of China's opening up to the outside world. After a long period of isolation, this led to an influx of all kinds of publications and other materials from overseas. Over the last decade and more, two forces have emerged as consistently useful in helping to raise the profile of Chinese lesbians and gays. One is the interest of groups and individuals outside China, and the other is the work of scholars, who can appear in the public eye as objective, fair-minded people with foresight.

As Chinese traveled outside and foreigners came in, the situation of Chinese lesbians and gays gradually became known to the outside world (Bullough & Ruan, 1993; Ruan, Bullough, & Tsai, 1989; Ruan & Chong, 1987; Ruan & Tsai, 1988). At the same time, the international lesbian and gay movement boosted the courage of Chinese lesbians and gays in demanding liberation. The International Lesbian and Gay Association, Amnesty International, and other human rights organizations have continuously brought their influence to bear on the Chinese government. Organizations concerned with AIDS, such as the World Health Organization, have also influenced the policies of this country towards gay men, and, in particular, towards public health policy. In the early nineties, for example, I witnessed the WHO negotiate successfully with the Chinese Ministry of Public Health for the inclusion of safe-sex education for men who have sex with men to be included as part of the country's medium-term plan on AIDS. And during the time of the International Women's Conference in Beijing in 1995, lesbian organizations were permitted to enter China, which without doubt promoted further improvements in the attitude of this country towards lesbians and gays.

As for the second major force helping to raise the profile of Chinese lesbians and gays, Chinese scholarly interest in homosexuality originated in the field of psychology. In 1981, the psychological health specialist Zhang Mingyuan wrote an article on homosexuality in the classical Chinese novel *A Dream of Red Mansions* for the Shanghai magazine *Mass Medicine.* Zhang wrote that homosexuality was extremely odd but that science had yet to make a final decision on whether or not it was an illness. This article did not mention whether or not there were lesbians and gays in China today, and, at that time, ordinary Chinese people certainly did not know that there were lesbians and gays in contemporary China. However, this essay was probably the first contemporary public discussion of homosexuality in China. Shanghai psychologist Liu Dalin told me in 1994 that the author received letters from more than one hundred lesbians and gay men in response.

As scientific and scholarly exchange proceeded during the 1980s, the existence of homosexuality became more widely known, and it became a topic of debate. One point of view believed homosexuality was a sickness from which people needed to be saved. The other felt that homosexuality was a natural part of humanity and that it should be treated equally. In 1985, the sexologist Ruan Fangfu wrote an essay under the pseudonym Hua Jinma entitled "Homosexuality: an Unsolved Puzzle" in *Good Health* magazine, later republished in the Chinese magazine, *Reader's Digest*. He wrote that homosexuality was legitimate and that it should not be subject to persecution, and he also pointed out that many lesbians and gays existed in contemporary Chinese society.

However, during the late 1980s, homosexuality was increasingly criticized as part of a larger move towards social conservatism, manifested for example in the movements against bourgeois liberalization and to prevent "peaceful evolution" (from socialism back to capitalism). This led to homosexuality being seen as a form of degeneracy found amongst Westerners and those Chinese influenced by the West, and it became an object of public condemnation. In his book *Critique of Sexual Freedom*, Liu Dalin stressed that it was reasonable that lesbians and gays should be subject to "the punishment of society." However, during this period, a few doctors also persisted in trying to help lesbians and gays by treating them medically as opposed to advocating punishment. For example, Dr. Liu Zhenni wrote an essay published in *Popular Health News* which called for helping lesbians and gays and which opposed moral punishment or accusations of criminality against them.

Entering the 1990s, the 1989 Democracy Movement was not able to block completely the concerns of the Chinese people, and especially the educated classes, for people less well off than themselves. The spread of AIDS and sexually transmitted diseases further stimulated the scholarly world to pay attention to homosexuality. Ironically, it also gave scholars a good reason for paying attention to homosexuality. Otherwise, people would have been worried that others would interrogate them about why they were not studying some other issue of major importance, but instead were focusing on a problem that few cared about and that was also morally dubious. Seminars, discussions, salons, psychological counseling hotlines and clinics, radio programs, and magazine articles have all helped to improve the understanding of homosexuality in our country enormously, and they have also influenced the policies of our government and legislators.

With this vast increase in public visibility and discussion, the existence of individual articles on aspects of homosexuality has become commonplace. However, the publication of three monographs devoted to the subject is noteworthy. In November of 1992, sociologists Li Yinhe and Wang Xiaobo published a study of gay male life in Beijing called *Their World*. In February of 1992, Zhang Beichuan's 700-page survey of materials from the ancient to the modern, the Western to the Chinese, and the medical to the cultural, entitled *Homosexuality,* came out. And in June of 1995, Fang Gang's *Homosexuality in China* was published.

PROBLEMS WITH THE LAW

Although homosexuality has gone from complete invisibility to widespread discussion in the mass media in a dozen years or so, only a very few lesbians and gay men feel able to come out yet. To understand why so few feel safe, we must investigate the law as it concerns lesbians and gay men in China and its impact upon their social status. Given a history where lesbians and gay men were not supposed to exist together combined with the ongoing critical debate about homosexuality, perhaps it is not surprising that the law is unclear and applied in many different ways. Also, the law has affected men and women differently. This is partly because some of the main statutes used against those who engage in homosexual behavior are those concerned with sodomy, which is not usually considered to concern women, and partly because in Chinese society, until recently, many people have not considered women to be agents of sexual desire at all.

However, at least as important as differences in the application of the law according to gender is an overall vagueness and lack of clarity concerning the status of lesbians and gays in relation to the law in China. The position of the lesbian or gay in mainland Chinese society is much the same as that of the "bad element" during the "Cultural Revolution." There is no law explicitly stating that homosexuality is illegal, but all kinds of criminal and administrative punishments have been and are applied against them.

Up until the 1980s, the moment homosexuality became visible, even if no illegal behavior was involved, the people involved were often sentenced to ten or more years imprisonment. In extremely serious cases, such as those concerning homosexual behavior between high school teachers and students, the sentence was sometimes life. For example, in 1975, a Beijing middle school teacher named Wang was sentenced to life in prison for having had a relationship with a male student (Ms. Zha Jianying of the Chicago Social Psychology Center, personal communication, March 31, 1993. Ms. Zha was Mr. Wang's neighbor and a former student of his at primary school level).

After the 1980s and especially the mid-eighties, as the scholarly and public debate mentioned above developed, homosexuality ceased to be subject to such serious punishment. However, its precise legal status remains unclear. This is from item 254 on page 188 of the *Criminal Law Handbook*, edited by the Criminal Law Office of the Working Party on the Law of the National People's Congress Standing Committee and published by the People's Court Press in January of 1994:

> Q: In the case of sodomy, what crime does one convict on and what is the punishment?
>
> A: In regard to what crime one convicts on and what the punishment is for sodomy, there are no clear stipulations in the criminal law. On the 25th of May 1984, the Law and Politics Committee of the Dalian City Council asked the Working Party on the Law's opinion on this matter. Following research, the opinion of the Criminal Law Office of the Working Party on the Law was as follows: this matter has been researched in the drafting of criminal law. Although this behavior is certainly harmful, it is not appropriate that it be listed as a crime in itself. This type of behavior can usually be dealt with administratively, but in serious cases criminal responsibility can be investigated under the terms of the crime of hooliganism.

This was an internally circulated opinion, to be referred to only by law enforcement agencies in the process of dealing with a case. However, the reply of the Criminal Law Office of the Working Party on the Law of the National People's Congress Standing Committee did not say whether or not homosexuality itself was illegal.

On November 2, 1984, the People's Supreme Court and the People's Supreme Procuratorate stipulated, in "An Explanation Concerning Certain Problems Currently Encountered in the Specific Application of the Law in Handling Cases of Hooliganism" ("84" Legal Research Notes, Item 13), that "sodomising children, forced sodomy of adolescents, the use of violence or force, multiple partner acts of sodomy, and severe cases" constituted the crime of hooliganism.

Back in 1987, during the wave of social conservatism that prevailed at the end of the 1980s, the Head of the Shanghai Municipal Committee on the Determination of the Administration of Psychiatric Justice, Zheng Zhanpei, made a clear reaffirmation concerning the administration of criminal justice in regard to homosexuality:

> because homosexuality violates public morality and therefore disturbs public order and affects the physical and mental health of young people, it clearly constitutes criminal behavior. (Zhang, B., 1994: 633)

In 1992 and 1993, signs of a period of relative tolerance of homosexuality appeared in China. The Chinese Public Security Bureau dropped the case against two lesbians charged with cohabitation, on the grounds that "under the present circumstances in our country where the law has no explicit regulations on what homosexuality is and what criminal responsibility may pertain, the situation you have reported cannot, on principle, be accepted to be heard as a legal case, and it is not appropriate that this should be submitted for legal punishment as an instance of hooliganism."

Despite this improvement, however, in an authoritarian country where the law is not impartial, the rights of lesbians and gays as human beings are repeatedly encroached on, especially during social crackdowns. Particular areas of concern can be specified and examples given.

First, in the midst of the ever greater amount of public discussion and debate around sexuality in general, there continue to be government-supported and public rejections of the rights of lesbians and gays. For example, between September and November of 1994, the National Exhibition on Sexual Health Education was held in Beijing at the China Science and Technology Information Center and later went on to tour the country. The text of the exhibition declared that homosexuality was a sickness, and that "promoting equal sexual rights for homosexuals and heterosexuals" was an expression of bourgeois "sexual license." The exhibition was also opposed to the individual possessing the right to sexual freedom.

Similarly, homosexuality and AIDS are often equated publicly even though, to this day, the Chinese government has not explicitly acknowledged the existence of lesbians and gays in China. For instance, an article by Zhao Zhonglong, in the July 1994 issue of *Health World,* lable to face their colleagues. For example, a friend of mine named Xiao Liu was recently expelled after years of training as a Beijing Opera performer after he was discovered having an affair with another student in the academy. His opera career in ruins, he now works on the Beijing metro.

Finally, lesbians and gay men are placed under a lot of pressure from their families to marry. On the basis of an informal survey I carried out in 1993 in Beijing, I estimate that over 90 percent of lesbians and gay men in mainland China have lived as heterosexuals or bisexuals. Living like this places them under great stress and many leave their families to become drifters or commit suicide.

In addition to family pressure, Chinese lesbians and gays feel pressured to marry because of the housing situation. Most people's housing is assigned by the state, which acts on the assumption that people live with their parents or in communal dormitories attached to their places of work until they are married. Generally speaking, it is impossible to get individual housing assigned as a single person. In a situation where there is no recognition of lesbian and gay partnerships, this makes it very difficult for most lesbians and gays to form long lasting relationships where they can live together with their partner.

AIDS EDUCATION AND GAY CULTURE

Li Jianquan's story, given at the beginning of this article, illustrates the particular difficulties and dangers of pursuing gay issues under the rubric of human rights, which is the subject of great political sensitivity in China. However, as indicated above, scholarly work is somewhat safer, and so it is not surprising that AIDS education has emerged as a particularly fruitful site for the development of gay culture. Nonetheless, as my own involvement in this work illustrates, this is also not without its vicissitudes, which are a concrete manifestation of the contradictions and ambiguities operating in China today and outlined above.

In January 1991, a project entitled "Investigation into the Knowledge, Beliefs, Attitudes and Behavior of Gay Men and AIDS Education Research" was set up in the China Health Education Institute. This Institute is an organization under the command of the Ministry of Public Health, and I had been working there since my graduation from Shanghai Medical College in 1988. It was decided that the head of the institute, Chen Bingzhong, would be in overall charge and would be responsible for social effects and all possible outcomes. I was to be second in charge, responsible for the design, implementation, and summing up of the project.

At the same time, the National AIDS Monitoring Center decided to launch research into the epidemic. Gu Xueqi of the Shanghai Health Education Institute volunteered to carry out surveys and distribute materials in Shanghai. Sexologist Pan Suiming took part in the early stages of the project. Sociologist Li Yinhe (one of the authors of *Their World*) volunteered to help mobilize people to work with us. The comrades in the Prohibitions Section of the Social Public Order Department of the Beijing Public Security Bureau (i.e., the police) offered their support and participation in our research.

Despite all this support and cooperation, I knew that this was a formidable subject to take on. In 1985, Da Dan of the Nanjing Railways Medical Institute had committed suicide because of his research concerning homosexuality, when he and two other researchers were asked to come in by the Public Security Bureau. In 1986, Zhao Min of East China Normal University in Shanghai had been subpoenaed six times by the Public Security because of his research into the treatment of homosexuality. The grounds given were that he had used videos in which people had appeared naked in the preparation of his treatment materials. At the end of 1990, I and Chen Yiyun had been criticized by a cadre in the Party branch for encouraging red light districts. This was because during our research into female sex workers, we had expressed sympathy for them and protested against crude crackdowns carried out against them.

Those of us working on the project had a few tacit understandings. We should not be gay, nor should we develop such a tendency during our research. We referred to gays as "them," and assumed that they were different from "us," alienated from society, that they might try to recruit "us," and that they were difficult to deal with. We assumed that our research project was in the public interest, and that it was also conducted with good intentions towards gays and, indeed, that it had to be in their interest. We discussed all kinds of research methods, but did not see gays as people who we could become friendly with. Our thinking was still caught between the new openness in China and the prejudices and fears of the past.

We also assumed that there were many secret police at gay meeting places and amongst gay circles and that our work would run into difficulties. We assumed that we had to have the support of the Public Security Bureau or at least their tacit permission for this research and education project to proceed smoothly. We were probably correct on this point, but the question of how to secure the support of the Public Security Bureau was even more important. The police officer responsible for dealing with us was very welcoming, and he welcomed research into social problems. However, because we were not familiar with each other and had not worked together a lot before, the following mistakes were made.

In April of 1991, some of the people involved in the research project held a work meeting. When talking about how to make contact with the gay community, everyone seemed to hold back as though none of us were too familiar with the situation. Then the police officer spoke. He suggested the police should take the gay men in, and then the researchers could do surveys and take blood samples for testing. He said the officers at the Mintong police station in the eastern district of Beijing were particularly experienced in taking in "rabbits" (*tuzi*, Beijing slang for gay men), and he estimated that they could probably get a dozen or more in one evening.

This shocked me, because we were not allowed to harm our research subjects in the course of our research. This was already written into the report on our project, and it is a basic rule in social research. But it was difficult for me to reject this suggestion because I was worried about damaging our new working relationship with the police. Therefore, I asked the social psychologists taking part in the meeting whether or not this suggestion could be taken up. One scholar expressed satisfaction with the idea. He said there was no problem with this method, because the police were simply doing their public duty, and we were taking advantage of the opportunity it afforded us to carry out our research. It was not as though the police were taking people in because we wanted to do our research.

I will never forget that meeting for the rest of my life. I felt very bad. Our aim was to help people, not to harm them. We were eager, but because of our lack of experience and our equivocal attitudes, we blindly went along with the habits of the police. I rationalized it to myself, saying that although this action would harm people and have bad effects, at least we might gain a better understanding of the circumstances and establish a good relationship with the Public Security

Bureau. Between May and July of 1991, I went through two unforgettable months. I spent three nights every week during that period at the Mintong police station in the eastern district. We worked hard with great willingness to help people, but they were harmed. The first evening, I felt so bad I did not want to go on. At the end of the first day's work, two of our assistants resigned. These two social psychology students said we were being fascist. At the end of the second day's work, I also demanded that we stop. That evening, an engineer in his sixties who had been detained had knelt before everyone weeping and saying that he was worthless. I feel a deep responsibility for what happened and cannot forgive myself even now.

In September of 1991, the World Health Organization held an AIDS Social Research Conference in Jinan at which I introduced our work and started to call for equality for lesbians and gays. Afterwards, someone in my work unit attacked me for supporting sexual freedom and liberation, but we pressed on. In November of the same year, a National AIDS Advice Workshop was held in Beijing. I chaired it and took charge of editing and translating the teaching materials. Letters attacking me were written the central authorities, to the Ministry of Public Health, and to the Institute's leaders.

Institute head Chen Bingzhong gave me a great deal of support and greater powers to initiate work myself. In January of 1992, we established a small group to begin working on an AIDS hotline, which opened on April 7th. On May 24th, our AIDS hotline counselors went to Dongdan Park in Beijing to carry out AIDS education work, handing out leaflets and brochures. We did this again seven or eight times in August. At first, people did not understand what we were doing and were even afraid of us, but later they actively sought out our materials and chatted with us. All this was reported in a feature article by Guo Jianyan in *China Youth News*, which also said lesbians and gays were like other people and should be treated fairly (Guo, 1992). A great deal more coverage followed, and I began to write articles myself.

In October of 1992, we held five meetings of a discussion group for gay men as part of our AIDS hotline activities. Attendance was highly variable. We discovered that discussing AIDS was not an opportunity for gay men, but that they found that it placed pressure upon them and inspired despair. So, on November 22nd we held the first meeting of the "Men's World" discussion group for gay men. This activity was soon reported on Chinese national radio, and following that, by other national and international media. For example, reports appeared in the *People's Daily* (*Renmin Ribao*), in *New World* (*Xin Shijie*) magazine (1993: 2), and on the BBC, Radio Australia, and Radio China. Other hotlines and discussion groups were set up in Shanghai, Kunming, and Shenyang in the following months. On February 14th 1993, Men's World held a Valentine's Day event at the Seahorse Ballroom at Xidan in Beijing. We distributed Valentine's Day cards and condoms. When this got into the media in March, the story was soon picked up and reported all over the country. Items appeared in *China Daily* on February 16, 1993, in *The Economic Evening News* (*Jingji Wanbao*) on March 31, 1993, and also in *Beijing Youth News* (*Beijing Qingnian Bao*), *The Consumer Times* (*Xiaofei Shibao*), *China Women's News* (*Zhongguo Funü Bao*), and in the reports of the China News Agency (*Zhongguo Xinwenshe*). This was probably the last straw for the authorities.

On May 10th of 1993, the Party organization in the Ministry of Public Health decided to stop my hotline work and to ban the Men's World discussion group. They criticized us for supporting homosexuality and human rights and for sympathizing with female sex workers in published articles, and they criticized Chen Bingzhong for having supported my work and my point of view. On August 10th, Chen Bingzhong was recalled from his position as head of the institute and asked to retire. During this time, the Central Propaganda Ministry criticized lesbians and gays and our work at several meetings, lumping lesbians and gays together with murderers, arsonists, poisoners, and drug pushers.

However, taking advantage of the new opportunities afforded by China's relative openness to the outside world and the development of autonomous non-governmental spheres of activity during the past decade and more, we had applied to the Elizabeth Taylor AIDS Foundation for support for AIDS work amongst gay men. In September of 1993, we heard that our application had been successful, and we were granted US$10,000 for our work. This proved to be a lifeline for me, too. For, in October of 1993, the new head of the Institute accused me of running up the flag of science as a front to carry out political activities opposing bureaucratism and corruption. He refused to sympathize with female sex workers and lesbians and gays, demanding to know what difference there was between lesbians and gays and murderers, arsonists, drug peddlers, and thieves. He demanded that I change my position and act together with him to eliminate homosexuals. Of course, I refused. My wages were reduced to 40% of their original level. From February 21 to March 1 of 1994, I was sent to work in Kunming. No reason was given. I have heard an order came from the Ministry of Public Health.

I returned to Beijing to visit relatives in March, and, at the same time, the funds arrived from the Elizabeth Taylor AIDS Foundation. We began work, continuing the activities we had carried out before in the Institute, but now as a non-government organization. In May, our AIDS Action newsletter was set up, and its distribution has helped us to establish a nationwide network of contacts and co-workers throughout the country.

COMING OUT IN CONTEMPORARY CHINA

From this previous section, you will have gathered that I had not publicly come out during my time at the China Health Education Institute. Indeed, my ability to carry out my activities there was dependent upon being in the closet. However, it went further than that. I was not at all sure of my sexuality at the time. So far, this article has focused on the public and material manifestations of gay culture in China and the various overdeterminations upon it, including a whole range of factors making it difficult for gay men and lesbians to come out or acknowledge their sexuality. However, it seems important to consider the personal and psychological effects of these unstable, contradictory, and rapidly changing circumstances. Therefore, I would like to close this article by recalling some of my own personal history.

For a long time, I did not seem to need to classify myself. In fact, it may well be that things really were like that. However, in a homophobic culture, this also made it appear that I was covering something up or that I lacked courage. I felt that refusing to classify myself was not helping me to stop thinking about my sexual orientation at all. In fact, it grew to the point where my personal life came to a halt, and I lost all capacity for happiness.

When I was studying in Shanghai in the early and mid-eighties, I was particularly eager to gain a better understanding of sexuality, partly due to youthful enthusiasm and partly because I was going through a great deal of mental anguish myself. Descriptions of homosexuality that I found were negative and medicalizing. In 1985, I bought a copy of the *Handbook of Sexual Knowledge*, edited by Ruan Fangfu, and read it together with my classmates in the dormitory, totally disregarding our examinations.

Afterwards, I continued to develop my understanding of homosexuality through reading books and articles and in class. Much of the information was very well meant, saying that although homosexuality was abnormal or deviant, it was not evil and it could be treated. In 1986, a Shanghai newspaper disclosed the location of gay public meeting places in an article I happened to spot. I was very curious and wanted to go take a look, but I did not, nor did this cause me to think about myself. During 1989 and 1990, when I was working as a volunteer for a psychological advice hotline, I sometimes handled calls from lesbians and gays. At first, most of these conversations concerned how to correct homosexuality or how to avoid being drawn by one's feelings. However, later, we spoke about how loving someone could not be seen as the same as hating someone, so why was it necessary to change? However, to connect myself with homosexuality still produced terror for me.

As I have just explained, I started to deal with sex education for gay men in 1991. I did not see myself as a gay man and told myself I should not get involved in gay life while I was doing my research. However, while meeting with gay men, I was also analyzing myself. I discovered that I did have gay feelings, hoped to be able to get rid of them, and tried to persuade myself that I was heterosexual.

Later, when I had the opportunity to speak about more personal things with friends, I acknowledged that my feelings were bisexual, but with heterosexual feelings predominating. However, I still did not dare to speak of sexual experiences. Homosexuality was still terrifying to me personally, and I was very uncomfortable.

Finally, in mid-December of 1994, by which time I was working completely independently of the China Health Education Institute, I told someone else about my own homosexual and heterosexual experiences for the first time. The other person was an academic who was studying the lives of single people. He had asked to interview me, and I told him almost everything. After breaking the taboo, I told more people about my gay experiences and my terror. As I spoke, I found I changed.

THINGS ARE STILL FAR FROM PERFECT

A final note of caution. I remember an Australian friend's words at a seminar on homosexuality held in Beijing on September 8, 1992. "I'm very happy that the existence of lesbians and gays is being acknowledged," he said. "In fact, this is also inevitable. Or maybe I should say that although the enthusiasm of everyone attending this seminar may not necessarily reflect the general situation prevailing throughout China, it does make me feel that it is unlikely that any anti-lesbian and gay laws or severe punishments will appear in China." I still remember that time as one of great political tolerance.

In 1994, first in Tianjin, then in Shanghai and Beijing, large scale arrests and detentions of gay men occurred. In 1995, during the UN Women's Conference in Beijing, lesbians from all over the world held meetings, went on trips together, and celebrated together. But China's lesbians remained silent, and China's gay men continued to be harassed. In August 1996, a Beijing writer came to interview me prior to traveling to Australia.

> Everything that is happening in China at the moment is very worrying, he said. Maybe one day someone will speak out against lesbians and gays, attacking lesbians and gays, and they may even be defended and encouraged by people in positions of influence.

Indeed, I recall a fervent nationalist railing against lesbians and gays not long ago. He said, "We won't have homosexuality in China! We should eliminate homosexuals!" Of course, these nationalists also attack the protection of human rights, democracy, and freedom.

REFERENCES

Berry, C. (1996). East Palace, West Palace: Beijing Begins to Come Out. *Outrage, 136* (May), 38-40.

Bullough, V. L. & Ruan, F. (1993). *Same-Sex Love in Contemporary China*. In A. Hendriks, R. Tielman, & E. van der Veen (Eds.), *The Third Pink Book: A Global View of Lesbian and Gay Liberation and Oppression*. Buffalo, NY: Prometheus Books. 46-53.

Fang, G. (1995). *Homosexuality in China (Tongxinglian zai Zhongguo)*. Changchun: Jilin People's Press *(Jilin Renmin Chubanshe)*. Hong Kong edition published by Cosmos Books *(Tiandi Tushu Youxian Gongsi)*.

Guo, J. (1992). AIDS–The Second Decade: Report from the AIDS Helpline (*Aizibing–Dierge Shinian: Lai Aizibing Qiuzhu Rexian de Baodao*). *China Youth News (Zhongguo Qingnian Bao)* 3. 29 August.

Hua, J. (1985). Homosexuality: an Unsolved Riddle (*Tongxinglian–Yige Mojue zhi Mi*). *Good Health (Zhu Nin Jiankang)*, 3, 14-15. Reprinted in *Reader's Digest (Duzhe Wenzhai)*, 1985 (11).

Li, Y. & Wang, X. (1992). *Their World: A Perspective on China's Gay Male Community (Tamen de Shijie: Zhongguo Nantongxinglian Qunluo Toushi)*. Taijuan: Shanxi People's Press (*Shanxi Renmin Chubanshe*). Hong Kong edition published by Cosmos Books (*Tiandi Tushu Youxian Gongsi*).

Liu, D. (1989). *Critique of Sexual Freedom (Xing Ziyou Pipan)*.

Liu, Z. (1987). Save Homosexuals (*Zhengjiu Tongxinglian*). *Popular Health News (Dazhong Weishengbao)*.

Richardson, P. (1995). Subcultural Revolution. *Attitude* February), 68-74.

Ruan, F. (1985). *Handbook of Sexual Knowledge (Xing Zhishi Shouce)*. Beijing: Science and Technology Literature Press (*Kexue Jishu Wenxian Chubanshe*).

Ruan, F., Bullough, V. L., & Tsai, Y. (1989). Male Transsexualism in Mainland China. *Archives of Sexual Behavior 18*(6), 517-522.

Ruan, F. & Chong, K. R. (1987). Gay Life in China. *The Advocate,* 470 (14 April) 28-31, 14.

Ruan, F. & Tsai, Y. (1988). Male Homosexuality in Contemporary Mainland China. *Archives of Sexual Behavior, 17*(2), 189-199.

Yangtze Development News (Changjiang Kaifa Bao). (1992). Our Country's Police Become Involved in a Law Case Concerning for the First Time (Woguo Jingfang Shouci Jieru Tongxinglian Anjian. 29 February.

Zhang, B. (1994). *Homosexuality (Tongxinglian)*. Jinan: Shandong Science and Technology Press (*Shandong Kexue Jishu Chubanshe*).

Zhang, M. (1981). Homosexual Phenomena in *A Dream of Red Mansions (Honglou Zhong de Tongxinglian Xianxiang)*. *Mass Medicine (Dazhong Yixue)*, (5), 42-44.

Zhao, Z. (1994). The Homosexual Disaster (*Tongxinglian Zaixing*). *Health World (Jiankang Shijie)*, 7, 6-7.

Mapping the Vicissitudes of Homosexual Identities in South Korea

Seo Dong-Jin

In the past few years, many have received a shock as homosexuality has been, for the first time, discussed openly in Korea.[1] Now, or one might say, at last, discussions of homosexuality can be held regularly. Indeed, Korean society has, in the past few years, become accustomed to discussions concerning homosexuality or homosexuals. It is as if the intellectual climate concerning homosexuals has turned to spring, and, with the thawing forces of spring, a torrent of discussions concerning homosexuals has appeared. In colleges, among intellectual organizations, and in the mass media, homosexual issues are being brought up.

I would like to take a look at what is behind the perplexing speed and strength of this new trend. It seems to me that the sudden increase in discussions concerning homosexuality is completely unrelated to the process of coming to terms with the ultimate significance of homosexuality. Of course, many people, in looking at the sudden increase in these discussions, think that Korean society is attaining a somewhat "better" or "correct" understanding of homosexuality. Many believe that more truths have been revealed concerning this issue. They imagine that as terms are batted about in the ongoing discussion, the truth concerning homosexuality will magically become clear.

This article was translated by Mark Mueller.

[Haworth co-indexing entry note]: "Mapping the Vicissitudes of Homosexual Identities in South Korea." Dong-Jin, Seo. Co-published simultaneously in *Journal of Homosexuality* (Harrington Park Press, an imprint of The Haworth Press, Inc.) Vol. 40, No. 3/4, 2001, pp. 65-79; and: *Gay and Lesbian Asia: Culture, Identity, Community* (ed: Gerard Sullivan, and Peter A. Jackson) Harrington Park Press, an imprint of The Haworth Press, Inc., 2001, pp. 65-79. Single or multiple copies of this article are available for a fee from The Haworth Document Delivery Service [1-800-342-9678, 9:00 a.m.–5:00 p.m. (EST). E-mail address: getinfo@haworthpressinc.com].

I would like to counter this fallacy. In so doing, I would like to bring forth the following objections to such a view. Although homosexuality exists in modern-day Korean society, it seems to be an entity whose meaning has been endlessly deferred. Paradoxically, one might say that in Korean society, "homosexuality" is a term without its own referent. The term seems to be used as a locus for the selves contained within sexuality which have had no opportunity for self-reflection. I call myself a homosexual and consider myself to be in possession of a homosexual identity. However, "homosexuality" and "homosexual identity" are differentiated by the constant occurrence of certain "incidents." The meaning of a term must possess endurance and repetition. Although they do not represent some fixed reality, homosexuality and homosexual identity must represent some truth that can be agreed upon. In modern Korean society, however, homosexuality does not seem to be "that love whose name one dare not utter" but rather "that love whose name does not refer to anything."

In my opinion, homosexuality, caught up in the suffocating pace of change affecting Korean society, is a symptom of the times. Obviously, it is not some isolated, individual monad. To the contrary, homosexuality is intertwined with the complex historical contexts of Korean sexuality, which has not been the subject of widespread conscious exploration and reflection.

My duty as a writer who must venture to describe homosexuality in Korean society is somewhat daunting. Unable to effectively describe any definitive object, it is as if I must bring to light some wispy phantom that I only know through its effects. Yet, I must still attempt to do so, for this must be discussed openly. After all, homosexuality possesses its own identity, and for myself and other homosexuals, who have confessed to our awareness of this identity, the one thing that is clear is how homosexuality has brought on the experience of unhappiness. Thus I must write this, for I feel that it is necessary that I, and many other homosexuals, must speak of homosexuality–the reason for our unhappiness–if we are ever to overcome this unhappiness.

In Korea, homosexuality does not have any social existence. That is to say, in public discourse aimed at forming the laws and regulations governing Korean society, homosexuality is not mentioned. In Korea, the "civil rights" of homosexuals are not threatened on account of their homosexuality. This is not due to tolerance of homosexuals. To the contrary, it is because they are not seen as representing members of the society who can exercise the power to effect social changes. In other words, their existence is ignored.

In modern society, whether it is the West or the Third World and regardless of the particular social formation, each social group, as the object of state regulations and controls, has at least had its existence defined negatively. In many societies, discourse concerning laws has defined how homosexuals in particular see themselves, and in accordance with the way they have been treated, they have developed their sense of themselves as an autonomous group. In other words, the way something is governed affects our understanding of it. However, this is not to say that homosexuals have continuously formed their identities exclusively through external pressures. Yet, it is true that through any form of government control and legal regulations, homosexuals have the opportunity to see themselves as a recognized group and by means of counter-discourse, they obtain the possibility of resistance. However, in Korean society, national or public authorities do not, strictly speaking, differentiate homosexuals.

In spite of this, homosexuals consider their lives to be painful. Although they do not exist as a significant social reality, they are, nonetheless, existential entities who suffer precisely because of their homosexuality. No matter what anyone says, it is clear that in our society, homosexuality is the cause of discontent. As a result, a "homosexual existence" implies change and resistance–a struggle for a better life. However, when social discourse claims that one does not exist, or in other words, when one is coerced into remaining a non-social entity, how does one effect changes regarding homosexuality issues? If a homosexual movement is only possible on the basis of a collective subjectivity, how do homosexuals form a significant social identity? How do they form the basis for a progressive communicative situation regarding homosexuality? How do Korean lesbians, gays, and other sexual minorities create a normative foundation for a brighter future?

As a progressive homosexual intellectual who has "come out" in Korean society, and as a critical homosexual who demands a better life for lesbians and gays, I believe that the above questions are of utmost importance. Below, I will describe Korean homosexuals and homosexuality in an attempt to provide some answers to these questions. Yet, it must be kept in mind that my description will not be entirely accurate. Even so, by putting together the array of homosexual identities in Korea, I hope to describe the cleavage between these identities. In order to do this, I will first attempt to map out the definitions utilized in this endeavor.

In Korean society, there are no official documents about homosexuality or related topics. Although some sources found in ancient or medieval Korean history suggest homosexual acts, these sources represent nothing more than historical footnotes, and even these brief accounts are exceedingly rare. In particular, there are no sources showing a significant link between the numerous social changes affecting Korea as it has transformed into a capitalist society and the emergence of a gay identity. Moreover, apart from the issue of homosexuality's significance, there has not even been an important person who has been able to unify the sexual identity of Korean homosexuals.

Needless to say, in a situation in which references to homosexuality have been officially non-existent, one cannot expect to see texts and documents concerning homosexuality. Even so, I believe that the modernity of Korean sexuality has formed within a concrete historical context that has given rise to homosexuals' subjective understanding of themselves, and their own subculture has been created based on this subjective understanding. Unfortunately, a collection and analysis of historical materials related to homosexual communities in Korea is still difficult due to the lack of research in this area. I am sure that a first-hand account of Korea's homosexual community will, at some point, be written. Some time ago, I had the opportunity to hear a transgendered person who had come to Korea from the U.S. give a personal account of the Korean gay community of forty years ago. In many ways, this amazing account overshadowed information on the gay community that I had been collecting for over ten years. This person later returned to the states, and I was unable to find anyone to explain about the homosexual community of this era.

I believe that Korea's present lesbian and gay subculture began around fifteen years ago. Defining a subculture as a group living in relatively close geographical proximity with relatively stable collective cultural rules, the Korean lesbian and gay communities have embodied a loose imagery of themselves from about this time. This is not to say that there weren't chance contacts between homosexuals before this time, but these were nothing more than individual events. In Korea, this subculture is only prominent in a few big metropolitan areas, such as Seoul and Pusan. For approximately the last fifteen years in Seoul, *Nakwon-dong* (a *dong* is district in a city) has been known as a cruising area. Initially, Tapgol Park and the theater behind it became a cruising area, and then a few bars began to open up in the surrounding *Nakwon-dong* area. These bars catered solely to gay males.

However, these places, at least up until a few years ago, were generally frequented by middle-aged gays of the upper-middle class. Even though these gays did not have any cultural signals, such as the handkerchief code used in the West, there were specific practices and language that indicated their membership in the gay community. Examples include feminine speech and gestures as well as special slang used to refer to sexual acts. As the community's slang developed, gays began to refer to themselves using words such as *pogal* or *iban* (often romanized as *ebahn*). *Pogal* is the backward reading of the word *kalbo*–the most vulgar term for a prostitute in Korea. Korean gays, denied access to traditional wedding vows or the norms of romantic love, are forced to resort to repeated chance sexual encounters. *Kalbo* is thus a term of self-degradation. However, the term is no longer used due to its odious nuances. It seems to me that the term not only indicates a situation in which gays were forced to live an over-eroticized existence, but also shows how, in the strict sense of the term, sexual behavior, reduced to sexual identity, is able to provide unique insights into the situation of homosexuals. Moreover, as the homosexual community has recently begun to see itself in a more meaningful context as "an oppressed minority" and has, therefore, spurned its erotic identities, the term *pogal* is interesting in light of its cultural and political function.

The term *iban*, which came into use after the term *pogal*, indicates a new consciousness of the homosexual community as a social group only vaguely differentiated from heterosexuals. *Iban* corresponds to the word *ilban*, which is used to refer to heterosexuals. In Korean, *ilban* means "universal" or "dominant." The homophonous word *ilban* can also be used to mean "first class." *Iban* can likewise be used to mean "second class," with the implication that homosexuals are a "second class" in relationship to the dominant first-class (heterosexuals). Thus, although this term does not indicate self-conscious reflection, it does show that homosexuals, to some extent, look at themselves as a unified social group. Even now, in cruising spots or other areas, homosexuals use this term to make themselves known to others or to refer to others that identify themselves as homosexuals.

Of course, besides these terms, the English words "homo" or "gay" have also been used. Yet, one must keep in mind that these words do not necessarily have the same usage that they do in the West. Although the word "homo" is occasionally used by homosexuals themselves, in the majority of cases, it is used by heterosexuals as a term of insult. In other words, the word "homo" has been used in a vague manner by heterosexuals to refer to someone who has a sexual interest in the same sex or who engages in homosexual acts. As sexology has become vulgarized and popularized, the contrived word "homo" has been used in Korean society to refer to what is believed to be a specific type of person.

Although the usage governing the term "homo" can be said to be somewhat similar to that of the West, the term "gay" has been used in odd ways. Up until a few years ago, the term was mainly used to refer to someone who had undergone a sex-change operation. However, this is not to say that a clear distinction was made between homosexual and transsexual identities.

In the case of the word "homo," the term has been used to refer to homosexuality as it relates to the sexual object. In the case of the term "gay," on the other hand, one would have to say that it is believed that the "gay" person has a masculinity that is different from heterosexual masculinity. From this, one may conclude that the former is based on the hypothesis of the sexual object and goal as mentioned in conventional sexology, while the latter is used to signify social gender roles centered around masculinity and femininity. Although the above terms for homosexuals have been used extensively in Korea, the most common term in both the past and present has been *tongsôngyônaeja,* which means "same sex lover." Since this term, taken literally, refers solely to erotic desire existing between members of the same sex, it is, in the strict sense of the term, distinct from matters of identity. The term indicates a tendency to see homosexuality in terms of various erotic desires. In the final analysis, homosexuality, instead of representing a consistent, unified social identity, is reduced to some perverted or shocking acts performed by a few people.

At present, however, homosexuals generally do not hesitate to call themselves gay, and, unlike before, from the time they first call themselves gay, they become aware of their own sexual identity. This is because a new homosexual community has arisen, and this community has used the term "gay" as the pseudo-standard appellation for homosexuals. In the past few years, the Korean gay community has witnessed explosive expansion and growth. Of course, this has been coincidental. After all, conditions have changed, granting homosexuals greater access to information and news related to their sexual identity. Moreover, the atmosphere that has developed has made it possible for homosexuals to have a more positive understanding of themselves.

First, more than anything else, the new arrangement of the homosexual community in Korean society in the last few years has been made possible by the emergence of several lesbian and gay organizations and the tremendous social repercussions that this has entailed. In April 1995 at Yonsei University, the leading private university in Seoul, I created a homosexual student organization called "Come Together." In brief, it would not be an overstatement to say that this was the first social movement through which homosexuals could effect changes in their lives. The movement went beyond the ghettoized and marginalized locales, such as bars, theaters and saunas, where homosexual cultural and sexual activities were performed. Needless to say, the movement caused a tremendous social reaction, and for the first time, there was social mention of homosexual identity and attempts to look at this identity from the standpoint of human rights.

After the founding of "Come Together," a student organization called *Maum001* was created according to the proposal of a Seoul National University student by the name of Yi Chôngu (He presently refers to himself as an *Ebahn* activist). Here, 001 represents the human rights conditions of homosexuals as figured on a percentage basis, and numbers are added as human rights improve; thus, the group is presently called *Maum003*. These organizations, each created by approximately ten students, held certain activities on campus, but, in the end, it wasn't their activities so much as their existence that stirred up social discourse on homosexuality. Moreover, these movements, in combination with other cultural changes affecting Korean society, caught the attention of the mass media. As a result, nearly every week and every month, leading organs of the mass media would compete to make reports and special articles on these new movements.

Yet, these organizations do not represent the beginning of homosexual organizations. In February 1994, the *Ch'odonghoe* organization was formed, and a month later, the organization split into the gay organization *Ch'in'gusai* (Between Friends) and the lesbian organization *Kkirikkiri*. *Ch'odonghoe* was originally founded according to a proposal by Chang Chinsôk, a Korean student who had been studying in the U.S. While in America, Chang became interested in Korea's AIDS situation. When Chang returned to Korea on a visit, he toured some gay bars and persuaded gays and lesbians to form a loosely structured group. (When he later returned to the U.S., he formed a group, also called *Ch'in'gusai*, for Korean-American gays in New York.)

In Korea, the *Ch'in'gusai* group was very loosely structured; yet, it did have a relatively firm understanding of its purposes. The organization proclaimed that the "transformation of *Nakwon-dong* Culture" was their goal, and they defined their organization as "a friendship group based on a dignified relationship between homosexuals." At this time, the term "*Nakwon-dong* culture," as a reference to Korea's gay subculture, signified casual sexual contacts between gays in bars, saunas, and theaters. Even so, *Nakwon* culture cannot be completely reduced to the forms of certain sexual behavior.

For example, certain cultural conventions are revealed in the current slang *uattôlgi* (putting on airs), such slang indicating a criticism of an aspect of *Nakwon-dong* culture. Since, within the current gay community, gays were limited in numbers and closed off, they developed certain ostentatious mannerisms aimed at manifesting and securing influence. Gays referred to this as *uattôlgi* (putting on airs). The gays in *Ch'in'gusai* criticized these practices, saying that they were dishonest and led to human relationships characterized by alienation.

Although public interest in homosexuality was not yet strong, there was a budding public concern over AIDS and gay sex. Unfortunately, in Korea, there are presently no exclusively lesbian or gay organizations focused on AIDS. In lesbian and gay groups, activities in this direction are limited to education on simple preventative measures. As a result, a flexible approach which views AIDS as not merely a disease, but as a complex cultural and political reality, has not yet come into existence.

In the aftermath of the founding of Come Together, the Korean Homosexuals Human Rights Association was formed as an umbrella organization unifying *Ch'in'gusai*, *Kkirikkiri*, and Seoul National University's *Maum001*. The organization, founded on June 28th in commemoration of the Stonewall Struggle, represented a decisive movement towards transcending the oppression and alienation that homosexuals experienced in Korean society. Moreover, the movement signified an initial step, however small, towards recognition of the human rights of sexual minorities. The founding declaration of the human rights movement for Korean homosexuals, which I wrote at this time, served as a program outlining the prospects and goals of Korea's homosexual movement. This is, therefore, the first full-fledged document associated with the movement.

Based on this, numerous homosexual groups spontaneously appeared in all sectors of Korean society. One of the most notable movements appeared in virtual space. Small lesbian and gay discussion groups began to form on the bulletin board systems of Korea's three major Internet servers: Hitel, Chollian, and Nawnuri. First formed in the summer and autumn of 1995, these BBS groups grew at a rapid pace, since they provided members with the opportunity to have anonymous and relatively diverse contact with a large number of fellow homosexuals. I would estimate that more than 2,000 to 3,000 lesbians and gays posted message on these bulletin board systems or engaged in real-time, on-line conversations using "chatting." Hitel's *Tto Hanaûi Sarang* (Another Love), Chollian's Queernet, and Nawnuri's Rainbow are names of these on-line discussion groups. As the names suggest, the homosexual intellectuals of this time were, to some extent, aware of the political trends and experiences of homosexual movements in America and other Western nations. Gradually, terms such as "coming out" (in Korea, the English term is used untranslated) and symbols of the lesbian and gay movement, such as the rainbow flag, began to appear. However, apart from these bulletin boards on domestic Internet servers, there have been no special servers solely for homosexuals.

Up until 1995, Korea's gay community had developed at a slow pace. There was only limited information concerning most of the gay groups that arose independently prior to this time, and this information had to be obtained via incidental rumors, exposés in third-rate magazines, or occasional reports on the radio. As a result, growth in the gay community occurred at a snail's pace. However, with the advent of the Come Together group mentioned above and the movements and social changes that appeared in its wake, there was a rapid increase in the availability of information. To an extent unimaginable previously, it was now possible to access information on the homosexual community and on homosexual identity.

It is interesting to note that in addition to the gay and lesbian groups of virtual space, loosely formed smaller groups and regional groups of gays began to form that connected via phone message recording services. These smaller groups usually formed for purposes of friendship, and, in addition to providing members with a rudimentary understanding of sexual identity, they served the practical function of helping people find sexual partners.

However, the university homosexual groups that formed in the wake of Yonsei University's Come Together and Seoul National's *Maum003* and the human rights organizations which these inspired, such as *Ch'in'gusai* and *Kkirikkiri*, have been unable to achieve any tangible, practical results. Unfortunately, these organizations have been groping in the dark for a lesbian and gay rights movement that is appropriate for Korean society. Moreover, even though many homosexuals generally recognize these organizations as advocates for the human rights of Korean homosexuals, they tend to show little interest in the activities or direction of the organizations and have little inclination to actually participate in organization activities. Since 1995, the Korean Homosexuals Human Rights Association has held a three-day "Summer Human Rights Camp" which provides rudimentary education in homosexual human rights while building solidarity between homosexuals. Although this camp is a step in the right direction, it must be pointed out that the association has an insufficient number of regular, organized activities.

However, this is not to say that that the organizations working for the human rights of homosexuals in Korea have a negative or skeptical attitude concerning changes to their situation. It is true that the vast majority of homosexuals find it difficult to consciously reflect on and assess homosexual identity as a cultural or political reality. These homosexuals have a vague sense of "social" injustice; yet, they are unable to understand the sociological causes of this injustice, and how, apart from sexuality, this injustice is related to the diverse power structure that constitutes social authority. Although there are minor publications put out by homosexual organizations on an irregular basis, there is still not a single public periodical with a mass circulation. In addition, no educational organs, let alone any colleges, offer courses related to homosexual identity. Courses on lesbian and gay studies have been unthinkable. The only published work on lesbian or gays studies is my *Nuga Sôngjôngch'irûl Turyôwôharya–Sông, Chôngch'i, Munhwayôn'gu* (Who Is Afraid of Sexual Politics–Sexuality, Politics and Cultural Studies, 1996). There is also a two-volume collection of essays by homosexuals. Volume I, titled "No Longer Sad or Ashamed," is a collection of articles by members of *Ch'in'gusai*. In these biographical essays, members discuss their sexual identity. Volume II, titled "Practice is Needed to Be a Scarecrow in Winter," contains an account of a gay man who tested HIV positive. These two works were published in 1994 and 1995, respectively. With such a lack of education and written sources, it is not possible for Korean homosexuals, as a group, to understand the sociological elements of their sexual identity, nor is it possible to counter social forces and institutions that deny and reject one's homosexual identity.

However, Korean homosexuals have continuously worked to organize themselves. In many of the other metropolitan areas besides Seoul, i.e., Pusan, Kwangju and Taegu, lesbian and gay groups have gradually begun to form, and lesbian and gay student groups have also been created in universities. Among these, the lesbian organizations are noteworthy as being very active. Although *Kkirikkiri* is the only lesbian group with a relatively stable organization, lesbians have begun to make their presence known on the Internet and other places. In Korea, opportunities to make sexual contacts are distinctly different for females and males. Even when menstruation and pregnancy are disregarded, it is very difficult for women to have a spontaneous attitude towards their own sexuality. Women could more accurately be called non-sexual entities, since, in Korean society, women are caught up in the double standard of a conservative sexual ideology that stresses motherhood, chastity, and virginity. In these circumstances, it is extremely difficult for lesbians to actively come to terms with their own sexuality. Even so, at least the lesbian identity of relatively refined, middle-class university students and unmarried graduates has begun to be understood. Although there is only one place so far, a lesbian bar (Lesbos) has now opened in Seoul, and *Kkirikkiri* membership is rapidly expanding. Even though the distinction between transvestite and exclusive lesbians in Korea must still be seen as various shades on a continuum, it has become possible to recognize the existence of lesbians as distinct from heterosexuals. In particular, terms such as butch, femme and dyke have come into use as an indication of the structuring of the community.

Yet it must be pointed out that these lesbian and gay communities are still centered around people in their twenties and early thirties, and most of these are middle-class people who have at least a four-year college degree. As a social group that can readily access the press, written works, or mass media, these people have the particularly free attitudes characteristic of the middle-class. In other words, these people identify with cultural ideals related to personal choice, individual preference, and freedom. In addition, as a result of being sensitive to ideological changes concerning cultural habits of the middle class, this group has been open to a diverse range of cultural information. As a result, these people have found it easy to obtain information concerning the latest lesbian and gay groups and have consequently formed associations with relative ease.

Lesbians and gays of other ages and social classes, on the other hand, have not found it easy to make contact with the homosexual community. In particular, those homosexuals past their mid-thirties, most of whom are married, are quite often completely unaware of the existence of lesbian and gay communities. Even if they are aware of these new groups, they tend to reject and avoid them. Instead of looking at their own homosexual identity as an "identity," these people have seen it as a shameful desire that constantly hounds them. In particular, homosexual fathers with children have found it difficult to go against expectations concerning their own social position. Especially in Korean society, one's economic livelihood is completely determined by family-based social structures, independent of one's particular social class. It follows that the livelihood of one's wife and children is almost totally determined by the man's economic ability. This dependence on the male breadwinner is seen clearly when we look at Korean society's economic structure, and, of course, is clearly evident in cultural patterns of behavior. In these circumstances, there will inevitably be clear differences between the homosexual identities of older lesbians and gays from a blue-collar background and that of the newly formed community of educated lesbian and gays from the middle class. Moreover, although it is still only a minor issue within the small homosexual groups now forming, this gap in identities is creating discord concerning cultural and social issues and matters of hegemony.

Of course, even lesbians and gays from middle-class backgrounds are not completely free in Korea's family-based society. They also dread coming out whether it be forced or of their own accord. (In Korea, only myself and several other lesbians and gays have publicly come out.) Although these homosexuals may find it relatively easy to come out among their peers, at school or work, etc., they would never think of coming out in front of their families. This can be credited to the strong psychological bonds that exist between parents and children and the fact that these bonds are reinforced in Korea's family-based society. In these circumstances, Korea's lesbian and gay movement inevitably finds it difficult to follow the example of Western lesbian and gay movements, which encourage liberation from heterosexual prejudices and pride in oneself. In other words, it is not easy for Koreans to view themselves as autonomous individuals and, on this basis, advocate their own freedom and dignity outside of the context of communities such as their family and relatives. Indeed, most Korean homosexuals consistently see family as the biggest problem troubling them. Moreover, they see the discovery of their homosexual identity by their family as the greatest possible calamity threatening their future. More than society's hatred and prejudice, these homosexuals fear the anxiety and stress that would result from the breaking of their familial bond. As a result of this psychological barrier, the Korean homosexual movement, unable to demand specific public activities from its members, must limit itself to private activities within the lesbian and gay communities.

However, it seems to me that too much can be made of this point. It would be foolish to reduce Korea's strong family values to "oriental," Korea's specific form of Confucianism and patriarchy. Not only Westerners, but even the majority of Koreans would support this stereotype. I see this attitude as a mere ideological fix for Korea, which has once more become aware of itself as non-Western after its recent confused race to Westernize. In a sense, this view could be called reversed orientalism. Unlike Western orientalism, this is a reproduced orientalism coming from the orient itself. Of course, sexuality and the family, the extended family system, and the Confucian ideology surrounding marriage cannot be ignored; yet, these concerns have developed into a mythology which seeks to explain the complex conflicts and changes that Korean society has undergone in trans-historical, abstract, and absolute terms.

The social reverberations that came in the wake of the founding of Come Together have nearly ceased to be felt. As a result of the group's efforts, many people have come to recognize the existence of homosexuals, and the term homosexual has definitely become part of the vocabulary of this generation. As the social turmoil surrounding homosexual issues has subsided, lesbians and gays have been busy searching for a life and a future within their communities. It seems to me that these trends will continue for a long time. As long as no major transformations take place, the extreme social reactions and debates surrounding homosexuals in Korean society will not reoccur.

Needless to say, in light of the recently changing circumstances, people have come to recognize the existence of homosexuals, that is to say, the existence of a type of person called a homosexual. Even so, when I look back on the quelled commotion surrounding homosexuality, I have a hard time looking at this as a firm victory or the beginning of positive changes that will guarantee a rosy future.

Personally, I do not like to think of homosexual identity as a biological result, i.e., a physical and psychological constitution or an inborn condition. At the same time, I oppose the view that homosexuality is simply the result of nurture or ideas acquired during the process of socialization. When one reflects on the changes regarding homosexual identity in Korean society, it is clear that homosexual subjectivity is a socially constructed complex process.

Yet, Korean society also has access to a half-century of discourse by Western homosexuals who sought to define homosexual identity. From the last century's attempts to understand homosexuality from a medical or scientific standpoint to the present "queer discourse" based on the fragmented point of view of post modern capitalism, there has been a plethora of competing views aimed at defining homosexuality in Korean society. One could say that in the West there has been a historical progression of views related to homosexual identity, whereas these views have appeared in Korea all at once. Thus, in Korea, there hasn't been a predominant view of homosexual identity. To the contrary, the various views on the matter have become little whirlpools, each with their own centripetal force. In these circumstances, no hegemonic discourse or master narrative has been able to develop. In Korean society, homosexual identity is merely the sketchy descriptions resulting from skimming through the various discourses on the subject.

I definitely believe that in the difficult process of developing homosexuals as a social group, lesbians, gays and other sexual minorities will, through their struggles, come to understand and explain themselves. Amidst the explosive increase in homosexual discourse, homosexuals will awaken to the power of language that does not lead to clarity about oneself but rather leads to absurdity. Yet the problem is not merely clarity about oneself; the problem is the tangled web of discourses that seek to explain and control homosexuals. To obtain freedom from this tangle, homosexuals must attain sovereign control of the power and language used in relation to themselves.

NOTES

1. Rapid social and political change has been occurring in Korea in recent years. In 1998, a queer film festival was held in Seoul, and the public awareness of lesbians and gay men has increased. A number of Universities now have gay and lesbian student groups, and the gay rights movement has received support from human rights and feminist groups. Gay issues have received publicity in recent months when a television star made his homosexuality know publicly.

REFERENCES

Kim Chunsôk (1994). *Tongsongaejaui sugi chip* Vol. I: *Ije tô isang sûlp'ûjido pukkûrôpchido anta* (A Homosexual Essay Collection: No Longer Sad or Ashamed), Seoul: Changjamot.

Kim Kyôngmin (1993). *Kyôul hôsuabido sanûn iren yônsûbi p'iryohada* (Practice is Needed to Be a Scarecrow in Winter), Seoul: Sôngnim.

Seo Dong-Jin (1996). *Nuga Sôngjôngch'irûl Turyôwôharya–Sông, Chôngch'i, Munhwayôn'gu* (Who is Afraid of Sexual Politics–Sexuality, Politics and Cultural Studies), Seoul: Munye Madang.

Seo Dong-Jin (1996). *Kûndae chabonjuûi sahoe esô tongsôngae chôngch'esôngûi sahoejôk kusônge kwanhan yôn'gu* (A Study of the Social Elements of Homosexual Identity in Modern Capitalist Society), Yonsei University Masters Thesis.

Tiptoe Out of the Closet:
The Before and After
of the Increasingly Visible
Gay Community in Singapore

Russell Heng Hiang Khng

THE BEGINNINGS OF A GAY SCENE

If one were to ask a socially active gay person today about his earliest memory of something related to homosexual life in Singapore, he is more than likely to recall Bugis Street. This was a road in the heart of the city where transvestite/transsexual prostitutes used to gather every evening to ply their trade, and it became an international icon of the exotic Far East. But most Singaporeans would be hard put to put an exact date or even the year when this street became a gathering point for the cross-dressing community. According to popular memory, the location became what it was sometime in the 1950s.[1] Anything before that was a blank, although it is likely that a more rigorous search of archival sources would be able to trace the development of homosexual life in Singapore further back into the island's history. This paper, however, is only meant to be a record based on the writer's memory and experience beginning in the 1960s.

Within Singapore, the cross-dressers on Bugis Street came to be known as "ah qua"–a Chinese Fujian dialect term particular to Singapore–which became a widely used pejorative term for all gay men.

[Haworth co-indexing entry note]: "Tiptoe Out of the Closet: The Before and After of the Increasingly Visible Gay Community in Singapore." Heng Hiang Khng, Russell. Co-published simultaneously in *Journal of Homosexuality* (Harrington Park Press, an imprint of The Haworth Press, Inc.) Vol. 40, No. 3/4, 2001, pp. 81-97; and: *Gay and Lesbian Asia: Culture, Identity, Community* (ed: Gerard Sullivan, and Peter A. Jackson) Harrington Park Press, an imprint of The Haworth Press, Inc., 2001, pp. 81-97. Single or multiple copies of this article are available for a fee from The Haworth Document Delivery Service [1-800-342-9678, 9:00 a.m.–5:00 p.m. (EST). E-mail address: getinfo@haworthpressinc.com].

Egregious as it may seem, this is the first known instance of homosexuality finding expression as a local idiom. By the end of the 1960s, the gay scene had expanded from the sex-trade of Bugis Street to include what was possibly Singapore's first gay bar, *Le Bistro*.[2] Its significance lay in providing gay men who did not cross-dress a place to meet and socialize without being treated as objects of curiosity. During the 1970s, the number of gay bars grew to three with the Treetops in what is currently the Royal Holiday Inn and the Pebble Bar in what was then the Forum Hotel. All these outlets were part of the cosmopolitan tourist-oriented night life that began around this time in the Orchard Road area. Homosexuality had made a territorial claim on the social landscape.

But it was a fragile claim. The homosexual venues still held trappings of the closet. In the Pebble Bar, the only one of the three places with a dance floor, dancing was not allowed among same-sex partners. So gay people sat in one half of the bar drinking and listening to the music, while watching the straight couples dance in the other half. A gay venue could also stop being gay because the proprietor decided it was not good for its image, as was the case with Treetops. Foreigners, largely Caucasian residents and tourists, were a major feature of this gay scene, which was dominated by a very set and dichotomized "local-foreign/Asian-Caucasian/dominated-dominating/bitch-butch" pattern of sexual pairing. This was limiting in some ways, but it also contributed to an awareness that living together with a man was not all that inconceivable even if it meant having to migrate out of the Singapore closet to a more liberal foreign country. The Singaporeans who could pursue this option were usually the Westernized English-speaking breed known as the "Orchard Road queens," but the great imbalance in numbers between the foreigners and Singaporeans limited this option. Thus the restrictions were more than just the lack of gay places to go to; they also included a mindset about clearly demarcated roles in gay sexual relations.

The late 1960s and early 1970s was a time when the gay liberation movement erupted in the West, and information about gay people getting together to affirm their identity, support each other, and struggle for their rights became available to Singapore homosexuals. However, the idea of activism in pursuit of such larger social and political goals was then unthinkable to them, and the interaction of gay people in those years amounted to no more than individuals seeking a network of friends. As such, it would be more appropriate to say Singapore in the 1970s had a gay "scene" but not a gay "community." That gay scene provided only two lifestyle options: the "Bugis Street ah qua" and the "Orchard Road queen."

1980s–THE CRITICAL DECADE

A sense of "community" started to take shape in the 1980s, and this must be seen in the broader context of how that decade was critical for Singapore society as a whole. It was a time of significant political and socio-economic changes. In politics, the 1980s saw a swing of 10 per cent of the popular vote against the ruling People's Action Party (PAP) and, with that, a breaking of the party's monopoly of Parliamentary representation. One explanation for this shift was that a new generation of better educated voters was coming onto the electoral roll, people who were less willing to stomach the authoritarian ways of the PAP. At the same time, economic growth by the 1980s had generated sufficiently broad-based affluence to create a middle class with yearnings for a more consolatory form of government. An indication of this was the beginning of non-governmental organizations pushing more forcefully their agendas on women's rights and environmental conservation. In a less obvious way, gay people also started to organize themselves. These movements were possible because the government realized it had to be seen to be less authoritarian and to accommodate a greater diversity of opinions that came with a higher standard of living.

As the social climate became more relaxed, gay people were also more ready to test the waters and sometimes got away with it. A benchmark event for gay life in Singapore was the opening of a disco called Niche in April 1983 where same-sex dancing was allowed. The gay scene also expanded from the elegant confines of the tourist belt to include cruising in public toilets, parks, and the beach. Cruising in public places has probably always been around but it was only the 1980s that saw the emergence of well-known places where there was extensive cruising. Examples would be Hong Lim Park near the financial district of the city and a stretch of beach along the East Coast Parkway. Essentially, this was a trend that had taken place in many Western countries and was being replicated in a small way in Singapore. But more substantive changes were taking place at other levels.

With economic development came more professions in which gay people felt comfortable, e.g., fashion and advertising. As the decade developed, the typecasting of gays in certain jobs gave way to the liberating notion that gay Singaporeans could be found in almost any walk of life. You could start thinking in terms of a gay policeman or truck-driver. In this, homosexuality was making yet another claim on Singapore society: it was breaking down class divisions, thereby expanding possibilities beyond the oppressive mindset that being gay had to mean being an "Orchard Road queen" or a "Bugis Street ah qua." An important corollary of this development was also the demise of the entrenched mentality of Asian-Caucasian/dominated-dominating relationships. Role demarcations were no longer central in a relationship. Here again, Singapore was probably experiencing a trend that was taking place in gay communities elsewhere.

Another commonality which Singapore homosexuals share with many of their counterparts in other countries is a representation in the arts out of proportion to their actual numbers in society. By the second half of the 1980s, gay writers started to explore the hitherto taboo area of homosexuality in their works, so much so that in 1988, three plays with gay themes were banned from performing.[3] From that starting point in the late 1980s to the present, homosexuality as a subject has found expression in books, paintings, and political essays. Collectively, this was another careful step out of the closet, a public expression of gayness outside the realm of the gay scene. These were the first instances of gay people finding a voice to speak about and for them; they marked an important step forward in the passage to a stronger sense of community.

The next step was taken when Singapore homosexuals responded to the challenge of AIDS. Following the first reported case of HIV infection in 1985, a group of people (both gay and straight) set up a non-government organization called *Action For Aids* (AFA), which provided support and counseling for AIDS victims as well as education on safe sex for the public. AFA is not technically known as a gay movement and has been careful to present itself as an NGO dealing with a public health issue. However, a significant portion of the energy and leadership behind it has been provided by gay people, and, in many practical ways, AFA has rallied homosexuals around a cause. The public education campaign on AIDS so far has not taken on a gay-hostile tone. But it should be noted that the Niche disco had its liquor license withdrawn in 1989 and was given only a week to close down; no reason was provided for the police action, but a person, personally involved in the running of the disco, believed it was a reaction to the first reported case of an AIDS death in Singapore. Anecdotal evidence also seems to suggest that after 1989 the police intensified surveillance and entrapment of homosexuals in public cruising areas.

Although the signals about officialdom's attitude towards gay life were mixed, the overall climate was still sufficiently encouraging. To put a rational construction to it, some gay people felt that the authority sought to limit the growth of homosexual activities, which had steadily increased in public profile, particularly the less discreet aspects of public cruising, but was not intent on eradicating all homosexual venues. At many levels, gay life went on unchecked. Although the Niche was closed, two other Sunday night discos for gays continued. This was a time when the political climate of Singapore was taking its most liberal turn in a decade, with a new Prime Minister, Goh Chok Tong, assuming leadership with a promise of a more relaxed and less authoritarian style of governance than that of his predecessor Lee Kuan Yew. A significant symbol of this "kinder and gentler Singapore" came with a gay subtext. The 1990 Singapore International Arts Festival staged a major production of David Henry Hwang's *M Butterfly*, which, coming in the wake of the proscription of three gay plays just two years earlier, was significant. This theatre piece about a male opera star's seduction of a French male diplomat in China was a watershed in more ways than one. It marked the first instance of total nudity in Singapore theatre. The impact was heightened by the local media, which, habitually sensitized to the political climate, highlighted members of the political elite seated in the front row taking in the spectacle with cultured nonchalance.

THE REVERSALS OF THE 1990s

A major development for the gay community in this decade was an attempt early in 1993 to start a support group to deal specifically with the issue of homosexuality in Singapore. This could be seen as the first time gay Singaporeans tried to organize. It began informally when three gay men explored casually the possibility of setting up such a gay movement in Singapore. In the months that followed, a few more people came into the discussions which were held in cafes and private homes, less like meetings than friendly chatting over cups of coffee. Two concrete concerns animated their conversations: the decriminalization of homosexuality and the registration of a movement with the Registrar of Societies (PLU, 1994). This desultory group grew bigger and called itself *People Like Us* (PLU), and it involved gay men, lesbians, and bisexuals. An event on 30 May 1993 provided the impetus for more focused organization and activity. That night, the police conducted a raid on Rascals disco in the Pan-Pacific Hotel (gay only on Sunday) and a number of people were taken to the police station because they did not carry identification papers. They were not charged, but this was clearly an act of intimidation. Raids on gay places were not new in Singapore but what was different this time was that a group of about 20 gay people sent a letter of complaint to the precinct police station. This must have surprised the police used to gay people being too frightened to protest against harassment, and they sent an apology, albeit only for the rude behavior of their men that night and not for the nature of the raid (PLU, 1994). The incident galvanized PLU into action to educate gay Singaporeans about their legal rights. This took the form of a monthly forum held in a public building open to anybody who turned up. At these sessions, a talk and discussion on gay or gay-relevant issues would be held. For the first time, gay Singaporeans had a forum to share their thoughts and raise grievances. The numbers coming to these meetings ranged from 20 to 80. PLU gradually developed sub-groups, such as Sanctuary for gay Christians, one for women to increase the lesbian participation, and a support group where more intimate personal issues could be discussed in small groups within private home settings. Then it began to organize regular social events, such as parties and picnics, drawing crowds of up to 200 people.[4] Despite this level of activity, a major problem remained that of legal status. In a country with highly discretionary laws about what constitutes illegal assembly for subversive purposes, many of PLU participants felt it should be properly registered as a bona fide society for its own good. However, PLU's organizers dithered for a long time over seeking registration, not confident that they would be successful. Their sanguine assumption was that in a society like Singapore, the authority would know about the existence of the group but was adopting a "leave well alone" approach so long as PLU kept a low profile and did not become too radical. The group's fear was that seeking formal recognition would disrupt this tacit understanding and force officialdom not only to turn down the application but to oblige the group to cease operating.

The first few years of the 1990s were encouraging for those Singaporeans who sought a more open political and cultural climate. A more liberal film censorship regime was ushered in with a film classification system so that adults can now get to see movies that would hitherto have been banned, and this would include a fair share of movies with gay themes. The first lesbian play, *Mergers and Acquisitions*, was staged. A novel, *Peculiar Chris,* was published which was a love story featuring a gay recruit who had come out to the military authority. An exhibition of homo-erotic paintings was staged by artist Tan Peng (*Out of the closet,* declared a positive review in the major English language daily *The Straits Times*). However, the stories of police surveillance of gay cruising places were increasing. Not only were gay people being entrapped, but their pictures were being published in the newspapers. There seemed to be an agenda to make examples of them. Six cases of entrapment led to caning sentences in court. This moved two performance artists to stage acts of protest. Their performance took place at a show in the wee hours of the first day of 1994. The official wrath it drew signaled the curtailing of the liberalizing trend in Singapore.

The two acts which so offended officialdom were induced vomiting in one and the scattering of some pubic hair on stage in the other. Whether or not these performances were good or bad art, or even art, need not be the concern of this paper. At worst, the artists should be regarded as no more than young people having some fun during a New Year's Eve party in front of a very small audience, most of whom were probably converts to their message. The official reaction, therefore, must be perceived as being out of all proportion to the incident. The belief was that when the event was sensationalized by the afternoon tabloid *The New Paper,* it generated a discussion within the cabinet. Condemnation of the show by senior political leaders and the National Arts Council lent credence to those rumours. The two artists were prohibited from performing.[5] Subsequently, the Ministry of Home Affairs, in response to this incident and other developments in Singapore theatre, issued new regulations to tighten control on what it termed "scriptless performance" and alluded to the latter's socially disruptive potential.

This event and a few others pointed to a political leadership that was viewing developments in the arts and the broader realm of lifestyle with a very attentive and suspicious eye. Those familiar with the ways of the Singapore government would assess this to be far more than just a few of the country's prudish leaders taking offense occasionally at the bohemian conduct of some of its citizens. What was in operation was a larger national ideology often articulated in strategic terms of a traditional Asian society fighting to preserve its essence against attrition by undesirable Western influences. Increasingly, the preservation of that essence is being presented as critical at least to economic well-being, if not to national survival. Two particular strands in this discourse continue to hobble the emancipation of gay people:

> (a) The views that the institution of the family is under threat from trends such as teenage pregnancy and notions such as radical feminism and the legitimization of "sexual deviance."

> (b) The notion that Western society has erred too far on the side of individual rights and that Singapore should avoid this at all cost. Asian societies should retain their traditional emphasis on responsibility. Recognizing the individual rights of homosexuals would, therefore, have to be weighed against the responsibility of respecting the moral standards of the larger society.

The year 1994 was witness to more constraints in public discourse, some of which were imposed directly by the government while others were the result of self-censorship as people became more nervous in the wake of the political climate growing more stern. This has had an impact on the fledgling PLU. In April 1995, a local English-language tabloid, *The New Paper*, wanted to do a story on it.[6] While the group had never operated on a clandestine basis, it was not yet confident enough to handle a potential publicity blitz by the media and, given the risky mood of the times, it decided to lie low for a while and rework its strategy. The big monthly forum was stopped for a while and energy was then focused on seeking registration. Such an interregnum was not helpful for a young movement trying to maintain a momentum of growth.

PLU made an attempt to register itself as a company rather than a society hoping to circumvent the need of declaring its gay identity in 1995, but this was turned down by the Registry of Companies and Businesses with an injunction that should the applicants proceed with incorporation, the Registry would exercise its powers under section 20(2) of the Companies Act (Cap 50). This particular law states:

> Notwithstanding anything in this Act or any rule of law, the Registrar shall refuse to register the memorandum of a proposed company where he is satisfied that:
>
> (a) the proposed company is likely to be used for an unlawful purpose or for purposes prejudicial to public peace, welfare or good order in Singapore; or
>
> (b) it would be contrary to the national security or interest for the proposed company to be registered.

This response from the Registry confirms the group's suspicion that the authority knows about its existence. With hindsight, seeking registration as a business was not a politic move because it created an impression that PLU was trying to be furtive, which invited suspicion. It was also against the raison d'être of forming an openly gay movement. The group then tried to register as a society, fully declaring its intention to address the homosexual issue. To do this, it needed a minimum of 10 people willing to lend their names to the registration process. By early 1996, it could only find nine candidates and meanwhile, many of the early supporters of the group and some of its founders had moved on. This indicated a dearth of stamina and a low level of confidence, which persist within the gay community. It also underlined a basic dilemma whereby gay people felt cagey about associating with an organization that had no legal endorsement, but were also too nervous to lend their names to get the movement registered. Meanwhile, the regular monthly meetings had been scaled down to smaller less-structured gatherings at a cafe, and the strategy was to maintain the group at this low profile until registration could be arranged. What kept PLU going was a core group of around five or six people.

Finally, PLU managed to gather 10 individuals (gay and straight) willing to put their names on the application to the Registrar of Societies, and the application was lodged on 7 November 1996. The group was never sanguine that registration would be that easily achieved but deemed it important to try. Even if it were bound to be rejected, it would be a way of getting an official explanation of why such a grouping had to be proscribed, and thus would initiate a form of dialogue between the State and the gay community. The registration went through the bureaucratic routine of being vetted by the Registrar of Societies and the police. The treatment it received from officials involved was business-like and courteous, but the application was still rejected on 9 April 1997. PLU followed up with a series of responses; first, they wrote to the registrar seeking the reasons for the rejection and, second, they appealed to the Minister of Home Affairs to review the registrar's decision. Again the emphasis was to get officialdom engaged in a dialogue even if the Minister turned down the appeal. Dialogue did not prove to be an easy quest, and, basically, the second round of answers was still a firm no. Technically, the appeal process should have ended at the Minister's office, but PLU took it further to the Prime Minister's office. The latter redirected the PLU's request to the Ministry, ending up with the same negative reply.[7] Clearly, the strategy to get a process of dialogue going with officialdom had not worked, and the situation was also illustrative of how constricted the scope for any form of political debate could be within an authoritarian polity dominated by one political party.

IMPLICATIONS FOR THE FUTURE

Viewed in perspective, homosexuals in Singapore have, within a generation of 30 years, progressed from the stage of just having a gay scene which served their entertainment needs to one where there was a nascent sense of community with an identified purpose of improving the status and welfare of gay people. If at one level, these gains have seemed impressive, at another, they remain precarious, determined to a large extent by how much the authority is prepared to suffer it and also how long the small core group of organizers will persevere.

The outdated law against homosexual acts is only one aspect of the challenge facing gay Singaporeans. Beyond the legality question is the larger issue of gaining legitimacy in the eyes of the larger public. Gay Singaporeans are far from overcoming both problems and all these serve to explain why stepping out of the closet is still being done cautiously on tiptoe. On this point, I quote Wong (1993: 114-119):

(a) Where legality is concerned, Singapore has very punitive laws against the homosexual act inherited from the British colonial government. This is written in Sections 377 and 377A of the Penal Code. The first of these imposes a penalty of up to life imprisonment for "carnal intercourse against the order of nature" which technically covers any act of sodomy or oral sex between gay or straight couples. Section 377A is more specific and prohibits "any male person . . . in public or private" from engaging in "any acts of gross indecency with another male person" and imposes a maximum sentence of up to two years imprisonment. Although life imprisonment has not been meted out to anybody convicted of homosexual acts and criminal prosecution has always targeted sex in public places and not in private, the laws are still psychologically intimidating. They expose gay people to police harassment for doing no more than drinking or dancing in a bar or sitting in the park. Defining homosexuality as a crime also makes it easier for the authority to close down gay places at their whim because the proprietors of these places would not dare to demand an explanation or challenge the action in court. The closing of *Niche* in 1989 was one such example. The laws make for a chicken-and-egg problem. In order to work towards decriminalization, the gay community has to get organized but organizing to defend a "criminal act" in turn makes gay people and their supporters cagey.

(b) Decriminalizing homosexuality would help the gay liberation cause in Singapore as it did elsewhere but it would not automatically guarantee legitimacy. Lesbians are a case in point. Singapore laws inherited from the British only specifically prohibit male homosexual acts and lesbian relations technically are not breaking any law. However, this does not make lesbians any less a target of social oppression and proscription by the State. In 1994 a bar on Boat Quay, a fashionable part of the city, decided to set aside a weekly night for lesbians. Billed innocuously as a women's night and advertised only by word of mouth, it became very popular. But it operated for no more than two weeks before the management received a letter from the police requesting that the establishment should ensure a better gender mix among its clientele. That put an end to the lesbian night.[8] Clearly, the lack of legitimacy is equally oppressive for lesbians as for gay men and the problem manifests itself in many daily situations, e.g., paucity and transience of gay-friendly places to relax, fear of family discovery and homophobic work environment.

Singapore's international image has been one of a highly regulated society, which tolerates not the tiniest infraction of its rules. But given the developments described in this paper, the reality of the gay scene can be perceived as being not all that confining to those living there. PLU's bid for registration may have failed, but it had existed for a good three years when it lodged its application, and, within that time, it had conducted a monthly public meeting without fail, and it put out a newsletter.

Singapore's gay community is also alert to the possibilities of the Internet. PLU did not succeed in getting the state into a dialogue on the homosexual issue, but made up for it by putting all the text of its exchange with the state on its WWW home page. As of December 1998, the page had logged more than 7 million hits since it was mounted on 15 December 1996.[9] This figure may be relatively modest by Internet standards, but viewed from another perspective, it is a figure more than twice the size of the Singapore population and, as such, would have a certain uplifting effect on the morale of those involved with the PLU endeavor. A few members of the PLU core group have also been preparing an alternative in expectation of failure to gain legal recognition; on 15 March 1997, they launched a newslist called the Singapore Gay News List (SiGNel).[10] To be sure, this is not the only cyberspace venue for gay Singaporeans to interact. Other newslists include SinGLe (Singapore Gays and Lesbians) and Singapore Pride, to name just two. Increasingly, gay Singaporeans are also becoming confident enough to set up individual homepages announcing their gay identity.

SiGNeL is useful as a forum for debate and a means of information dissemination. It, therefore, helps create an intellectual climate of openness and mutual support. SiGNeL has not remained purely as chatting in cyberspace. Subscribers have used it to organize large meetings in restaurants, trips to concerts, and school reunions for gay alumni. Thus the list has contributed substantively to community building. More significantly, in a society where many gay people are, firstly, anxious about the exposure of their sexuality, and, secondly, nervous about political activism, SiGNeL has provided the critical publicity for those members of the gay community who had set examples by taking bold individual public action to challenge hostile socio-political norms against homosexuality. Two cases should be mentioned in this regard. Joseph Lo, one of the founding members of PLU, took the opportunity of his attendance at a government-organized conference to raise the issue of the rejection of PLU's registration without any explanation, and he challenged the government Member of Parliament chairing the conference by arguing that any state claim to wanting to consult citizens in decision-making would amount to no more than platitudes in view of the summary rejection of PLU.[11] The second case was Andrew Lee's protest against the Anglican church's homophobic policy by attending a service at Saint Andrews Cathedral carrying the rainbow flag and a placard that read: "God loves all Bisexual, Gay, Lesbian and Transgendered Persons too!"[12] These acts signal a new mood of unprecedented activism, even though it is still far from the militancy and defiance that gave birth to gay liberation movements in the West. Nevertheless, it is a harbinger that the threshold of activism is slowly but steadily shifting to a willingness to confront authority on the gay issue rather than be satisfied with the status quo.

According to the SiGNeL list owner, there were 564 subscribers by October 1998. In numerical terms, it was reaching out to far more people than the monthly PLU meeting where attendance usually stayed below a hundred. However, the more activist members of the gay community also understand that cyberspace interaction with the occasional party event is not a substitute for the focused association which is critical for a gay political movement. Furthermore, for the 500 that could be reached through email linkages, the vast majority of the gay constituency remained unreached because they had no access to computer facilities. So at some future date, another effort must be made to continue where PLU left off, whether this is done by some of the old PLU core-group or by a new set of people.

Several developments in the legal field also gave gay Singaporeans reasons to hope for a less draconian and more just approach to non-mainstream sexual behavior:

(a) A landmark decision on 5 April 94 by the Singapore High Court in the case of Tan Boon Hock v Public Prosecutor saw the Chief Justice Yong Pung How allowing Tan to appeal against an excessive sentence of imprisonment and caning which was meted out after he was arrested during a police gay entrapment exercise. The accused was first charged in the subordinate courts with having used criminal force to outrage the modesty of a police constable under section 354 of the Penal Code (Cap 224). The Chief Justice drew a distinction between a situation where the modesty of "an unsuspecting and vulnerable victim of the fairer sex" was outraged and one, which involved a young male police officer on an operation, designed to entrap homosexuals. In the latter case an element of consent was evident if the police were out to entice and so his Honor felt that the accused should never have been charged with the offense of outraging another's modesty under section 354. He substituted a fine of $2000 for the sentence of imprisonment and caning. Apart from the lighter sentencing, this would make it difficult for the police to use section 354 to charge future entrapment cases. (Hoe Lun, 1995)

(b) In August 1995, Justice Lai Kew Chai, presiding over a case where heterosexual oral sex took place, ruled that oral sex between two consenting adults as a prelude to natural sex was not an offense. This was a lenient reading of Section 377 of the Penal Code and, by the judge's own admission, a judgment arrived at after "many sleepless nights, thinking of the evidence again and again." When asked about oral sex between two consenting adults who did not proceed to have natural sex, he said: "What is wrong with that?" Counsel then wondered if the court was saying that so long as it was between two consenting adults, it was not an offense, and the judge's reply was: "Let's cross the bridge when we come to it" ("Justice Lai clarifies when oral sex is not an offence" *The Straits Times*, 30 August 1995). Justice Lai's open-ended answer to the query was more encouraging for the cause of homosexual rights than if he had distinctively proscribed it. Whether or not this ruling will influence future court cases remains to be seen, but it still has a larger significance of indicating a certain amorphous relaxation of judicial and, possibly, social attitudes towards variable sex acts between consenting adults in private.

(c) A third development illustrates a certain benign capacity within the State to initiate legal reforms even when it implies a certain official acceptance of sexual unorthodoxy. This was the proposed amendments in January 1996 to the Republic's Women's Charter to remove a legal technicality which had made it impossible for transsexuals to get married since 1991 ("Sex change and marriage" *The Thing* Issue 20, March 1996, Singapore).

Given the above scenario, an optimistic reading of the situation would acknowledge the following:

(a) A generational change has taken place over the last 30 years which has produced a critical mass of gay citizens, who are no longer content with being allowed to meet discreetly in a few bars to hunt for sex partners, but who seek a louder voice to articulate their grievances and negotiate better treatment from society. This is what made efforts like that of AFA and PLU and SiGNeL possible. It is part of the larger trend of a country becoming more affluent, its citizens better educated, better traveled and better informed. These are liberalizing influences and all indicators are that they will grow in Singapore in the foreseeable future.

(b) Sufficient numbers of gay people feel that they can negotiate with and modify the regime they have been living with–notwithstanding the uncertainty and risk that the process may run into.

(c) Violent homophobia in the form of gay bashing does not find significant expression in Singapore society.

Be that as it may, the relationship between homosexuals and the state will continue to have its share of suspicion and uncertainty. Improvements are going to evolve over a long haul, and the gay movement in Singapore is unlikely to move in the direction of the radical activism and large-scale mobilization that was witnessed at the birth of gay liberation movements in countries such as the US or Australia. The reason is simple: the gay struggle in most western societies took place within well established liberal democratic polities where there was a strong tradition and acceptance of political activism. Street protest or even civil defiance enjoy both legitimacy and a measure of protection by the law. Even then, the advancement of gay rights (e.g., decriminalization) in the West took years. In Singapore, which basically is still an authoritarian country, these liberties cannot be taken for granted. Top down institutional tolerance for dissent, or its lack of, is only half the problem. The other half is the lack of a constituency, with possibly a

majority of gay people still being uncomfortable about a more assertive form of gay activism. Those who are pushing the political agenda
can not count on a critical mass within the gay community who are
willing to go public with their support. In other words, bottom up
grassroots pressure for improvement to the status and welfare of homosexuals remains weak. Singapore's gay movement is in the early
stages of finding its own form of activism. The deliberations of this
movement should also not be seen in isolation. It is part of the larger
pattern where many other constituencies, e.g., racial minorities,
women, journalists, artists, etc. are seeking more socio-political space
for themselves. Collectively, they will have to soften up the political
climate before any significant change can take place.

NOTES

1. The earliest published description I could find of Bugis Street as a place of
great gender diversity was Ommaney (1960: 39-45). Ommaney did not specifically
date his description of the street, but his book makes it clear that he was in Singapore
from 1955 to 1960. The "sex bazaar" character of Bugis Street came to an end in the
mid-1980s when an urban redevelopment project turned the area into restaurants and
nightspots minus the old risque image.

2. *Le Bistro*, as far as many gay Singaporeans can recollect, was the first gay bar
in Singapore. A retired New Zealand serviceman, in a chance encounter, claimed that
in the early 1960s when he was stationed in Singapore, there was a Golden Venus bar
in the Orchard Hotel on Orchard Road. This claim has not been collaborated by Singaporeans. The old Orchard Hotel has since been reconstructed beyond recognition.
Golden Venus and *Le Bistro* are no longer extant.

3. The plays were Eleanor Wong's *Jackson on a jaunt*, Chay Yew's *As if he
hears*, and Russell Heng's *Lest the demons get to me*. The first two plays were subsequently staged in 1989/1990 after negotiations with censorship authorities. The third
was staged in 1992 after Singapore's culture policy was liberalized by its new prime
minister, Goh Chok Tong.

4. Much of this information comes from the writer's own involvement in PLU.

5. Legal action was taken against Josef Ng, the artist who displayed his pubic
hair. He was fined by the court.

6. The gay community was generally wary of *The New Paper* because of its sensational coverage of homosexuality. It was the paper that splashed on its front page a
picture of the performance artist Josef Ng snipping his pubic hair offstage, which
caused the furore over the event.

7. PLU has posted all its correspondence with various government departments
on the matter of registration at the website *<http://www.geocities.com/WestHollywood/
3878/#Letters>*.

8. This incident was recounted by lesbian friends in PLU. In 1998, there were a
few commercial venues where lesbians met on a few nights each week.

9. The PLU homepage is at: <*http://www.geocities.com/WestHollywood/3878/*>.

10. For details of SiGNel, see <*http://www.geocities.com/WestHollywood/9803/#what*>.

11. The conference on 15 October 1998 had the theme, "Consultation and Consensus versus Decisiveness and Quick Action," and was meant by the ruling party to solicit public opinion on how it could be more consultative in policy-making. The government Member of Parliament (MP) was Lim Swee Say but also present was Nominated MP Simon Tay. A Nominated MP, as the title indicates, is an MP who is appointed from the ranks of eminent citizens rather than elected–the idea being to provide non-partisan critical opinions in a parliament overwhelmingly controlled by the ruling party. In response to Lo's challenge, Lim reiterated the government line that homosexuality was illegal in Singapore, but Tay was more sympathetic to PLU's problem and volunteered to seek an official explanation for PLU as to why its application was rejected. A description of the proceedings was posted by Lo on SiGNel on 17 October 1998.

12. Lee's action on 30 August 1998 came in the wake of the Lambeth Conference anti-homosexual stance in which the Singapore Anglican church played a leading role. On a subsequent Sunday, Lee's action led to a confrontation where he was denied the right to take communion unless he renounced his homosexuality. He publicly refused. Accounts of both incidents were posted on SiGNeL by Lee on 30 August 1998 and 7 September 1998.

REFERENCES

Lun, Hoe (1995). "Guilty or Not Guilty?" *People Like Us* Newsletter Issue 15. February. Singapore

Ommaney, F. D. (1960). *Eastern Windows*. London: Longman

Ong, Wilfred (1993). "Decriminalizing homosexuality." *Commentary* National University of Singapore Society. 11(1):114-119.

PLU (1994). "The history and herstory of PLU." *People Like Us* Newsletter. Issue 7, June. Singapore.

Culture, Sexualities, and Identities: Men Who Have Sex with Men in India

Shivananda Khan

INTRODUCTION

This essay arises from a specific context of working with sexual health issues among males who have sex with males in India, where HIV/AIDS has become an urgent issue. Over the past few years, The Naz Foundation (formerly The Naz Project)[1] has sponsored several consultation meetings, worked with local male sexual networks and organizations, and helped develop locally based service projects in Calcutta and New Delhi focusing on the sexual health needs of males who have sex with males and gay-identified men. The Naz Foundation has also been involved in a variety of research and ethnographic studies among male sexual networks and has published a variety of reports on the cultural, religious, and social frameworks of males who have sex with males in India. It is our belief that understanding frameworks of sexual behavior is the first step towards developing appropriate strategies for encouraging behavioral changes towards safer sex practices.

This perspective has also arisen from my work as founder of Shakti, the South Asian lesbian, gay, and bisexual organization formed in 1988 in the UK. Working with this network and articulating its concerns to the broader lesbian and gay communities was to lead me to question some of what I considered the fundamental assumptions that

[Haworth co-indexing entry note]: "Culture, Sexualities, and Identities: Men Who Have Sex with Men in India." Khan, Shivananda. Co-published simultaneously in *Journal of Homosexuality* (Harrington Park Press, an imprint of The Haworth Press, Inc.) Vol. 40, No. 3/4, 2001, pp. 99-115; and: *Gay and Lesbian Asia: Culture, Identity, Community* (ed: Gerard Sullivan, and Peter A. Jackson) Harrington Park Press, an imprint of The Haworth Press, Inc., 2001, pp. 99-115. Single or multiple copies of this article are available for a fee from The Haworth Document Delivery Service [1-800-342-9678, 9:00 a.m. - 5:00 p.m. (EST). E-mail address: getinfo@haworthpressinc.com].

configured these communities. It led me to read, listen, and learn about constructions of sexuality and their historical and contemporary significance.

This essay is a part of that learning process, a process whose focus continues to be primarily on developing appropriate strategies to promote male sexual health. As a part of this process, The Naz Project was involved in two significant events in India. The first was a seminar held in December 1993 on Alternate Sexualities, organized by Sakhi (a lesbian resource center in New Delhi founded by Gita Thadani[2]) and sponsored by The Naz Project. The second was a consultation meeting on sexual health for men who have sex with men and gay identified men held in Bombay in December 1994, organized by The Humsafar Trust[3] and The Naz Project.[4]

This essay focuses on men who have sex with men, and gay men. This is because most of the research and analysis conducted so far by The Naz Foundation has been on the male to male sexual behaviors as a significant factor in STD/HIV transmission in India. This is a different matter than the construction of men's sexualities.[5] While considerable work has been done on female bonding and friendships, gender constructions, and female social roles, very little research has been conducted on female to female sexual behaviors and constructions of lesbianism in India. I fully acknowledge the weakness this lack brings to this essay.

SOME EXAMPLES

Prem[6] is 26, married, and has a young son. He works in a large family business in Calcutta, where his family are prominent members of Calcutta society. He has fond memories of his first sexual experience with another boy at the age of 13. He has continued to have sex with other men, even after his marriage, albeit less frequently because of the lack of opportunity. His sexual interactions with other men have always been fleeting, "pick-ups." He has never wanted to form a relationship with another man because this would increase the risks of discovery for him. Such a discovery would be disastrous for him in terms of his family and his social standing. He would prefer not to be married. He doesn't love his wife, but feels he performs his husbandly duties adequately.

Islam is an auto-rickshaw driver in Pune where he lives in one of the small shanty villages on the outskirts of the industrial area. He is married with four children. He says that sometimes he just has to go out and find a man to have sex with, although he is happy with his wife. This usually happens about once every two months, and he feels that he can't control his desire for this. He finds men at the many contact points around the city. He doesn't call himself a homosexual; the word gay he doesn't understand, not having access to English. Nor does he see anything wrong in what he does. He is just "messing about." The terms "homosexual" or "bisexual" cannot refer to him, he believes, because he is happily married with children. He remembers his first sexual experience with his uncle back in his home village. He was 12.

Arjit is 19 years old and is a student at New Delhi university studying English literature. He is from a well-to-do family in the diplomatic service. He calls himself gay and would like to "come out" to his family, but he is deeply concerned about their possible reaction and rejection of him. They might cut him out of the family, and he would lose everything! He has always known about himself ever since he can remember. He was always attracted to other boys. His first experience with another boy was when he was 11. Now he visits the various "gay" haunts around New Delhi where he can find "plenty of action."

Ranjan is a male prostitute, a young man of 16 who plies his "business" in Central Madras near the railway station. He has done this since he was 13, when he ran away from home because of the beatings of his father. He never wants to go back home. He says that he enjoys his "work" because it gives him a lot of money, even though sometimes his clients are rough. He is saving money to buy a small business. He doesn't call himself a homosexual, even though he enjoys the sex. It is only business.

Mohammed, 42, is married with three children and works in a hotel in Pune. He visits a local female prostitute once a month after payday. He also has sex with some of the male guests and other staff at the hotel. He says, "I am always 'hot.' I want a girl, but they're too expensive. So when I am hot and I don't have enough money, then I know several men who I can have *maasti*[7] with. A lot of my friends do this."

Arun lives with his lover Kamal near a railway station in Bombay. They have lived together as lovers for the last five years. Both work as municipal sweepers. That is how they met. Both have had sex with other men prior to their meeting. They say they want to stay together as lovers. They don't consider themselves as different. They know many men who enjoy sex with other men. They don't play husband and wife roles, thinking it rather silly as both are men. Neither read nor speak English. They both left school at 13.

BEHAVIOR AND LANGUAGE: IDENTITY AND COMMUNITY

In the field of HIV/AIDS prevention strategies, discussions on heterosexuality, bisexuality and homosexuality, "straight" or "gay" are often used to refer to clear cut categories in terms of sexual behaviors, and these are often conflated with sexual identities, i.e., that one's self-concept as a sexual being is consistent with one's sexual behavior, and that sexual identity is fundamental to the sense of self. The lesbian and gay "movement" has been globalized (e.g., see Sullivan, in this volume, or Adam, Duyvendak & Krouwel, 1999) and so in India several gay and lesbian groups have been established, such as Bombay Dost, Sakhi, G.A.Y, Counsel Club, and Friends India (see Appendix 1 for contact details). Many cities have well-established social/sexual networks of lesbians and/or gay men. For men, as "owners" of public spaces, almost all major urban areas will have well defined "cruising areas," where casual sexual partners can easily be obtained.

Within these groups, formed more often than not by those from the English speaking middle classes, Western terms are used almost exclusively, and the context of discussions relate to Western understandings of gay identities, gay rights, and gay lifestyles. You may hear a term such as *hamjinsi* or *samlingi*,[8] but these are contemporary transliterations of the word homosexual. You may also hear the phrase, "he is a gay" or "he has gay sex" or "he likes "homosex," but these refer to sexual acts more than to an identity category.

Who is gay in an Indian context? What is a gay? Who is a homosexual? About three-quarters (72%) of truck drivers in North Pakistan who participated in a recent survey published in AIDS Analysis Asia admitted that they had sex with other males, while 76% stated they had sex with female sex workers. Are these 72% gay? Homosexual? There is sufficient anecdotal evidence to indicate that in the other countries of the sub-continent, similar levels of male to male sexual behaviors exist as a part of a broader sexual repertoire. Are these males bisexuals? Does the use of these terms carry the same meaning and significance as it does say in New York, London, or Sydney? In the context of developing and delivering sexual health services for males who have sex with other males, these questions become extremely relevant, for any answers given will determine the shape and content of the delivery of such services.

In working with sexual health issues in India and in listening to the rhetoric of UNAIDS representatives, international donor agencies, the Indian medical profession, and many Western and Indian gay men, an assumption is often made that same-gender sexual behaviors must mean the person is a homosexual, or gay, while male to female sexual behavior must mean that the person is a heterosexual. In these discourses, procreative "heterosexuality" is seen as "normal," while other behaviors are seen as perverse and foreign. However, these constructs seem to have very little contemporary or historical validity in India (and even to some extent in the West). This reductionist ideology is a recent invention from the 19th century, which has consequently acted to reduce the rich diversity of alternate sexualities (Foucault, 1978; Weeks, 1986; Katz, 1995; Herdt, 1994). Closer analysis of these debates seems to me to indicate a confusion among the terms sexual behavior, gender, identity formation, and cross-cultural validity, and within such confusion there may well be elements of neo-colonialism, racism, and Western imperialism (Khan, 1994c; Hyam, 1990).

I am not arguing that there are no women or men with lesbian or gay identities in India. This is patently untrue. What I am putting forward is that too often language and terminology are used inadequately outside the cultural context in which that language is used. In India, over 80% of the population do not understand English. Use of Western terms easily leads to misunderstandings, inappropriate terminology, and as a consequence (particularly with reference to HIV/AIDS work), Indians can often state that there is no indigenous homosexuality.[9] This easily leads to the proposition that there is no, or very little, "homosexual" behavior, which, therefore, means there is no need to invest in HIV prevention programs for males who have sex with males. It is clear that we need to explore what "homosexuality" is and to distinguish between it and "homosexual behavior," which also needs to be defined for the South Asian context.

This exploration is particularly urgent in India, with its increasing rate of HIV infection, in order to ensure appropriate and adequate access to sexual health services, and to address human rights violations. We need to recognize that behaviors and identities in India are constructed within differing cultural frameworks and to acknowledge that contemporary Western understandings of lesbian and gay identities are beginning to be imagined, to emerge and to develop among some men and women. But in what form? For whom? In what context? And in what language?

These debates have involved a growing number of Indians (and other South Asians) who, in living in Western countries, have "come out" as self-identified lesbians, gay men, and bisexuals and who have formed specific self-help and support organizations, such as Trikone in the United States, Khush in Canada, and Shakti in the UK (see Appendix 2 for contact details). A question can be posed as to whether these diasporic lesbian and gay organizations act (or acted) as instigators of the development of a "queer" India? *Trikone*, a lesbian and gay magazine for South Asians, was first published in the United States in 1986 and *Shakti Khabar* in the UK in 1989. *Bombay Dost* appeared in 1990. On their frequent journeys "back home," members of lesbian and gay diasporic groups carry with them their newly wrought identities and a passionate discourse on lesbian and gay rights, lifestyles, and identities, which they sometimes convey to their fellow Indians still living under the hegemony of Indian traditions and cultural values. These discourses are, of course, most often conducted in English, and those Indians privileged enough to access these discourses may then try to attempt to fit them into their lives, amid arranged marriages, children, and joint and extended family systems (Ratti, 1993).

Ashok Row Kavi and Giti Thadani are two people who have fought against homophobic traditions and cultural values, and have spoken in public in India many times about lesbian and gay issues. They have worked tirelessly to address the concerns of emerging sexual identities and helped establish a public arena where lesbians and gay men in India can articulate identity issues. They are being joined by a growing band of women and men who are willing to challenge "the system." However, it still needs to be recognized that the vast majority of these groups, networks, organizations, and individuals are privileged to be a part of an English speaking, urban elite, who have more options and choices than the vast majority of people whose same sex desires and acts have to be bounded within tradition, custom, and culture, and who often do not have language to articulate their sense of desire and difference (Spencer, 1980; Khan, 1994b).

I was interested to hear Dede Oetomo, a gay activist in Indonesia, say at the Vancouver International AIDS Conference in July 1996 that perhaps "importing" Western constructions of gay identities into Indonesia was creating a social tension whereby local homoaffectionalist and homosocial[10] structures were being destroyed for the fear of being labeled "gay."

The debate on sexualities and identities may even at times be perceived as a form of sexual neo-colonialism whereby Western sexual ideologies have "invaded" Indian discourses on sexuality and identity by professionals, laypersons, "straights" or "gays," and where indigenous histories and cultures become invisible. What we, as diasporic Indian "lesbians" and "gay" men, often do is to try to fit Indian sexual and cultural histories as well as contemporary behaviors and identities into a Western sexual discourse. Thus we have the discourses on Indian "queer" histories.[11] This often means that we urgently seek "evidence" for a lesbian and gay history within India to validate ourselves as lesbians and gay men of Indian origin living outside of India. The politics of ethnicity and racism in the West often force those of us in the diaspora to seek self-justification not only among the larger numbers of white lesbians and gay men, but also within our own communities. This may often be the rationale for the formation of groups such as Trikone, Khush, and Shakti. Labeled "the other" in our countries of residence by our color, culture, and country of origin, and by both "straight" and "gay" society, we seek admittance into a self-affirming social club to be with others who are like us both in terms of color and identity (Khan, 1994b).

Indian histories are replete with evidence of homosexuality. Mughal (15th century onwards) paintings and poetry are often explicitly homoerotic. There is an abundance of Hindu temple carvings and iconography that show same-sex sexual behaviors (Thadani, 1996). Konarak, Khajaraho, and other sites become places of pilgrimage for the diasporic Indian lesbian or gay man. *The finger points. Here is the evidence. Yes, there were lesbians and gay men in our past.* But how much of this is valid? As contemporary self-identified Indian lesbians or gay men (whatever those terms mean to us personally), we shouldn't need self-validation based on a presumptive past. Our existence is our own validation, however we may label ourselves. Western discourses on sexuality appear to have placed sexual desire and a sexual sense of self as the center of a personal self. This perhaps arises from the historical development of the concepts of individuality; the rights of the individual; the individual as a distinct entity separate and separated from his/her family, kinship group, and social milieu; and the medicalization of sexual behaviors.

For the majority of males who have sex with males in India these notions of sexuality are considerably less significant than the often clear distinctions between concepts of "active" and "passive," concepts of "discharge," "pleasure," and "desire," or even concepts of "real sex" (in marriage between husband and wife, where sex is defined by procreation and duty), and *maasti*. It is very common for both "active" and "passive" male partners to engage in sexual relations with women and to be married with children, as well as having sex with other men. This does not mean that all same-sex relationships fall into this characteristic of "active" and "passive" role/stereotype activity. Much same-sex sexual activity involves non-penetrative varieties, mutually indulged in frameworks of friendship and sexual play, while in other situations urgent sexual discharge and sexual "need" is the significant factor.[12] Indeed, same-sex sexual behavior may play a relatively insignificant role in the construction of an identity. Being a husband, a father, or a wife or mother often carries greater weight.

None of these frameworks are fully synonymous with Western lesbian or gay constructions. While most "active" partners in male same-sex interactions do not consider themselves either to be homosexuals, gays, or even bisexuals, male "passive" partners in sexual contexts with other males often see themselves as "feminized" men (as "not-men"), but only in this context. What they do does not have a central significance as to who they perceive themselves to be, which tends to be oriented more towards family and marriage.

In discussions in a number of Indian cities with males who visit "cruising" sites for sex, a constant refrain was that their sense of self in the "cruising" site was differently constructed than that outside the site. As one English speaking person in Calcutta told me, "Look, inside the park I am a gay. Once I leave the park and go onto the streets that changes. Outside the park, I am a good Hindu, a married man with a good family." Identities shift, change, and shape themselves according to context, place, social situation, need, and desire. There is often little sense of continuity, but one of fluidity.[13]

The act of sexual penetration is not so much a definer of identity, but one of phallic power. For many Indians, the "penetrator" maintains a sense of "manliness," while the "penetrated" will be seen as "not-man." There is an assumption that exclusive anal intercourse is the behavioral definition of homosexuality and that exclusive vaginal intercourse is the definer of heterosexuality. Of course, what is forgotten is that non-penetrative sex plays a substantial role in same-sex sexual behaviors and that men also anally penetrate many women.

In India (and in other countries of the sub-continent), *hijras*[14] are a specific social, religious, and cultural group who are often said to be transsexuals, transvestites, or "passive" homosexuals. None of these descriptions are particularly valid. *Hijras* are often said to constitute a "third gender." Sexual desire, poverty, and pre-adolescent sexual penetration by older men all play roles in the development of a *hijra* identity.

In many of the largely sex-segregated regions of South Asia, young boys, who are neither seen as men nor women, have been historically defined as sexual objects desired and penetrated by men. The "beardless youths" of much Arab and Mughal literature reflects this construction and practice, which continues to the present in some situations (Rahman, 1989; Schild, 1990; Baldauf, 1990).

In India, a peron's position in the joint and extended family, being married and having children, are central to his/her social definition and personal identity. In other words, who we are arises from where we are in the extended family network and what family obligations and duties that position creates. Individuals have a family and community identity to which personal identity is subsumed. The focus of the self is not upon individuality but upon kinship. Concepts of individuality, of a personal self separated from others, are weak. And in the context of identities and behaviors, they all have a central impact on the social constructions of actual sexual behavior.

Family, social, and cultural pressures on individuals to marry and have children are intense and unavoidable. In that sense, "a procreative sexuality" can be seen as a social compulsion, as a familial and community duty. Men who would prefer to form sexual relationships and partnerships with other men still feel obliged to marry and produce children to honor family and community obligations. The following statement made to the author by a self-identified gay man in Bombay is typical:

In the end I got married. It was the only way to get back to my family. My parents continuously harassed me for three years, as did my uncles and aunts. Marriage is everything. And if I didn't obey my parents and accept their choice, where would I be?

Such men will look outside the marriage for sexual and emotional fulfillment (Khan, 1990).[15] Where marital sex is seen as duty, sex outside marriage (for men!) becomes a source of pleasure and discharge:

I can't tell my wife about myself. It would destroy my family and her. I can't have a divorce because of the shame it would bring to our families. I go out maybe several times a month, pick up some guy for quick sex in the park or toilet. (Khan, 1990)

The fluidity of many South Asian males' sexual experiences and behavior reflect the socio-cultural frameworks in which they live. Factors such as sexual invisibility, gender segregation, joint and extended families, homosocial and homoaffectionalist culture, male ownership of public space, shame cultures, izzat (honor) in the community, compulsory marriage and procreation, gender constructions where male and female roles are based upon duty and obligations as much as upon biology, and where adulthood is as much defined by duty as by age frame Indian cultures and, therefore, identities.

There are specific understandings of what it is to be a man or a woman which are defined by socio-cultural duties and obligations to the marriage partner, family, and community. Men and women are not seen as adults until they are married and, in the case of women, have produced a child (often this could mean a boy). To be a single person after a certain age is seen as shameful, bringing dishonor to the family, and is often seen as an aberration or sickness. Being alone is judged negatively. Many men who have sex with men report that they are constantly asked by their parents, "But who will look after you when you are old?"

Indian languages do not have specific words for homosexuality, heterosexuality, and bisexuality as nouns or adjectives in the same way that these terms are understood in the West. What exists are terms that express differing forms of sexual behavior that are gendered or those that refer to particular sexual acts.[16] These terms are often abusive and male dominated, referring to specific acts of penetration. In these constructions, who does the penetrating in a sexual act becomes important for male self-definition and prestige.

Descriptions of sexual behavior are not necessarily coterminous with personal identity. For many men, sexuality often becomes a matter of combining duty, opportunity, access, cost, and a self-absorbed need for sexual discharge.

Contemporary sexual behavior and understandings do not preclude different practices and comprehensions existing in the history of Indian cultures. The sub-continent has experienced many differing invasions from pre-Vedic times through the Muslim invasions to the British Raj, bringing with them their own social constructions and frameworks of identity. These have undoubtedly had an impact upon ideologies of gender, sexuality, and sexual behavior in contemporary India. However, the denial of variations in history in many Western and Indian discourses has given rise to a prevailing construction of sexuality, where a "procreative and penetrative" sexual ideology is the only "sexuality" that is seen as relevant. Perversely, any other form is categorized as deviant and Western. This dominant sexual ideology has claimed precedence over all others as a system of social control, which enables male power to take on a singular and patronizing social role. At the same time, the construction of patriarchal social systems, the enforcement of compulsory marriage, and the necessity of producing male heirs has created a pattern of destruction, marginalization, and denial concerning alternate frameworks of sexualities and their histories in India.

Alternate histories existing as traditions of the periphery are being lost due to the dominance of procreative and marriage ideologies. Older, alternate mythologies and histories are manipulated, deformed, and mutilated to suit rural male patriarchal ideologies. This creates rural economies where there is gender segregation of labor, boy children as social capital, and control of land, economic and cultural resources by men. These social relations are recreated in urban spaces and form the basis of a sexual ideology which serves the interests of rural men, and which are romanticized in urban discourses as traditional and authentic.

Sex is either defined as penetrative and gendered, or, in order to maintain male power, it is defined as play or discharge: for example, at times of "body tension" and sexual urgency, when sexual arousal occurs during play or body contact, or when opportunities are created for sexual contact in the dark, under a blanket, in shared beds. Opportunities like these are frequent and mean that significant amounts of male-male sexual behavior occur within family environments and networks, between male relatives and friends. But this is not seen as real sex! This is *maasti*, invisible and denied. The recognized object of desire is still a woman, but because she is unobtainable, another male will do. This is not to deny expressions of romantic and passionate love among males. Intense friendships between males in a homosocial and homoaffectionalist culture create boundaries that are easily crossed in sexual play. But the goal of marriage and children remains.

Male sexual behavior becomes self-absorbed. It is reduced to one of discharge, to the act itself, rather than being based upon a desire for the other person. Sexual behavior becomes depersonalized. In this, the sex act becomes brutalized whether it is between male and female or male and male. For example, in a survey I conducted of 35 men who have sex with men in Calcutta, the average time for a penetrative act from insertion to discharge was between 3-5 minutes. One respondent commented, "There is no time for foreplay. They just shove it and pull out."

Sexual behavior becomes indiscriminate in circumstances where high levels of sexual repression leads to sessions of urgent sexual release. For example, at a particular truck stop in Bombay, several young men reported that on average they experience more than five acts of penetration by truck drivers in any given night. Truck drivers have also reported that when they are on the road, they "need" at least four to five sexual encounters per night to release their tension.

In this situation, concepts of personal choice and privacy become lost. There can be no development of individuality. The following comment made to me by a man in New Delhi captures the context of much sexual expression in India:

> Privacy? What privacy? I share a room with my three older brothers, and I have had sex with all of them. The other room is where my parents and grandparents sleep. There is no lock on the door. In the hallway, my uncle and aunt sleep. It's like this everywhere in India.

There is no social, psychological, or cultural space to resist a closeted and schizophrenic state of being for men who have sex with men, and whose sense of desire and self articulates a yearning for a "life-style" or some sort of safe "identity" that expresses "gayness." The following statement made to me captures this:

> I was married at 11 and I finally had sex with my wife when I was 16 years old. I had no choice. My family arranged every-thing. I first had sex with my [male] school teacher when I was 12 and this continued until I was 16, when I left school. I have always longed for a man to be with, you know, who will care for me. But how can I find such a man? How can I leave my wife and children? What am I? I don't know. I just know what I feel sometimes when I see a handsome man.

This man tries to assimilate into society through marriage and by having children, yet expresses alternate sexual desires which can only be realized in darkness, shame, and silence.

Among the educated middle classes, there is a small, but growing, movement of people whose sense of personal identity is separate from that of their family, kin group, and community and who are beginning to create new forms of sexual identity. Many of these may well call themselves lesbians, gay men, homosexuals, bisexuals, and even het-erosexuals.

In the main, these evolving and emerging identities are arising with the growth of urban, industrialized, and commercial cultures, concom-itant with which is a rising sense of individuality, personal privacy, and private space. This cultural change appears to be associated with the development of nuclear family lifestyles, the expansion of educa-tion, and the power of the English-speaking middle-classes to access Western literature and to make more choices about their lives. It is mostly people from these backgrounds who meet, socialize, discuss and debate (usually in English) issues of sexual identities and "com-ing out." Gay activism in India is growing and has begun to challenge laws which criminalize homosexuality and which were inherited from the British Raj. It remains to be seen whether these emerging identities will reflect (or perhaps imitate) Western constructions and whether those who adopt these identities will attempt to live these out within Indian cultures, or whether differing identities will be constructed.

NOTES

1. The Naz Project was established in October 1991 to develop and provide culturally and linguistically appropriate HIV/AIDS services for the South Asian, Turkish, Arab, and Irani communities in Greater London. It rapidly became one of the leading ethnic minority HIV/AIDS and sexual health agencies in the United Kingdom. By January 1996, associated organizations had been established in India through The Naz Foundation (India) Trust, which provides HIV/AIDS-related services in New Delhi and Calcutta. In June 1996, The Naz Project changed its name to The Naz Project (London) and continued to deliver HIV/AIDS services in the Greater London area. The Naz Foundation provides HIV/AIDS services elsewhere in the UK and abroad.

2. Gita Thadani's book (1996) is a valuable text which provides a lesbian perspective on Indian history by reference to sanskrit texts, ancient iconography, and temple statues.

3. The Humsafar Trust is a HIV/AIDS and sexual health agency based in Mumbai, India. It provides sexual health outreach and support programs for gay men and men who have sex with men in Mumbai.

4. I am indebted to all the participants at these meetings for the hundreds of interviews and discussions that I have been privileged to have with men who have sex with men and gay men, both in India and the UK. I am also grateful to Shakti participants, Giti Thadani and Ashok Row Kavi, who founded The Humsafar Trust and *Bombay Dost*, the first legally-published gay newsletter in India. Gita Thandani and Ashok Row Kavi are among the few lesbian and gay rights activists in India.

5. Though terms such as sexual behavior and sexuality are often used interchangeably, I draw a distinction between them as follows: In contrast to sexual behavior, sexuality refers to self identity in reference to sexual desire and gender. For example, in many interviews with men who have sex with men in India, I was told by informants that they sexually desire women. Others said that they were interested in the sexual act itself more so than the person with whom they had sexual intercourse. I refer to this as "discharge sex." It is clear that in many instances, factors other than sexual desire play a role in the sexual partner choice.

6. The case studies related at the beginning of the essay come from a collection of personal stories related to the author over the last four years during training workshops, research, and casual meetings. Names have been changed.

7. *Maasti* is a Hindi term which means mischief and often has sexual overtones when it is used between young men.

8. *Hamjinsi* is an Urdu word, while *samlingi* is a Hindi term. Both refer to a man who has sex with other men.

9. At a number of HIV/AIDS meetings in India and internationally, a number of professionals have made statements such as: "There are no homosexuals in India"; "The level of homosexual behavior is very small"; or "Homosexuality is a Western import brought in by the British Raj." At a meeting in December 1995 in Colombo, Sri Lanka, a consultant for the United Nations Development Programme, who had visited Chennai and Mumbai to collect information for a report comparing HIV/AIDS non-governmental agencies, publicly stated that there were only 3000 homosexuals/gay men in Mumbai (population approximately 13 million) and some 1500 homosexuals in Chennai (population some 3-5 million).

10. Following Hardman (1993), I use homoaffectionalism to mean social acceptance of the public display of male/male or female/female physical affection. I use the term homosocial to mean a social framework of strong male or female bonding, and gender segregation of social spaces. For example, in India it is very common to see two women or two men holding hands or putting their arms around each other or sharing a bed, and so on. Public space is socially owned by males. Homoaffectionalism and homosexual behaviors are not the same (Khan,1996).

11. For example, an attempt to organize a "Queer Trip of India" in 1994 was made by a disaporic group of South Asians living in San Francisco, which produced a T-shirt with the slogan "India - The Queer View." A gay and lesbian film festival was planned as part of the tour, as were visits to a number of cities meeting up with the local lesbian/gay groups and tours of temple sites where there is iconography and statues of same-gender couplings. Interestingly, the T-shirt was saffron–a color which for many, carries associations with the BJP (a nationalist political party based on recovering so-called Hindu values and prejudice against minorities).

12. Many truck, auto-rickshaw, and taxi drivers have stated that their bodies get "hot" from the engines and this produces a need for sexual release to cool their bodies down. They state that "body tension" produces mental or sexual tension.

13. Based on my experiences working with Shakti and The Naz Project, I have found that as people of color, Indians, Pakistanis, or Bangladeshis living in the UK have multiple frameworks of identity which shift and change according to the context or space they are in. For myself, "I am an Indian male among Indians, a South Asian among South Asians, a gay man among gay men, and a black person within the general society. Who I present to myself and to the outside world depends on who I am with. None of these identities are central to my sense of self. Each reflects a different need and context."

14. Hijras are "males" who dress as women. They are often castrated as a sacrifice of malehood to the goddess Renuka Devi. They can often be seen aggressively begging on the streets in Bombay, Varanasi, New Delhi, and other cities. Some engage in sex work. They are often called to the birth of son or to a wedding because of the belief that their blessing will bring prosperity and good luck (Nanda, 1990).

15. An unmarried man from Orissa who has sex with men stated that when he fucks a male he thinks of it as practise for when he eventually gets married. His body is "hot," and he believes it is much better to "fuck" than to masturbate. A common Indian belief about masturbation is that each drop of semen is equivalent to 40 drops of blood. To masturbate is to weaken the body.

16. *Khusra* and *gandu* are terms meaning a "not man" who is fucked by a man. The term in Hindi for anal sex is *gand marna* which approximately means, "to beat the butt[ocks]."

REFERENCES

Adam, Barry, Duyvendak, Jan W. & Krouwel, Andre (Eds.). (1999). *The Global Emergence of Gay and Lesbian Politics: National Imprints of a Worldwide Movement*. Philadelphia: Temple University Press
Baldauf, I. (1990). "Bacabozlik -Boylove, folksong and literature in Central Asia." Paedika, Autumn, Vol 2, No. 2.

Cohen, L. (1995). "The pleasures of castration: The post-operative status of Hijras, Jankhas and Academics." In Abramson, Paul & Pinkerton, Steven D. (Eds.). *Sexual Nature/Sexual Culture.* Chicago: University of Chicago Press.

Foucault, M. (1978). *History of Sexuality Volume 1.* London: Allen Lane.

Hardman, P. D. (1993). *Homoaffectionalism.* GLB Publishers.

Herdt, G. (1994). *Third Sex Third Gender–Beyond Sexual Dimorphism in Culture and History.* Zon Books.

Hyam, R. (1990). *Empire and Sexuality–The British Experience.* Manchester University Press.

Kakar, S. (1989). *Intimate Relations–Exploring Indian Sexuality.* Penguin Books.

Katz, J. (1995). *The Invention of Heterosexuality.* New York: Dutton.

Khan, S. (1990). *KHUSH report,* Naz Foundation.

Khan, S. (1991). *KHUSH: A Report on the Needs of South Asian Lesbians and Gay Men in the UK.* Naz Publications.

Khan, S. (1994a). *History of Alternate Sexualities in South Asia: A report on a 3-day seminar.* New Delhi, India: Naz Publications.

Khan, S. (1994b). *Contexts–Race, Culture and Sexuality: A Report and Needs Assessment on South Asian Communities.* Naz Publications.

Khan (1994c). *Contexts–Race, Culture and Sexuality.* A Naz Report.

Khan, S. (1995). *Conference Report: Emerging Gay Identities in India–Implications for Sexual Health.* Naz Publications.

Khan (1996). "Under The Blanket." In *Bisexualities and AIDS.* London: Taylor and Francis.

Nanda (1990). *Neither Man nor Woman–Hijras of India.* Wadsworth.

Rahman, A. (1989). *Boy love in the Urdu Ghazal.* Paedika, Summer, Vol. 2, No.1.

Ratti, R. (1993). *A Lotus of Another Colour.* Boston: Alyson Publications.

Schild, M. (1988). "The irresistible beauty of boys–Middle-Eastern attitudes about boy-love," *Paedika,* Winter, No. 3.

Sharma, S. K. (1993). *Hijras–The Labelled Deviants.* New Delhi: Gian Publishing House.

Spencer, K. (1980). *Man Made Language.* London: Routledge.

Sullivan, Gerard (2000). "A New Innings or a New Game? Gay and Lesbian Identities and Communities in Asia." In Sullivan, Gerard & Jackson, Peter A. (Eds.). *Gay and Lesbian Asia: Identities and Communities.* New York: The Haworth Press, Inc.

Thadani, G. (1996). *Sakhiyani: Lesbian Desire in Ancient and Modern India.* London: Cassell.

Weeks, G. (1986). *Sexuality.* London: Routledge.

APPENDIX 1
Lesbian and gay and HIV-related organizations in India

Bombay Dost, 105A Veeena Beena Shopping Centre, Mumbai 400 050, India
   (gay magazine)
Counsel Club, c/o Pawan Post Bag 10237, Calcutta 700 019, India
Friends India, Post Box 59, Mahanagar, Lucknow 226 006, India
Humsafar Trust, c/o Bombay Dost (HIV/AIDs agency for gay men)
Naz Foundation (India) Trust, Calcutta Project, 468A Block K, New Alipore,
   Calcutta 700 053, India or New Delhi Project, P.O. Box 3910, Andrews
   Gunj, New Delhi 110 049, India (branches of an HIV/AIDS organization
   promoting male sexual health programs)
Sakhi, P.O. Box 3526, Lajpat Nagar, New Delhi 110 024, India (lesbian resource
   center)

APPENDIX 2
Lesbian and gay and HIV-related organizations located in North America or England oriented toward people of South Asian ancestry

Atish, Box 345, 1027 Davie Street, Vancouver, BC V6E 4L2, Canada
Khush, P.O. Box 6172, Station A, Toronto, Ontario M5W 1P6, Canada
Naz Project (London), Palingswick House, 241 King Street, London W6 9LP,
   UK (an HIV/AIDS service agency for the South Asian, Turkish, Arab, and
   Irani communities in Greater London which provides a sexual health
   program for men who have sex with men)
Masala, P.O. Box 1182, Cambridge, MA 02142, USA
SALGA, P.O. Box 50, Cooper Station, New York, NY 10276-0050, USA
Sangat, Box 268463, Chicago, IL 60626, USA
Shamakami, P.O. Box 460456, San Francisco, CA 94146-0456, USA (lesbian
   magazine)
Shakti, P.O. Box 93, 28A Seymour Place, London W1H 5WJ, UK
Trikone, P.O. Box 21354, San Jose, CA 95151-1354, USA
Trikone-Atlanta, P.O. Box 18638, Atlanta, Ga 31126-0638, USA
Trikone-Los Angeles, c/o The Center, Admin Box 400, 1625 Scrader Blvd.
   Los Angeles, CA 90028, USA

Survival Through Pluralism: Emerging Gay Communities in the Philippines

Michael L. Tan

It is the eve of Queen's Day in Amsterdam and I am at a party on Herengracht–one of the canal streets–in a bed and breakfast owned by a Filipino gay man and his Dutch lover. The Filipino now has Dutch citizenship, as do most of the dozen or so Filipinos attending the party. Some are with long-term partners, others with recent boyfriends, and still others, alone. Many have lived in Europe and the United States for several years now. I hear Tagalog and Cebuano–Filipino languages–mixed with English, Dutch, German, and French.

Occasionally, there is talk about returning to the Philippines. Those who have been "home" recently talk about their visit, complaining about the heat and the traffic and about how little has changed with the gay scene, how it has remained so terribly commercial with mainly brothels and massage parlors flourishing. A few days after Queen's Day, I, too, return home and wonder: Where indeed is the gay scene in Metro Manila, this vast metropolis of 9 million people? There are a few watering holes in three cities–Manila, Quezon City, and Makati–but even on a weekend, they seem quite empty. In fact, at least one gay bar I knew of–which used to be so packed patrons had to stand outside on the sidewalk–had closed down.

The Library Foundation, a gay organization doing HIV/AIDS work, used to have weekend workshops twice a month and rap sessions

[Haworth co-indexing entry note]: "Survival Through Pluralism: Emerging Gay Communities in the Philippines." Tan, Michael L. Co-published simultaneously in *Journal of Homosexuality* (Harrington Park Press, an imprint of The Haworth Press, Inc.) Vol. 40, No. 3/4, 2001, pp. 117-142; and: *Gay and Lesbian Asia: Culture, Identity, Community* (ed: Gerard Sullivan, and Peter A. Jackson) Harrington Park Press, an imprint of The Haworth Press, Inc., 2001, pp. 117-142. Single or multiple copies of this article are available for a fee from The Haworth Document Delivery Service [1-800-342-9678, 9:00 a.m.–5:00 p.m. (EST). E-mail address: getinfo@haworthpressinc.com].

twice a week, with a gayline counseling service in a large old house rented as a drop-in center. But funds for gay groups are drying up–the foundation moved to a smaller center and then gave this up as well in January 1996. It now works out of borrowed space from other NGOs. The weekend workshops have stopped while the rap sessions attract a few men each week. (In January 1996, the foundation gave up this smaller center as well and now borrows space from the Remedios AIDS Foundation.)

In the early 1990s, I felt gay organizing had finally arrived in the Philippines, but such hopes may have been premature. It has taken time for me to understand that maybe these "boom-and bust" cycles are to be expected in emerging gay and lesbian communities, ever unpredictable, ever paradoxical. What comes to mind are Gagnon and Parker's (1995: 3) views about sexuality research: "This is such a time in the human sciences–a time of epistemological doubt, when the issues are not solely how do you know or what do you know, but whether you can know."

Can we "know" then if there is an emerging gay and lesbian scene? I know that I can write about what I know, but that it is from a certain "gaze" of someone in his 40s, who has been part of a diaspora of Filipino gay men, often more at home in Amsterdam than in Manila, but driven to return to Manila for many reasons–"nationalism" (I cringe at the word but cannot find an alternative); aging parents; even a masochistic attachment to the anarchy of a Latin culture–none of which relate to being gay. I am aware, too, of the dangers of attempting to write about "others," of gay men of different generations, of men who do not necessarily self-identify as gay, and of the still largely invisible lesbians and bisexuals. In earlier papers (Tan 1995a, 1995b), I described the range of "homosexualities" and "bisexualities" in the Philippines, with detailed descriptions of what people "do" and "think." Preparing this paper was more difficult because I had to shuttle between the micro- and macro-levels of individual "coming out" as well as of communities that seem to be emerging.

I write as an academic person challenged by the ambivalence of movements and processes. Because of this background, my paper will focus mainly on communities of gay men. I feel I have no right to describe the emerging lesbian communities at great length. There are lesbian organizations that have been quite active; in fact, in December 1996, three lesbian organizations convened a First National Lesbian

Rights Conference with more than a hundred participants, an unprecedented event in Philippine gay and lesbian history/herstory. The lesbian movement is itself an enigma, given its low profile (compared to gay men's groups) and yet it is able to move with such unity (again, in contrast to gay men's groups).

I write, too, as an activist working with NGOs on health and development issues, and with strong feelings about "relevance" in research–thus the final section is entitled "So What?". In all candor, even as I put the finishing touches to the article, I still wonder if I have answered that part adequately. That is the part that I will never know.

SOCIAL HISTORICAL BACKGROUND

Before we go specifically into the issue of gay communities, I feel it is necessary to present a brief sociohistorical overview of the Philippines. The Philippines went through more than three hundred years of Spanish colonization and half a century of U.S. colonial rule. Among Asian countries, the Philippines is perhaps one of the most westernized, and in many ways seems to be a chunk of Latin America that ended up on the wrong side of the Pacific.

As with Latin America, most Filipinos will profess to being Roman Catholic. The Roman Catholic Church is quite powerful, but people generally practice a syncretic form of Catholicism blending in precolonial animism. The sexual culture reflects this eclecticism: many Filipinos will say that sex between two men is a sin, but will also agree that homosexuality is probably just another alternative lifestyle and then qualify again that this is all right as long as it is not a brother or son who's gay.[1]

Understanding Filipino sexual culture also means understanding its political culture. The Philippines went through martial law and the Marcos dictatorship from 1972 to 1986, a period that brought the country to the brink of economic disaster. While other Southeast Asian countries went through rapid economic development as "little dragons," the Philippines was called "Asia's sick man." In fact, if it had not been for Filipino overseas workers, now numbering about 4.5 million (out of a population of 70 million), the economy would probably have collapsed many years ago.

Even after Marcos' ouster, the Philippines continued through a period of economic and political instability. In the last few years, there have been rapid economic changes occurring under the neo-liberal government of former President Fidel Ramos, with an open-door policy on foreign investments, deregulation, and privatization. A middle class seems to be emerging, partly because of domestic changes but also partly because of the continuing deployment of overseas workers.

The country's economic and political past are important factors that influence Filipino sexual cultures. A colonial past and a native landed elite created a very feudal culture based on authoritarian values, which, in a way, predisposed the country to the Marcos dictatorship. At the same time, the excesses of the dictatorship–more than 100,000 Filipinos died from the armed conflicts, arrests and torture–have also created a distinct political culture. Public debating is common and spills over into all kinds of issues, including those related to sex and sexuality.

A final word: until recently, much of Filipino economic, political and cultural life centered on Metro Manila, also known as the National Capital Region. This area consists of 17 cities and towns including Manila, Quezon City, Makati City, Pasig City, and others. Most Filipinos will refer to Metro Manila simply as Manila, and it is only in the context of conversations that one makes a distinction, e.g., *"Taga-saan ka sa Maynila"* (Where are you from in Manila?) is a question asking which city in particular you are from.

This article centers on Metro Manila, although I also refer in passing to developments in other areas of the country, developments which will probably speed up in the next few years as the government pushes its policy of distributing investments to areas outside the capital.

WHAT IS EMERGING?

What/who is emerging? *Bakla*–identified mainly as cross-dressing effeminate men–have been organized for many years, usually as neighborhood associations in cities. Members of these associations have been mainly low-income *bakla,* also sometimes called *parloris-tas* because they usually work in beauty parlors. The *parlorista* associations function mainly to provide entertainment, usually around May when fiestas are held for a neighborhood patron saint. The entertainment consists of beauty pageants and/or Santacruzans–a Roman Catholic religious procession where *parloristas* come out in drag, with male escorts, representing different characters from early Christianity, from Mary Magdalene to Queen Helen of Constantinople.

The neighborhood *parlorista bakla* have specific niches, not just as beauty parlor workers but also as domestic helpers, market vendors (vegetables, fruits, fish, but never of meat), and in the entertainment industry. The *parlorista* have also served the function of servicing sexual needs of young and not-so-young male victims of the Philippines' madonna/whore culture: raised in a society where they cannot access their girlfriends, but neither can they afford female sex workers. Older married men are also known to seek out the services of the *parlorista,* who can perform, to use the words of one middle-aged woman I was interviewing for a research project, "unspeakable dirty sex."

In the beginning, then, there were only *bakla* and *lalake,* the "real men." A proper *bakla* would never have sex with another *bakla* for that would have been tantamount to lesbianism. A *bakla* was a "girl," and "girls" go for "real men."

The *bakla parlorista* is clearly associated with urbanization. While the government defines a location as urban once it has an "industrial establishment" (e.g., a factory), two types of service establishments seem to be more indicative of urbanization in the Philippines: beer houses (a hybrid of a bar and restaurant) and beauty parlors. Beauty parlors attract rural *bakla,* who can find there social mobility and a degree of acceptance. The parlors tend to sprout in clusters, along specific streets. This usually starts out with one *bakla,* who then hires younger *bakla* migrants. The younger apprentices eventually save up enough money, or fight with the older one, and start their own establishment. Despite rivalries and intramurals, the *parlorista* will inevitably form a neighborhood association. In some cases, a richer *bakla* in the community becomes a *ninang,* a "godmother," by extending financial and logistical support for the activities of these groups.

The community associations are important, too, in allowing some form of intergenerational passage. One example of such an association is SKRF or the Sining Kayumanggi Royal Family (literal translation: Brown Arts Royal Family, "brown" used to refer to Filipinos), which was established in 1968 and holds annual parties that include several drag beauty pageants, including one called Golden Girls–from the American sitcom about older retired women living in a house in Florida–for older *bakla* still interested in competing.

Canell (1995) gives an extensive description of the "culture of beauty" in a Filipino town outside Manila, describing the importance of the *bakla* in mediating and creating this culture, both as make-up artists (beauticians) and as made-up women in drag beauty pageants. Canell also describes how these activities become major town activities, attended by townsfolk and with boards of judges composed of government officials and other local celebrities. In recent years, such beauty contests have become quite popular, launched by *barangay* (village) councils as fund-raising activities. Late in 1996, for example, I visited the southern city of Zamboanga and saw banners all over the city announcing a Miss Gay Zamboanga beauty pageant sponsored by the provincial council and the Save the Filipino Youth Movement.

Many *bakla* groups are small and localized. In recent years, two national organizations of hairdressers and parlor workers have been set up. One of these groups, HACAP (Hairdressers and Cosmetologists Association of the Philippines), has at least 15,000 *bakla* members, and, although they also have women members, the large number of *bakla* members probably makes them, in a sense, the country's largest organization of cross-dressers. The other national organization, Fil-Hair, has been active in self-help programs, offering vocational training classes in dressmaking and cosmetology, which attracts many young *bakla*. Showing its political clout, the former First Lady, Amelita Ramos, often attends Fil-Hair's functions, which also mobilizes the organization for fund-raising activities.

The *bakla* does not cross-dress for special occasions: cross-dressing is standard daily wear for the shop and for the streets. In many ways then, the *parlorista bakla* was out long before the terms "out" and "outing" were even coined. The local term for coming out, *magladlad ng kapa*, has a literal translation of unfurling one's cape and was clearly coined in the context of the *parlorista bakla*.

There are some parallels to the *tomboy*, loosely equivalent to the butch dyke in western societies. If the *bakla* is a man with a woman's heart (*may pusong babae*), the *tomboy* is constructed as a man trapped in a woman's body. Like the *bakla*, the *tomboy* has particular stereotyped occupational niches, mainly as security guards and bus conductors.

The high public visibility of the *bakla* and *tomboy*–complete with cross-dressing in varying degrees–is often interpreted as public tolerance, even acceptance, of homosexuality in the Philippines. The few published articles on male homosexuality in the Philippines, written by Westerners (Hart 1968; Whitam and Mathy 1986), focus on the *bakla* and this acceptance. This interpretation is not quite accurate: "acceptance" is conditional, as long as the *bakla* remain confined to certain occupational niches and fulfill certain stereotypes, of the man with a woman's heart, of the village entertainer, of the outlet for male sexual drive. Some professions–nursing, for example, and even medicine–have some space for *bakla*, but generally, a gay professional finds it more difficult to come out publicly. Somehow, and this becomes clearer later in the paper, "gay" means *bakla* and *bakla* means being entertaining and funny and an outlet for male libidos.

GAY AND LESBIAN?

There can be no doubt that the "gay" movement in the west had some impact on the local scene. In the late 60s, local newspaper articles were already referring to "gay bars" in Manila. The "gay men" were usually from the elite, men who had studied and lived in the United States and Europe. The gay scene was associated with the "rich and the beautiful," with approval from the authorities. The former First Lady, Imelda Romualdez Marcos, was the ultimate fag hag, traveling with a retinue of couturiers and hairdressers and extending her patronage to the "arts" and to "cinema," fields that had attracted many of those who were now self-identifying as "gay." The Philippines was under the Marcos dictatorship from 1972 to 1986, but upper income gay men were generally apolitical, spending weekends in discos with names like Velvet Slum and Coco Banana, places that also became chic for straight men and women. Cross-dressing was common in such places, but this was clearly camp drag, not daily-routinized *bakla* drag. Not surprisingly, "gay" became associated with the elite. Gay men who joined the political anti-Marcos underground at this time still remember how "comrades" would talk of homosexuality as "bourgeois decadence" and as an import from the west. Such views were grafted on to older norms. For example, at public rallies, one had to contend with comments such as, *bakla ang speech* (The speech is *bakla*), meaning it was too weak. The *bakla*, and by extension gay men, were weak and soft.

While the terms gay and lesbian came into common use in the 1970s–now part of Taglish, a hybrid of Tagalog and English used in many parts of the country–interpretations of the terms still vary. Generally, even among gays and lesbians themselves, the terms are interchanged with *bakla* and *tomboy* and used in the traditional sense, i.e., one could not be *bakla,* or gay, if he was not effeminate, and one could not be *tomboy,* or lesbian, unless she was masculine. This is reflected in the media, including the letters of young men and women writing to agony aunts asking why they are attracted to persons of the same sex, but have no desire to cross dress.

The emerging gay scene was, in many ways, an amplification of social expectations and construction of the *bakla.* A Filipino "gay bar" was not a cruising bar where one could meet other gay men. With a few exceptions, gay bars were establishments where *bakla* could pick up *lalake,* "real men," and pay them for sex. At the same time, some of the gay men from the 1970s were now talking of what was forbidden for the *bakla,* having sex with each other.

We see here that "gay" and "lesbian" take on very specific but varied meanings. In the late 70s, there were gay men called *Kakasarian* (of the same sex), who set up at least one middle-class group, but this lasted less than a year. *Kakasarian*'s members were mostly middle-class professionals espousing a kind of gay activism that did not catch on because of the argument, coming from *bakla* themselves, that there was no need to fight for "gay rights" in the Philippines. "Gay" did take on an organized form: it was there, visible but amorphous.

While this first wave of organized gay groups disappeared in the 1980s, the "gay scene" did evolve, drawing in more people from the middle-class, many of whom had never traveled outside the Philippines. The exposure to "gay" was, therefore, a mixture of international media as well as local reinterpretations from gay men who had lived overseas. The emerging middle-class gay men sought relationships with other gay men and not with "straight" men. These were men, too, who generally did not want to cross-dress and who talked of themselves being "decent gays" as opposed to cheap *bakla*–Philippine society's class stratification was now being reproduced in the gay scene.

It was not until the 1990s that we see another wave of emerging gay and lesbian organizations. This wave is significant, with different "currents" that compose distinct gay politics. Examples of such groups are The Library Foundation, Katlo, Pro-Gay, LesBond, Lesbian Collective, Can't Live in the Closet, Amaranth and Sulo Davao (now Iwag Davao). Most of these are based in Manila, but there are also associations in other larger Philippine cities. While none of these groups were formed specifically to respond to the AIDS problem, several did eventually become very active in HIV prevention work, in fact, surviving through financial grants for HIV programs. (Conversely, as with The Library Foundation, several face possible closure as donor fatigue begins to hit the AIDS industry.)

Also distinctive was the establishment of student gay organizations. Let me describe some of these organizations at greater length since their emergence again parallels wider social trends. At the state-owned University of the Philippines (UP), which has over the decades turned into an elite university because of the difficulties in hurdling its entrance requirements, there has been only one gay organization, UP Babaylan, *babaylan* being cross-dressing religious functionaries from the pre-colonial period. UP Babaylan's rhetoric comes closest to that of the queer movement in the United States, its members going around in camp drag and wearing T-shirts with statements like: *Bakla Ako. May Angal Ka?* (I'm *bakla*. Any objections?).

At the Polytechnic University of the Philippines (UP), another state-owned university with students coming from middle- and low-income families, the main gay student group is Pro-Gay (Progressive Organizations for Gays). Pro-Gay is a militant nationalist organization that has joined public rallies and demonstrations in protest of government decisions, such as increases in oil prices, the imposition of new taxes or plans for a national identification card. Pro-Gay's statements do not mince words, hitting the government for being a lackey to imperialism or for being fascist.

At the Far Eastern University (FEU), a private university, there are two large gay organizations. One is called BANANA, a whimsical name that has a more ponderous meaning: *Baklang Nagkakaisa Tungo sa Nasyonalismo* (Bakla United Toward Nationalism). BANANA, like Pro-Gay, participates in protest actions against the government. One member of this group describes their role as "*pangharang sa pulis, kasi hindi kami babanatan*" (We block the police, because they won't hit us). The description is striking because the use of the *bakla* as front-liners plays on Filipino society's construction of the *bakla* as women, who are not to be subjected to violence. Yet, as with women, *bakla* are in fact quite often objects of violence, usually in more private and domestic settings.

The other organization at the Far Eastern University is called SHE or Society of the Homosexual Encounter, which organizes gay beauty pageants. Some of its members actually attend classes in drag and one attempted, unsuccessfully, to join the university's Miss Accounting, a beauty contest for female students.

We see here that in the 1990s, the *bakla* is reincarnated in various forms. Middle-class gay men consider the term insulting when they hear it from non-gay men, but consider it a term of endearment when used among themselves. At the same time, there are also middle-class cross-dressers, as with university students, taking on militant "queer" roles, although again in different forms.

In 1994, Pro-Gay organized the country's first gay and lesbian march, coinciding with the 25th anniversary of the Stonewall riots in New York City, which is usually invoked as the beginning of "gay liberation" in the United States. The Pro-Gay march drew about 50 participants, and as many media people eager to cover the spectacle. The event made it to the front page of newspapers and into the evening primetime newscasts. That same night, Blue Cafe, a mixed bar in Manila with a largely gay clientele, sponsored a party to commemorate Stonewall and gay and lesbian pride. A hundred people showed up, again with good media coverage.

The following year, there was no gay and lesbian march, but Blue Cafe sponsored another street party, again drawing a crowd. In 1996, several organizations came together to organize two events publicized as gay and lesbian pride celebrations: a march in the afternoon and a street festival that night. The newspapers reported about 5000 showing up for the events. Gay pride, it seemed, had finally arrived in the Philippines

COMMUNITIES?

Can we speak of gay communities in the Philippines? "Community" takes on many political meanings and functions. Certainly, one cannot speak of a gay community, or even of a *bakla* community. In fact, one can even speak of conflicts in the ways these subcultures are constructed. On the surface, some of these conflicts seem to be drawn along boundaries of "traditional" cross-dressing "fem" roles and the more "western" standards of masculine gay identity. The distinctions can be artificial, often overlapping with class differences. For example, an upper class queen is "chic" while his working-class counterpart is considered cheap. *Parloristas* hold many yuppie gay men in contempt, accusing them of being closeted. A common retort from the *parlorista* would be: "*Sino ang niloloko niya? Naaamoy naman ang kaniyang matris*" (Whom is he trying to fool? You can smell his uterus).

The tensions can be found even with the "gay pride" groups. On the one hand, there is the influence of the queer movement from the west, pushing for "butch" (read closeted) types to come out and camp up, sometimes with a nativistic agenda of returning to a mythical past of "gay" shamans and healers. (Cross-dressing shamanic healers were common throughout the Southeast Asian region. My view here is that they are an important link to the past, but that it would be inaccurate to call them "gay" or even *bakla*.) On the other hand, there is the dissonance that comes with middle-class gay pride groups, "proud" yet cautious. During the gay and lesbian pride activities in 1996, several organizers appeared in print and television interviews and referred frequently to the problem of "stereotyping," which was equated with "screaming faggots." The reference to "screaming faggots" is telling, in a sense excluding one group from among "the different faces of homosexuality."

This exclusion process comes through even more dramatically with a university gay student group called PLM Avant-Garde. (PLM is the Pamantasan ng Lungsod ng Maynila, a university run by the city government of Manila for low- and middle-income students.) In 1993, a local newspaper (*Manila Bulletin,* September 1993) interviewed several members of this group. One member of the organization's board of trustees stresses: "Entry to the organization is not at all simple. One has to be personable, talented, dedicated, and most importantly, above average in intelligence. . . . " He added that members are not allowed to use hair-dye, have long hair, and, certainly, "no girlie attire." His explanation for these policies was that the organization "strictly adheres to a social norm of being straight. This straightness is measured in terms of physical projection to solicit a certain respect within the academic community and outside."

What we find then are attempts to mainstream, to "solicit" respect. Gay "activism" here takes on the role of wanting to mainstream, of conforming to heterosexual norms, to be "accepted." This is perhaps "logical" when we look at the class dynamics. The "emerging" gays and lesbians are middle-class. Should it be surprising that the 1996 gay and lesbian pride activities drew a motley group of sponsors that included the Department of Tourism, condom manufacturers, straight bars, and a beer manufacturer? Ten years ago, it would have been unthinkable for such commercial interests to support any gay or lesbian event. But then ten years ago, in the mid-1980s, it would have been impossible to have any kind of gay and lesbian event, period. It is clear that the emerging "community" comes, too, with an emerging middle class that includes gays and lesbians with some disposable income, a potentially profitable market. Thus, a newspaper such as the *Evening Paper* had, for a few months, a weekend section called Gayzette, which includes articles such as reviews of recent American gay fiction. Earlier, a popular magazine for teenagers and young adults, *Mr. & Ms.*, began featuring a gay column as well, one which has been sustained for more than a year now. This column responds to reader inquiries while featuring articles about the local gay scene.

Is there "a" gay and lesbian community then? Not in the sense of a homogeneous "group." No one can presume homogeneity, even in the use of terms like *bakla*. The middle class *bakla*, invoking ancestral links to transvestite shamans, is very different, in terms of language and values, from the low-income *parlorista bakla*. Likewise, the emerging "gay" movement is fluid and includes some middle class *bakla* as well as the *parlorista bakla*–plus so-called yuppie gays. I say "so-called" because even "yuppie gays" can be quite diverse. For example, one group of "yuppie gays," the so-called "Makati gays"–Makati being the financial district–are often described as being either in banks or in advertising. Indeed, but the "bankers" are quite different from those in advertising, the staid bankers cautiously avoiding the more flamboyant advertising people when they meet in Makati's streets during lunch breaks. During one workshop for gay men, I actually heard one "banker" apologizing to an advertising executive, "I'm sorry, but there will be times when we meet in Makati and if you say hello, I'm going to have to pretend I don't know you."

Class differences can be quite significant. The Library Foundation, composed of mainly middle-class men living in Metro Manila, has been conducting HIV education programs with *parlorista bakla* in different cities. Each time a workshop is conducted, the Manila-based workshop facilitators come back almost as if they had come from another country, or another world. Even "gay slang" is different across the subcultures, from one class to another and from one city to another. The differences can be so significant that a pre-workshop team is usually sent ahead to draw up a glossary of important terms.

Beyond semantic differences, we also find significant differences in the construction of gay and bakla sex and sexuality. Most amusing is the way the Manila visitors become "the other," objects of curiosity, as local *parlorista* marvel at how a *bakla* can go to bed with another *bakla* or how a *bakla* can be a *bakla* without cross-dressing. At the end of one workshop conducted by The Library Foundation, one *bakla* from Olongapo–a city about 100 kilometers north of Metro Manila–exclaimed: "Now I can go back and tell my friends it's true, that in Manila the *bakla* do date and fuck other *bakla*."

The terms "gay" and "lesbian" and "communities" run the risk of becoming monolithic, often constructed out of middle-class experiences. Filipino men and women often grapple for a politics of identity based on models from the United States, yet are goaded by postmodern arguments that identity is meaningless in sexual domains. We grope for terms: men who have sex with men; men who love men; homosexually active; homosexually experienced. Recently in Davao, one gay academic told me that "someone" (he could not remember who) had done a survey in an urban poor community and found that 85 percent of the men had had same-sex experiences. What does this make them? Gay? Bisexual? Homosexually active? Homosexually experienced?

Quite often, too, there is an element of wishful thinking, a desire not just to reach but to surpass the mythical Kinsey 10 percent figure (I refer here to the influential 1940s survey of male sexuality in the United States, or the Kinsey survey, where around 10 percent of informants were said to lead predominantly homosexual sex lives at some period of their life). Many Filipino gay men and *bakla* will declare that all Filipino men are bisexual. Perhaps reflecting the emergence of lesbians, I have also started hearing from lesbians that all Filipinas are latent lesbians. A movie gossip columnist–himself *bakla*–writes about an actress who was the target of rumors of lesbianism. The columnist quotes the actress as saying, "*Hindi ako tomboy,*" a literal translation of which should have been "I am not a tomboy" but which the columnist translates as "I am not a butch." One could go into a lengthy discussion of the meanings of what the columnist meant, but my point here is that the terminology is affected both by globalization and by local currents.

Bakla and *tomboy* become glosses, appropriated and reappropriated, presented and represented. The *parlorista bakla* beauty pageant, for example, has become popular with the middle-class as well and has been transformed through this expropriation. For example, the beauty pageants used to be for local titles like Miss Manila or even Miss Tondo (a district within Manila) but today are more often modeled on Miss Universe contests, complete with a Parade of Nations where the contestants represent such countries as Malawi and Bosnia. The beauty pageants, too, are interesting in that a question-and-answer portion–to test for "brains as well as beauty"–is conducted in English. While pandering to the prestige status of English, there is also a humorous play on English as low-income *bakla* intentionally go into well-rehearsed stereotypical opening lines, such as "An intelligent question deserves an intelligent answer, so it is my opinion that . . . " (Others, more practical, will ask for an interpreter).

Generational differences are also strong in creating divisions within the "community." Few Filipino gay men over the age of 30 continue to go out. They seem to disappear, eventually marrying women and setting up families or retiring to a semi-celibate life for as many reasons as there are older gay men (I'm too old; they're too young; I don't like the music; they don't like our music; I'm not pretty anymore; they're too pretty). The few who do remain "in circulation" do not usually date, acting instead as "den mothers" (a term I have actually heard in use) who provide advice and support to younger gay men. It is interesting, too, that the few older men who do remain in circulation are more often Caucasian expatriates who say that they are more appreciated in the Philippines than in their own countries. Older Filipino gay men, on the other hand, say that Filipino gay culture is much more oriented toward youthful "beauty" than in the West and that there is more of a social life for the "gay and gray" in North America or Europe.

Many other "variables" can be named here as significant in shaping and differentiating gay "communities." Ethnicity is an example: gay men from the south (Visayas or Bisaya) are perceived as being less inhibited and more carefree by their more staid counterparts from Manila and the northern regions. The cohesive nature of the Filipino gay "community" in Amsterdam, for example, has been attributed to its being mainly "Bisaya." One Tagalog–the only Tagalog man in fact at the Queen's Day party I attended–told me: "Only a Bisaya can throw a good gay party."

What can we conclude then? Certainly, the emergence of a Filipino nation-state means that there is a crossing of ethnic lines among gay men, *bakla,* lesbians, and other sexual minorities. At the same time, I have shown how other variables–class in particular–can persist in setting several communities apart. These divisions are reflected in clothes, gestures, language, and, more importantly, in "values" (e.g., what is "masculine" or "feminine," what is "decent" or "vulgar").

WHO ARE WE? POLITICIZING IDENTITY

The evolution of the diverse categories *bakla,* gay, tomboy, lesbian, bisexual, *silahis* (local term for bisexual) shows how, too often, "we" have been named by "them" much like "tribes" and "natives" were given names by colonizers. My own choice of *bakla* and *silahis* as the only words to italicize also reflects this process, for we are confronted with only two "indigenous" terms. Who are we then in the Philippines?

In mid 1995, I received a letter from a Manila-based social marketing researcher who wanted to assess the demand among gay men for lubricants to go with condoms. He asked if it would be safe to accept the "3 percent figure" for gay men in the country. I was puzzled: what was this "3 percent figure?" I realized shortly after that this had been lifted from a recently concluded national Young Adult Fertility and Sexuality Study conducted by the University of the Philippines. The social marketing researcher had depended on media reports. I finally tracked down the unpublished statistics. (The full report has yet to be published.) The more specific figures, and the context of the figures, was that 3.3 percent of both male and female young adults had had sex with a person of the same sex. Disaggregated by sex, the figure was 5.1 percent for males and 1.8 percent for females.

In this example, we see how the academe and the media have clearly been drawn into the reinventing of the Filipino *bakla* and tomboy. The condom distributors are convinced that the gay men form 3 percent of the population because a survey–and the media–say so. The focus of course is on sex acts, which tells us nothing about sexual identities or, more importantly, identities in flux. The survey actually had a separate section on "homosexual attraction." About 9.7 per-cent–so close to that older magical 10 percent–of the young adults said they were attracted to persons of the same sex.

Numbers numb. The non-governmental organization I work with, Health Action Information Network, found that as many as 25 percent of students in midwifery schools said they were "not sure" about their sexual orientation. When we pretested the questionnaire, which was used for various health science institutions, there were nursing stu-dents who asked what a heterosexual was. No one asked what a homosexual was–that was clear to the respondents (most probably as an effeminate cross-dressing male, or the *bakla*), but heterosexual was something else. There is no word or even a gloss in any of the Philip-pine languages for the heterosexual. We often forget that heterosexual is a western construction.

But after all the figures are in from surveys such as those I have described, we are left with more questions than answers. I will not go into research methodologies and questions of validity and reliability. My point is that an emerging research culture in the Philippines con-verges with other discourse from the media, religion, medicine, and the diverse popular cultures of "us" and "them." The discourse mixes the old and the new: how many *bakla* are there? The question of course comes from varied sectors with different agendas. *Bakla* them-selves want to know: "how many of us are there?" Straight people want to know: "how many of 'them' are there?" "Straight" curiosity is not always benign: the newspaper's advice columns often feature letters from parents wondering about their children; sisters wondering about brothers; women wondering about their husbands or boyfriends. And, always, the question is not just how many are there, but is there a way of "telling?" Detection is the goal in a society where disclosure remains difficult.

Research now names us, lumping all together under academic cate-gories that both represent and contradict the "real" world. Thus, the middle-class yuppie gay man fumes about "stereotyped" media repre-sentations. The 1996 gay and lesbian pride statement notes: "As gay men, we are portrayed as limp-wristed weaklings who crumple in the face of danger. We are also shown as sex-starved effeminate sissies who exploit minors. As lesbians, we come across as macho thus prone to violence." Yet, the organizers seem to forget that it was the "limp-

wristed" men and "macho" women who had the courage to come out
to the media at the march and at other events.

The rhetoric about gay rights needs to be grounded. I prefer to talk
about space: are we being given space, or are we appropriating space?
Recently, I caught a newscast feature, "Youthspeak," which was
quick interviews with adolescents about particular topics. That night,
they asked about "the third sex." Most of those interviewed were
"accepting" in the tradition of "they're people too." "We're people
too," I hear a few days later when some *bakla* are interviewed on a
television show. But I feel restless with such "they (or we) are people
too" statements. Following the American tradition, Philippine television is filled with talk shows, and it is not uncommon to have at least
one talk show featuring gay men or lesbians talking about homosexuality. In most cases, the host's distanced curiosity always comes
through, as he or she asks questions such as "How do you people look
at yourselves?"

Taking this analysis a step further, gay organizations are also featured in the media. It would, of course, be factitious to assert that all
this proves that a gay community exists. To borrow from Durkheim,
organic solidarity does not seem to exist. If anything, we find an
underground movement, with occasional public appearances, occasions for a cautious test of public sentiment, some bolder than others.
When a cartoonist attempts a caricature of gay public school teachers
by drawing them in drag with fishnet stockings, Danton Remoto, a gay
university professor and writer, dashes off a letter to the editor: "We
do not wear fishnet stockings. They are no longer in vogue." One can
almost hear thousands of gay readers applauding, but the applause is
muffled and private, as is gay and lesbian space. Perhaps the muffled
applause comes, too, in the ways gay space is so often interstitial,
overlapping and intruding with "straight" space.

SO NOW WHAT?

With the HIV/AIDS epidemic, there is a real danger of gay men
being the targets of scapegoating. There are already signs that this is
happening. Dr. Margarita Gosingco Holmes, a clinical psychologist
who once had a sex advice column, has compiled letters from and
about homosexuals and lesbians in her book *A Different Love* (Holmes

1993). The book includes several letters with scathing remarks about "perverts" and AIDS.

Borrowing from the American tradition, the term "men who have sex with men" was introduced to pinpoint a population for "targeted interventions." The term "men who have sex with men" has been rejected by at least one gay writer, who says that this allows closet cases to remain in the closet. It is an argument that really falls back on a form of essentialism, almost as if a proclaimed "gay identity" is required to be truly gay.

What we do miss out on is a more vital issue, that of the rubric "men who have sex with men" having been created by a biomedical establishment which focuses on the behavioral component. This draws from a new public health ethic that looks into risks, risk factors, and risk populations. "MSM," as "men who have sex with men" has come to be abbreviated, is not meant as a substitute identity or as camouflage. A creation of epidemiologists, "MSM" has become, on one hand, a new identity for surveillance, one of six "sentinel groups" that are targeted by the Philippines' Health Department and USAID (U.S. Agency for International Development) for periodic blood-collecting and occasional social research. In USAID-commissioned behavioral survey in 1995 with the "general population," there is actually a question: "Have you ever had sex with men who only have sex with men?"

Yet, when wielded by gay men's groups, MSM becomes a floating descriptor that is necessarily temporary but that has its uses. I have, for example, started hearing people asking: "Hey, don't you think he's cute? Do you think he's an . . . MSM?" Or, people describing a recent sexual encounter: "Oh, I don't think he was gay. Just another MSM."

There have been attempts to popularize terms like "homosexually active," but words like "homosexual" and "gay" remain loaded and alienating. MSM, used as MSM and in English (in Filipino it becomes intimidating: *lalakeng nakikipagtalik sa kapwa lalake*), is tentative, an introduction used in workshops where we can't be sure. Certainly, it is a term that is completely useless when we deal with the *parlorista*. The *parlorista* can be *bakla*, the *parlorista* can be gay, but the *parlorista* can never be MSM. *Babae kami, hindi lalake* (we are women, not men) parloristas protest. In the last year, attempts have been made to fit the *bakla* into the category of transsexual, again for "targeted interventions," but the term is again tenuous and inaccurate. Most of the *parlorista bakla* have no intentions of getting "the" operation. *Banal ito* (this is sacred) several tell me, as they point to their crotch. (But nature's sacrality is relative: many have put themselves on hormones. Diane, an anti-acne preparation with estrogen, seems to have replaced oral contraceptives as a favorite to grow breasts.)

We return to the word "communities." I am conscious of my own cognitive filters, filters that need to be given a temporal context. Together with another generation of *bakla,* I mourn the loss of *the* Coco Banana, which was a bar, a coffee shop, and a disco. We talk of Coco days, of a mythical past of better days, pre-AIDS, pubescent innocence. I say "mythical" because the nostalgia for Coco Banana is partly based on a reconstruction of what did exist in that establishment: a choice of dancing, watching a show, or just talking; the relative absence of male sex workers; a mixing of locals and expatriates. Older gay men like myself describe Coco Banana whenever we complain about the lack of "good" gay places to go to, places where one had a sense of community. In retrospect, Coco Banana was actually quite elitist, with its high admission charges and expensive drinks. Nevertheless, there was a strong sense that it was a "truly" gay bar where even straight men and women were seen as "visitors" that one could "tolerate," rather than the other way around.

But maybe times have changed and no one wants to go into an exclusively gay place. People go instead to straight places and take over the dance floor for half an hour–or the left half, or some corner. I see it happening not only in Manila but also in Iloilo, Cebu, Davao. In far-flung Puerto Princesa, a frontier town, I walked into a raunchy, smoky bar one night and realized half of the customers, all dressed in jeans and shirts, were women. Again conscious that my notions of "space" are created from having lived in the west, I begin to wonder if perhaps this is the "Filipino way." Even in fairly large cities like Cube and Davao, everyone knows everyone. You cannot walk into a gay bar and not be seen and talked about. Going into a straight place–with a gay corner–seems to offer, paradoxically, more security because there is still room for doubt, i.e., maybe he is straight and was just saying hello to gay friends. Perhaps again it reflects a middle-class construction of gay scenes, where one can actually be quite courageous in taking over space, and yet be cautious by carving the space within a straight world and by conforming to some of the straight norms.

I will give one more example here to show this process. In 1996 there was a lot of talk, even a formal announcement, about a new gay and lesbian magazine to be launched. It was to be called *Wednesday*, because of Wednesday nights being popular night outs for gay men, a kind of mid-week relief. The magazine would have come out every two months–clearly a test case–and would have sold for P80 each or about US$3 (the same price for upmarket Filipino glossy magazines). The magazine was never launched. Officially, the financier had backed out, but gay yuppie men also talked about how such a magazine would not have worked out. It was not just the price, I would hear in coffee shop discussions, but the idea of "a" gay magazine. Who would dare write for it? Who would dare buy it?

But even as the middle-class gay men debated about *Wednesday*, several new weekly magazines had in fact been launched early in 1996, all featuring beefcake photographs of young aspiring actors. The magazines sold at P18 each (about US$0.75), still quite expensive by Filipino standards but fairly affordable to the middle class. The magazines are on newsprint, with barely tolerably readable type, but they sell quite well, with print runs of about 150,000 each, higher than many newspapers. The articles are written tabloid style, mainly news about movie stars with "juicy" headlines like, "Has so-and-so ever had sex with another male?" or "Would so-and-so mind if someone peeked while he was peeing?" There is a page for readers' letters (mostly letters of unrequited love for another male) and a pen-pal page, with an interesting selection of photographs of cross-dressed *bakla* and men in swimming trunks.

What has happened here? The magazines, with titles such as *Chika-chika* (gay slang for talking); *Controversial,* and *Hot Spot* inserted themselves into the market for movie gossip magazines. They are sold next to the "straight" gossip magazines, with obvious differences in the covers: showing actors instead of actresses. The magazines do not say they are gay magazines; in fact, one magazine actually featured the following disclaimer: "We are the magazine for your uncle and your aunt, your brothers and your sisters. We are the magazine for everyone, and not just *bakla.*"

Perhaps dramatizing how the channels for gay culture can be diverse and unpredictable, I found out about these magazines nine months after they were launched from a Filipino based in Chicago who had heard it from other Filipino gay men through an Internet chat group. Yet, almost a year after the magazines first came out, I was still running into middle- and high-income gay men who had never heard of the magazines and who would be shocked (but titillated) when I would show them copies. A yuppie Wednesday magazine probably would have flopped. *Chika-chika* was doing well a year after, conforming to tight censorship rules, mindful of discrimination against gay men and *bakla*. Its articles may be "trashy," but magazines like *Chika-chika*, clearly a *bakla* magazine, have created gay space. I find the magazines are sold throughout the country, even in the more remote areas, and am no longer surprised to find them in run-down beauty parlors as well as in plush condominiums (not in the living room, of course). And, I found out recently from my Filipino friend in Chicago that the magazine is now sold in a Filipino grocery near his place, "for only US$2 each."

Creating space also means crossing boundaries. The class boundaries remain the strongest, and this is where we confront the many frightening facets of marginalization taking place within an already marginalized sector. I can never forget the look on a gay professional in one of the southern cities when he responded to our offer to conduct HIV prevention workshops: "Oh, not for us professionals. We don't need it. Maybe for the lower class *bakla?*" Elitism takes many forms and is particularly dangerous when it enters AIDS education.

"Western" standards are too easily borrowed by a middle class that projects its own perceptions and interests to a larger population. I have seen too many variations of such projections, including the more benign forms such as, "Oh, we have to reach the uneducated ones." Such perspectives fit perfectly into the agenda of mainstream public health with its focus on "AIDS surveillance." Not surprisingly, programs like those of The Library Foundation–emphasizing interpersonal workshops–are dying out from lack of funding. The little money that goes into gay or *bakla* programs is limited to one-shot outreach activities that have quite often been co-opted by public health authorities as a way of getting more samples for HIV antibody testing. It is the same tactic used all too often for sex workers, reflecting the power relations where the powerless become the objects of interventions and of surveillance. The HIV epidemic shapes gay "communities" in more ways than might be readily apparent, all too often duplicating structures of oppression and discrimination.

UNITY?

Given that we have diverse communities, is there any basis for unity? Or is it pushing it to argue for unity at this point or ever? There is arrogance and elitism in imposing one view, in setting one standard because, as Weeks (1995) points out, sexual identities embody power relations. There is power in naming an identity; but there is also arrogance in proclaiming that one identity should be superior to all others, or that there should even be just one identity. A kind of internal colonization and marginalization takes place, minoritizing what may actually be a majority, as is happening with the middle class gay disparagement of *parlorista bakla*.

My concern is that we may be looking for unity when such unity, in an organic or formal sense, may not be necessary. The diversity of communities is important because this allows for a constant revalidation, for want of a better term, of what might be a community experience, situated in history. This necessarily includes men and women who do not self-identify as gay or lesbian or bisexual or even MSM. One major achievement in The Library Foundation's workshops was the way such activities brought together different "gay" men: from different classes and including "butch" and "femme" types. It was also striking how, at the start, there would be a clear distinction between the two groups even in seating arrangements. By the end of the workshop, new friendships had been made that cut across the lines, with both groups still teasing the other for being too effeminate or being too butch, but understanding that the differences were not half as important as the similarities.

For want of a better term, I would use the term "cultural expression" to refer to "gay," "*bakla*," "lesbian," "tomboy," "*silahis*," and "men who have sex with men," reflecting the myriad ways in which individuals respond to social conditions. These conditions vary not just from one city to another but even within a geographically contiguous area. Class, ethnicity, and even age need to be considered if we are to understand the many evolving subcultures. We have seen, too, how this evolution occurs as "gay" and "lesbian" Filipinos move in space, searching for and creating space. The diaspora will be especially important in the years to come, given that about 4.5 million Filipinos–including many *bakla*–now work overseas on contracts lasting one to three years. This is not the same diaspora of the 1960s and

1970s–which tended to involve elite families. The current wave involves more middle-class Filipinos.[2]

It is important to consider how *bakla* ideology interacts with other sexual ideologies. The all pervasive idea that the *bakla* is a man with a woman's heart (*pusong babae*) now competes with other discourses, as in the example of the university student gay group "adhering to a social norm of being straight . . . to solicit a certain respect . . . " and the dismissal of the "screaming faggots." The *bakla* is constructed as having a female heart and is, therefore, not *macho*. In fact, resentment of the *bakla* is often qualified as resentment of the *baklang agresibo* (aggressive *bakla*), a violation of the construction of *pusong babae* or a woman's heart. An example comes from a young adolescent girl interviewed in a Health Action Information Network project on young adult sexuality. Here, she describes the *agi*, the Ilonggo (a local language) term for *bakla*:

> *Kasi may maraming klaseng agi diyan. Mga agi na baboy, at saka yong agi matitino. Baklang baboy 'yong you know they chase guys nga ganon tapos they have sex with them . . . 'yong baklang matino, they just feel like a girl . . . tapos.* (There are many kinds of agi. There are the pig agi and there are the decent agi. The pig agi are the ones, you know, they chase guys and then have sex with them. The decent agi, they just feel like a girl . . . that's all.) (F17AB)

The passive "girl" *agi* is, therefore, acceptable. Notice, though, how the *agi* becomes acceptable after he is de-sexualized.

Conversely, we find *macho* ideologies defined in contrast to the *bakla*. This starts with the most trivial (being too gentle or "soft" in one's movements) and this is totally arbitrary, differing from one class or region to another and can bring accusations of *bakla*. One, therefore, learns to cross his legs or hold a cigarette in the "correct" *macho* style. In other instances, *machoness* takes on more serious implications. A young man who retains his virginity (i.e., does not have sexual experiences with women) is teased or taunted as *bakla*. Here, the pressures to be "baptized" (*mabinyag*)–initiated into sex through a female sex worker or a causal pick-up–can be tremendous.

It is interesting how this construction of being *lalake*–one where sexual experience marks man-hood–takes on a different dimension among the *bakla*. Peer pressure on the *bakla* to have sexual experiences with another male is not as strong. This struck me in several of The Library Foundation's workshops, where there would be such "virgins" attending. One can be *bakla* and remain a virgin, just as women's femaleness is not tied into her sexual experience.

Bakla ideology (or, more precisely, ideologies) is central but understanding *bakla* will mean teasing it out from its social matrix, including its interface with other sexual ideologies. To be more specific again, even "gay" relationships in the Philippines quite often borrow on heterosexual ideologies, for example, in duplicating "male" active and "female" passive roles in courtship. Thus, one aspect of HIV/ AIDS programs has been teaching "passive" gay men and *bakla* to challenge this stereotype, particularly in negotiating for safer sex.

I will not go into details of *bakla* ideology. My point here is that "being" gay in the Philippines draws from a *bakla* ideology that finds different expressions. Unless we recognize this, we will continue to deceive ourselves in pretending that we can create what Weeks (1995) has called "fictional unities." These fictional unities, often-fictional deceits, can become barriers precisely because, in its fraudulent claims to unity, it becomes part of a politics of exclusion and discrimination.

This is not to say that there is no room for community organizing. I recently talked with someone who had just returned from working overseas, and he said it was important to have been "exposed" before leaving. When I asked what he meant by "exposed," he mentioned the books of Margarita Holmes (the collection of letters to her newspaper column) and "Remoto" (referring to Danton Remoto, one of the co-authors of *Ladlad*, the anthology of gay writing). Apparently, such books represented "gayness," not quite Filipino, but not alien either. The images need to be drawn in, reinterpreted until it becomes part of "Filipino" "bakla" "culture." Perhaps some of these definitions come as we define ourselves in relation to the "other." One is struck by Richard Fung's (1995) article on "Asian" "gay" consciousness, of how this develops "under conditions of white racism, either expressed here in the diaspora, or through Western colonialism and imperialism in Asia." It is this political context that often disappears in the artificial attempts to create "gay" pride or solidarity in countries like the Philippines, for being Filipino and gay also means understanding what is not-gay and not-Filipino. The notions of solidarity do exist and sometimes take on global qualities, as in the idea of gay pride being connected to Stonewall–25 years ago, in a place thousands of miles away.

But much of what it means to be gay is shaped locally, sometimes by very practical considerations. I think, for example, of gay yuppie friends earning more than US$1000 a month (in a country where the average monthly household income was $227 in 1994) but who still live with their families, sometimes even sharing a room with a sibling. Some of the limitations of such living arrangements are obvious–such as not being able to bring home a boyfriend–but other limitations are subtler, yet important. One friend, for example, told me he could not watch any of the talk shows featuring the gay and lesbian groups after the march because to even watch the talk show at home would have been "suspicious."

In contrast, the low-income *parlorista* are quite often independent of their families, having moved out or been forced to move out. The Filipino yuppie gay male, on the other hand, could move out but does not. It is, in a way, a choice, and it is a choice that will, for better or for worse, determine the trajectory of "gay communities" in the Philippines. The dilemmas of describing emerging gay communities are obvious. The communities are diverse, built out of consensus as well as dissonance; shuttling between assimilation and de-assimilation; between globalization and localization.

NOTES

1. In surveys conducted by Health Action Information Network (HAIN, unpublished data) among medical and nursing students, it is not uncommon to find agreement with statements like, "Homosexuality is a sin," as well as with statements like, "Homosexuality is an alternative lifestyle."

2. Another indicator of this growing importance of a "*bakla* diaspora" comes with two incidents in 1996 in the Middle East. The first case involved the flogging and deportation of 26 Filipinos in Saudi Arabia for "homosexuality." The second case, in Kuwait, involved the deportation of seven Filipino hairdressers accused of using their beauty parlors as a front for massage services.

REFERENCES

Cannell, Fenella. (1995). The Power of Appearances: Beauty, Mimicry and Transformation in Bicol. In: Vicente Rafael (Ed.), *Discrepant Histories: Translocal Essays on Filipino Cultures,* Manila: Anvil Publishing. 223-258.

Fung, Richard. (1995). The Trouble with "Asians." In: Monica Dorenkamp and Richard Henke (Eds.), *Negoitating Lesbian and Gay Subjects,* London: Routledge. 123-130.

Gagnon, John H. and Richard G. Parker. (1995). Conceiving Sexuality. In: John H. Gagnon and Richard G. Parker (Eds.), *Conceiving Sexuality,* London: Routledge. 3-18.
Garcia, Neil C. and Danton Remoto (Eds.) (1994). *Ladlad: An Anthology of Philippine Gay Writing.* Manila: Anvil Publishing.
Hart, Donn V. (1968). Homosexuality and Transvestism in the Philippines: The Cebuan Bayot and Lakin-on. *Behavior Science Notes* 3(4): 211-248.
Holmes, Margarita. (1993). *A Different Love.* Pasig, Metro Manila: Anvil Publishing.
Johnson, Mark. (1995). Transgender men and homosexuality in the Southern Philippines: Ethnicity, political violence and the protocols of engendered sexualities amongst the Muslim Tausug and Sama. *South East Asia Research* 46-66.
Manalansan, Martin IV. (1995). Speaking of AIDS: Language and the Filipino "Gay" Experience in America. In: Vicente Rafael (Ed.), *Discrepant Histories: Translocal Essays on Filipino Cultures.* Manila: Anvil Publishing. 193-221.
Tan, Michael L. (1995a). From Bakla to Gay: Shifting Gender Identities and Sexual Behaviors in the Philippines" In Richard Parker and John Gagnon (Eds.), *Conceiving Sexuality: Approaches to Sex Research in a Postmodern World,* New York and London: Routledge. 85-96.
Tan, Michael L. (1995b). Tita Aida and Emerging Communities of Gay Men. Two Case Studies from Metro Manila. In: Gerard Sullivan and Laurence Wai-teng Leong (Eds.), *Gays and Lesbians in Asia and the Pacific: Social and Human Services,* New York: The Haworth Press, Inc. 31-48.
Weeks, Jeffrey. (1995). History, Desire, and Identities. In: John H. Gagnon and Richard G. Parker (Eds.), *Conceiving Sexuality,* London: Routledge. 33-50.
Whitam, Frederick and Robin M. Mathy. (1986). *Male Homosexuality in Four Societies: Brazil, Guatemala, the Philippines and the United States.* New York: Praeger.

Gay and Lesbian Couples in Malaysia

Ismail Baba

INTRODUCTION

The term "homosexual" has different connotations in different cultures and also has different meanings for individuals who perceive themselves as gays or lesbians (Blumenfeld & Raymond, 1993; Moses & Hawkins; 1982; Murray, 1992). A homosexual refers to someone who is primarily sexually attracted to people of the same sex (Oxford, 1992). However, Moses and Hawkins (1982) argued that in order to understand homosexuality, we should be able to differentiate the three elements of sexual identity: gender identity, gender role, and sexual orientation. According to Moses and Hawkins, gender identity refers to one's perception of himself or herself as male or female. Gender role is involved with a set of role behaviors that are expected of females and males. For example, women are expected to be "feminine," gentle, and nonaggressive, whereas men are expected to be "masculine," and "macho." In sexual orientation, the individual's preference for partners, whether of the same sex, opposite sex or both sexes, is based upon sexual and affectionate relations.

Kinsey, Pomeroy, and Martin (1948) claimed that when it comes to sexual orientation, human beings could be categorized from exclusively homosexual to exclusively heterosexual, with most people falling somewhere in between. Whatever homosexuality is, it is too complex

[Haworth co-indexing entry note]: "Gay and Lesbian Couples in Malaysia." Baba, Ismail. Co-published simultaneously in *Journal of Homosexuality* (Harrington Park Press, an imprint of The Haworth Press, Inc.) Vol. 40, No. 3/4, 2001, pp. 143-163; and: *Gay and Lesbian Asia: Culture, Identity, Community* (ed: Gerard Sullivan, and Peter A. Jackson) Harrington Park Press, an imprint of The Haworth Press, Inc., 2001, pp. 143-163. Single or multiple copies of this article are available for a fee from The Haworth Document Delivery Service [1-800-342-9678, 9:00 a.m.–5:00 p.m. (EST). E-mail address: getinfo@haworthpressinc. com].

143

to be understood by any definition or model. Sexuality touches on issues such as basic biological sexual functions, attitudes, norms, beliefs, values, taboos, rituals, customs, and sexual practices. No matter how we label the way others behave or act sexually, sexuality remains both individual and personal (Blumenfeld & Raymond, 1993).

This article looks at three case studies of two gay men and one lesbian couple in Malaysia. The study addresses some of the common psychosocial issues in this community, such as self-acceptance, social isolation, role models, and the socialization process. It should be noted that these three couples are not representative of gay and lesbian life in Malaysia, but they reflect some aspects of gay and lesbian relationships in the country.

METHODOLOGY

Several criteria were used in selecting these three couples. The first criterion was the long-term commitment and dedication of each couple to one another. All three couples have been in their relationships for at least seven years. This commitment should help them to reflect back on the challenges of maintaining their relationships. Second was the heterogeneity or diversity of these couples in terms of their ethnic background, religion, education, values, sexual identity, and lifestyle. This helps highlight the impact of various cultural factors and reflects how complex it is to arrive at common definition of homosexuality. The author knows the three couples; therefore, they can be considered as convenience sampling. Since "coming out" is still an issue for most gays and lesbians in Malaysia, by selecting these couples, I have ensured that they may feel more comfortable discussing their own experiences and struggles in maintaining their relationships.

GAYS AND LESBIANS IN MALAYSIA: A BRIEF VIEW

"Gays" or men having sex with men and "lesbians" or women having sex with women exist in Malaysia even though at present they are not socially and politically accepted. Gay and lesbian behaviors, lifestyles, and desires exist in Malaysia and are a feature of Malaysian life. It is interesting to note that there are no strictly equivalent words for "gay," "lesbian," or "homosexual" in Malay. The terms *pondan, mak nyah, darai, bapok*, and *kedi* are derogatory and heavily focus on men who are effeminate. They are often used for cross dressers, transvestites, transsexuals, and transgenders and are more appropriately translated as transvestites or, usually, transsexuals. When the English term gay is used, it is associated with *pondan*. For the purpose of discussion, the words *pondan* and *mak nyah* are used interchangeably in this paper.

In general, *pondan* are not well accepted by their families nor by Malaysian society. Well-adjusted *pondan,* in particular more mature or elderly ones, are less afraid to display their own identity to some of their family members, friends, neighbors, or community. In that sense, those who are close to them accept them. Because of the fact that they have been living all their lives as *pondan* and are unable to meet others' expectation of being "normal," they eventually learn to come to terms with their own sexual identity.

The young emerging *pondan* are still as likely to suffer from social prejudices as their matured counterparts. For this reason, many prefer to join together in big cities or small towns in search of moral support, acceptance, and even employment, especially in the sex industry (Rahman, Hashim, & Ariffin, 1984; Nagaraj & Yahya, 1995).

The concept "gay" in Malaysia refers to a stereotype of men who are effeminate. Although men who appear to be "masculine" and do not fall into this stereotype are somewhat free from being labeled as *pondan,* many, nevertheless, live in fear of being identified and constantly suffer some form of stress. The stress is associated with concern over what would happen if their family, friends, colleagues, and neighbors knew that they are gay. There does not seem to be any traditional concept of lesbianism.

In Malaysia, when people come to know of men who prefer men, they may also refer to them as *pondan*. In the gay and lesbian community, gay men who appear to be "masculine" are often referred to as *jantan*, meaning "macho" or "manly." In some instances, gay men also refer to each other as *nyonya* or *nyah*, a short form of *mak nyah*.

This paper will not try to stick to the term "gay" or "lesbian" as defined by the western world. The paper uses the term "gay" to mean men who see themselves as women and behave accordingly, such as *pondan,* but also uses its modern manifestation of homosexuality with no gender reversal. In general, these two groups do not socialize and share very little or no interest in each other. Furthermore, it is not the intention of this paper to focus on *pondan*, although they are a sub-culture of the gay and lesbian community in Malaysia.

Culturally, many Malaysians consider that gayness and lesbianism is a product of the western world (Baba, 1995; Junet, 1991; Rahim, 1991). Religious and cultural norms consider sex between people of the same sex as morally wrong. Malaysian laws forbids the practice of homosexuality even between consenting male adults, and homosexual intercourse and activity can result in imprisonment for up to twenty years (Humana, 1992). However, there are no reported individuals who have been imprisoned for being gay or lesbian. With these views and laws, gays and lesbians in Malaysia not only learn to lead hidden lives, but also feel obliged to get married so that they can be "accepted" by the society. In general, Malaysia has not been very positive when responding to gay and lesbian related issues (Baba, 1995; Harian Metro, 1995; Rahman et al., 1984; Md. Ali, 1996; Nagaraj & Yahya, 1995). But in the early 1980s the Ministry of National Unity and the Community Development, formally known as the Ministry of Social Welfare, began to show some concerns towards *mak nyah* or transvestites. The Department of Social Welfare, for instance, views *mak nyah* as "handicapped" and regards them as "men" who are impotent and unable to have a family. In light of this rationalization and the fact that they are not well accepted to the mainstream of Malaysian society, the Department has created job-training programs, such as sewing and hairdressing skills, so that they can earn their living honestly and not as prostitutes or sex workers. The Ministry even encouraged *mak nyah* themselves to form their own group and to register as a non government organization (Abd. Rahman, Mohd. Hashim & Ariffin, 1984; Baba, 1995; Lamat, 1984). Although the Ministry is trying to be helpful, its approach does appear to be stereotyped. Many transvestites would like to be accepted as they are and to choose a profession that interests them (Lamat, 1984). However, even this limited effort by the Ministry is counter to the general public's view.

Many adult *mak nyah* live with each other in big cities, such as Kuala Lumpur, Johor Bahru, George Town, and Alor Star. In the cities they have their own social support system and are free of pressure from their families, relatives, and neighbors. By living in the cities and small towns, they also feel less discriminated against (Rahman et al., 1984).

As for the other segment of gay and lesbian community, at present, there are no formal social services at the government level to cater to them. The Pink Triangle (PT) is the only organization that deals with gay and lesbian issues in Malaysia. The organization was formed in Kuala Lumpur, the capital city, in 1987 by a group of concerned gays and lesbians. Its main mission is to address issues that are related to the gay and lesbian community. But since HIV/AIDS has become a major concern in the nation, PT's tasks have very much focused on helping gays and the general public to understand HIV/AIDS, even though the number of HIV/AIDS cases in Malaysia among gays remains relatively small (Ministry of Health, 1996). By focusing on HIV/AIDS-related issues (such as hotline, talks on HIV/AIDS for both government and non-government organizations, counseling for HIV/AIDS, programs on positive living for those who with HIV/AIDS), members of PT feel that they can still render some social services indirectly to its members without being too visible about it.

Since PT was the first non-government organization (NGO) to address HIV/AIDS issues in Malaysia, it has been recognized by the government as one of the most active organizations to fight HIV/AIDS. This has resulted in PT obtaining a government grant, through the Malaysian AIDS Council (MAC, 1996), to further their HIV/AIDS activities. Ironically, the government is fully aware of the nature of the organization but has been silent about its existence. Furthermore, they would not support PT activities in educating members on gay and lesbian related issues.

Since PT has been busy with HIV/AIDS related issues, some members of the organization claim that they have not been fully effective in helping the gay and lesbian community for fear that they may be banned. According to one former member of Pink Triangle, the organization is reluctant to play an active role for fear of political and social repercussions.

Unfortunately, because of its location, PT caters mostly to the gay and lesbian community in Kuala Lumpur. Even then, only those who are comfortable enough with being gay or lesbian would be more likely to utilize the services or use the center for socializing. Others go to the one gay disco in Kuala Lumpur, the streets, shopping complexes, gay friendly nightclubs, or simply home parties to socialize and meet gays. For gays and lesbians outside of Kuala Lumpur, similar meeting places exist in larger towns, but there are no specific gay bars where they can socialize.

The Malaysian mass media, such as local newspapers and magazines, often look down on gays and lesbians. Teenagers who write to local newspapers about being gay or lesbian are often advised not to pursue their sexual orientation for the simple reason that it is unnatural and considered abnormal behavior. The Malaysian Islamic Department and Islamic priests or scholars often condemn this behavior by stating that Allah will curse such behavior. Other religions in Malaysia, such as Christianity, Hinduism, and Buddhism, also disapprove of same sex activity. Thus in Malaysia, it is very difficult for gays and lesbians to come out in the open (Baba, 1995; Rahman et al., 1984; Md. Ali, 1996; Safar, 1994; Nagaraj & Yahya, 1995).

Despite all these constraints, gays and lesbians can be found almost anywhere in Malaysia, especially in the large cities, such as Kuala Lumpur, Penang, Ipoh, Johor, and in most big towns, such as Melaka, Kuching, Kota Baharu, and Alor Star. However, they are not easily identified. They go to "straight" (heterosexual) discotheques and cruise around in shopping complexes and parks. Many gays and lesbians are only comfortable being at home in the company of a small group of friends. Since it is difficult to be openly gay or lesbian, many of them learn to live and cope with their lives without help from anyone. Some have managed to identify other gays or lesbians to act as support group. Due to societal and family pressures, many gays and lesbians are unable to remain single and, therefore, get married. At the same time, these individuals lead double lives and secretly continue having gay and lesbian sexual relationships.

The following case studies highlight some aspects of gay and lesbian relationships in Malaysia. This study shows that despite all of the psychosocial problems faced by the gay and lesbian community in Malaysia, it is still possible for some to have "meaningful" and long lasting relationships.

As mentioned above, the selection of these three couples was based on their long-term commitment. The participants are in the age group between 35 and 45 years old and are of different ethnic background: four Malays, one Chinese, and one European. Four are professionals, one has a blue-collar job, while the remaining one is self-employed. Five of the participants come from families of economically disadvantaged status.

In discussing these three case studies, pseudonyms are used for confidentiality. However, their stories and struggles are real, and they continue to be an integral part of Malaysian society.

CASE ONE

Susan and Rokiah have been together on and off for the last 16 years. They met in the early 80s when Susan first came to Malaysia. Rokiah worked as a cabaret dancer in the city when Susan first met her. Although they have never lived together, their relationship continues until today.

Susan is a 36-year-old middle-class European woman, a university graduate, and is very open about her own sexual orientation. She does not know other lesbians in Malaysia and interacts with a few gay men in the city. Having lived in Malaysia, Susan learned to be somewhat discrete about her sexual orientation. Her openness in the past has caused her some forms of rejection from those to whom she had reached out. For example, Susan has unveiled to a few of her heterosexual friends that she is a lesbian and, in a few instances, they were very upset and refused to see her. Susan is very liberal in her outlook and not afraid in demonstrating her love to Rokiah.

Susan is a tolerant person. She speaks Malay very well and is well adjusted to the Malaysian way of life. Susan would like very much to live with her partner, but that is difficult because Rokiah is fully committed to her family and would never reveal to them that she is a lesbian.

Rokiah is a 55-year-old Malay woman from an economically disadvantaged group. She had a few unsuccessful marriages and is now a single parent with four grown up children. To stay married is expected in Malaysia, especially for women. In most cases, the woman is the one blamed when a marriage breaks up. Being a cabaret dancer was already "immoral" enough for a Muslim woman and being single even more so. Therefore, it was important for Rokiah to stay married even if she did not feel it necessary.

Three of Rokiah's children are married, and Rokiah has four grandchildren. Rokiah does not understand what lesbianism means and is very afraid of others finding out about her relationship with Susan. As a Moslem woman, Rokiah does not think her religion and community accept her being a lesbian. She loves Susan very much but is often confused as to how to live with her religious beliefs and cultural norms. Rokiah is very afraid of revealing to others that she is having a sexual relationship with Susan. These unresolved issues continue to be obstacles in Rokiah and Susan's relationship.

Rokiah only had four years of schooling in a Malay elementary school. She reads and writes Malay but does not speak English. She is very industrious and has independently brought up her four children. Rokiah earns her living now by running a small stall selling food. In the past, Susan did help Rokiah financially.

According to Susan, one of Rokiah's daughters suspects that Rokiah and Susan are having an affair. The daughter actually caught them embracing each other when Susan used to be allowed to visit and sleep at Rokiah's house regularly. According to Susan, since then, she has been barred from entering Rokiah's house and was labeled as *perempuan jahat* or a bad woman. It has become more difficult for Rokiah and Susan to meet, and Rokiah does not feel comfortable visiting Susan because she is living with a straight couple. They meet regularly in town and occasionally have managed to sneak out of town for a couple of days. According to Susan, Rokiah has to come up with all kinds of excuses to her children whenever they are out of town.

CASE TWO

Roslan (age 36) and Lee (40) have been involved a relationship since 1989. They met at a gay discotheque and have been living together ever since. Roslan has a diploma in social studies and was married when he first met Lee. He knew that he was gay; he had been involved in a few sexual relationships with men, but he got married because of societal pressures. He has a six-year-old son who is now living with his ex-wife. Roslan spent most of his time with his partner, Lee, even when he was still married. He used to give all kinds of excuses to his ex-wife, such as business meetings and business trips, in order to be with Lee.

Roslan comes from a working class Malay family and has a good relationship with them. According to Roslan, he thinks that his family suspects that he is gay, but Roslan is not ready to disclose his sexual identity to his family. According to Roslan, there was a man with whom Roslan was involved prior to Lee who actually told some members of his family that he is gay, but Roslan denied this. Roslan actually did marry after that incident.

Roslan works as an administrator at one of the higher learning institutions. He has a good job and enjoys socializing with others, such as going to the disco, movies, and concerts with his partner Lee. Within the gay community, Roslan is very open about his sexual preference. Both Roslan and Lee entertain and attend gay social gatherings as a couple. They also have straight friends who accept them.

As a Muslim, Roslan prays five times a day and attends the weekly Friday prayer as is required for adult male Muslims. He also observes the fasting month of Ramadhan. Like most devoted Muslims, Roslan believes that homosexuality is "wrong," but he feels that as long as he is praying regularly, Allah may be able to understand his needs.

Lee is Malaysian Chinese and a graduate from a local university. He accepts himself as being gay but is somewhat troubled by the pressures from his parents and relatives to get married. According to Lee, at one stage, he avoided going home to his parents because they often hinted to him that they would like to see him married. At work, Lee also faces some pressure from his straight counterparts. Sometimes, said Lee, he lied to his colleagues that he was married with two children just to shut them up.

Within the gay community, Lee is well adjusted but is unable to deal with his family about being gay. Lee is very close to his mum and dad but would never hurt them by informing them that he is gay. According to Lee, his parents suspect that he does not like women but do not want to confront him directly with the issue.

Being the only son in a Chinese family, culturally, he would be expected to continue the family name. This has caused Lee a lot of stress. He is not religious and is easily influenced by new ideas or fads. Lee has had a few gay relationships in the past. Two of Lee's previous partners have ended up married but continue to actively have ongoing sexual relationships with other men.

CASE THREE

Azlan (38) is a Malay civil servant and a college graduate. His partner, Ramli (40) is a high school graduate and a mechanic. They have been in the relationship for a total of ten years. Azlan and Ramli first met at a restaurant about a year after Ramli divorced his second wife.

Azlan has never been married. He comes from a working class family and was raised in a small village. He never knew the word "gay" but has realized since childhood that he was different. As a young man, he moved to the city and discovered that gay life existed in Malaysia and identified himself quite comfortably with the gay community.

Azlan comes from a family of eight brothers and sisters. According to Azlan, a few of them, especially the elder ones, suspect that he is gay, but Azlan has only ever discussed his gayness with one of his younger brothers, who has since accepted him. Although all of his sisters and brothers are married, they never pressure him to be like them. He suspects most of his brothers and sisters know about him, but he feels there is not a need to inform them at this stage. They all know that Ramli and he live together, and Azlan feels either they accept it or they see it as normal for two single men to share a house together.

Azlan appears to be well adjusted socially and psychologically and has some straight friends who know about his sexual orientation. Some of his colleagues suspect that he is gay, but he has never been ill-treated. Azlan had a few boyfriends in the past, including a few expatriate men. He had a few long-term relationships for about five years each before living with Ramli. Azlan is a Muslim and sees religion as an individual choice that should not be imposed on others. He believes that there is nothing wrong in being gay and sees any act of love between two men or women as the work of God. He is a very liberal and open-minded person.

Ramli comes from a working-class family and has had three unsuccessful marriages. His father passed away when he was seven years old, and he is not at all close to his family members. Ramli has a son that he has never seen from his first marriage and a 15-year-old daughter from his second marriage. Ramli never claims that he is gay. He loves Azlan at the moment and does not believe that he should be considered gay. Ramli has had some sexual experiences with men prior to his relationship with Azlan. They both have their own set of friends with whom they socialize separately. However, Ramli socializes mostly with straight men but has become quite friendly with a very few of Azlan's gay friends.

Ramli finished secondary school and has never been exposed to gay life. According to Azlan, Ramli does not feel comfortable around gay men, and he suspects that Ramli does not want to be labeled as being gay, since he does not thinks that he is. Nonetheless, Ramli is well accepted in Azlan's family and very comfortable in their company.

Ramli is a Muslim but not religious. Others easily influence him on matters that relate to religion. The relationship with Azlan was disrupted when Ramli decided to get married for the third time. Nonetheless, his marriage only lasted for about three years, and, eventually, Ramli moved back in with Azlan. Ramli never really met all the women that he has married; friends arranged the marriages. He felt that heterosexual marriage is expected of Malay men, and he did it out of duty. According to Ramli, he realized soon after his third marriage that he was not happy but was not able to do anything about it because he did not want to be an irresponsible husband. Nevertheless, after three years, they decided to divorce.

PSYCHOSOCIAL ISSUES FOR THE GAY AND LESBIAN COMMUNITY IN MALAYSIA

The above three case studies portray some of the gay and lesbian situation in Malaysia. This section of the paper looks at some of the psychosocial issues that can be drawn from these three studies. They all touch on issues of self-acceptance, social isolation, role models, and the socialization process.

Self-Acceptance

Self-acceptance and the process of coming out have been an ongoing issue in the gay and lesbian community (Blumfield & Raymond, 1993; Eichberg, 1990; Signorile, 1994). According to Eicherg, being able to admit to someone that one is gay or lesbian is the first phase of coming out. However, coming out or learning to accept that one is gay or lesbian can be a life long process that depends upon several factors. These include:

a. how much the person considers that being gay or lesbian is a normal phenomenon,

b. how willing one is to take the risks of telling someone, and

    c. how receptive or comfortable the environment is for the person to be openly gay or lesbian (Cass, 1979; Khan, 1991; Lewis, 1984).

All these factors play an important role in the process of coming out.

In Malaysia, there is a trend for people to be more open with their own sexual identity. The Malaysian mass media are slowly trying to educate its public on gay issues by importing gay and lesbian materials. Recently, one of the Malaysian television channels screened an American film titled *Consenting Adult*, a movie about a young adult coming out to his parents. In addition to that, local newspapers are also trying to portray a more positive image of being gay (Chesterfield, 1994; *News Straits Times*, 1995). However, all of these articles are western stories and are written by westerners reinforcing the belief that this is only a western phenomenon. So far, there has not been positive image written by a Malaysian author about gays and lesbians in Malaysia.

In these studies, self-acceptance appears to vary from individual to individual. Some are somewhat comfortable about being gay or lesbian. This is true in the case of Susan, Azlan, Lee, and Roslan. All of them appear to be somewhat comfortable with their own sexual orientation, especially within their own community. Higher education, media influence, and city living appear as common social factors that can contribute to their level of coming out. All four have completed their education at the university level with the exception of Roslan, who is a diploma holder. Their higher education may have served as a tool for them to be more rational in their own thinking and assessment of what is right and wrong about being gay or lesbian. Exposed to the urban environment, as well as being in touch with gay friends constantly, perhaps made it easier for them to be out.

The "coming out" process for the individuals concerned in the three case studies appeared to start with their telling other gay men, trusted friends, and eventually family members about their sexual identity. As it is, perhaps most gays and lesbians in Malaysia are much more comfortable coming out this way as opposed to having to march or to make a public statement about their sexuality. Well, at least this has not happened yet in Malaysia.

For the others in the studies, coming out has been more difficult. In the case of Rokiah, even though she has been with Susan for more than 15 years, she has refused to accept herself as being a lesbian. Similarly, Ramli is reluctant to admit that he is gay even after having being involved with Azlan for about ten years. Rokiah and Ramli's levels of education are lower as compared to the other four individuals. This may play a factor in terms of one's own self-awareness. Furthermore, both individuals appear to be confined to their traditional social milieu which could mitigate against their coming out. For Rokiah and Ramli, coming out to their partners perhaps is good enough without having to tell others. Both see that being lesbian/gay is a private matter between two consenting adults.

Whatever the degree of self-acceptance, all three couples are able to continue with their relationships despite their individual differences. The fact that they are able to retain their long term companions shows that they are committed to their relationship. From the three cases, it can be said that self-acceptance may not be a requirement for gay and lesbian couples to maintain long-term relationships. It appears that commitment to one another plays an important role.

Social Isolation

The gay and lesbian community is considered a minority group in any society, especially in a country where they have been denied civil and legal protection (Blumenfeld & Raymond, 1993). In Malaysia, men who have sex with men and women who have sex with women may want to see themselves as a minority group. But since there is very little effort at the moment from the government or society to help them come out, they may have to stay in isolation for a while. Although there is a trend in educating the Malaysian public about gays and lesbians, on the whole, the general perception towards these individuals remains negative, which keeps them socially isolated. This would be indicated by the case of Roslan and Ramli. Roslan intentionally got married to avoid gossip that he was gay while Ramli repeatedly got married because of strong pressures from his straight friends.

In three studies, all have been living in isolation from the so-called mainstream society. In the cases of Azlan, Lee, Roslan, and Susan, although they are somewhat well-adjusted within their own community, they are very much restrained from living openly among their heterosexual counterparts or even with their own family members. In the case of Ramli and Rokiah, both are much more isolated, since their contacts with the gay and lesbian community are confined exclusively to their partners. As a couple, Susan and Rokiah are the most isolated with no contact or supportive help from their lesbian counterparts.

Social isolation is associated with the willingness of gay men and lesbian women to come out and with how much they want to tell the truth about themselves (Eichberg, 1993). It is also related to how conscious they are of their own sexual orientation (Cass, 1979; Coleman; 1981-82). Given the fact that the social environment in Malaysia gives very little opportunity for gay men and lesbian women to come out openly and also because of limited positive awareness that has been created for this group, all three couples have learned to live adequately in isolation. Although problems do occur in trying to balance their dual roles–being gay or lesbian and behaving as straight–they are able to cope and maintain their long-term relationship despite the socio-cultural obstacles.

Social isolation will continue to exist in these couples' lives as long as they are not made to feel welcome being out. Nonetheless, this does not stop them from maintaining an acceptable relationship regardless of the situation.

Role Models

Role models refer to "positive" examples of how gays and lesbians can act, think, and behave (Blumenfeld & Raymond, 1993). Lacking in positive role models or what appear to be acceptable norms in being gay or lesbian can lead to role confusion.

In the past, gay men and lesbian women relied on their heterosexual counterparts as role models. Being unable to form their own identity, some gay men perform the so-called "butch" role while the other takes on the feminine role. Whatever it is, with the women's and gay liberation movements that took place in the West, gays and lesbians in the Western world are becoming more comfortable now with who they are and are creating their own identities (Blummenfeld & Raymond, 1993).

In Malaysia and throughout the Malayo-Polynesian world, there is a long history of homosexuality and transgenderism (Murray, 1992). *Pondan* have provided some sort of role model for those with unconventional sexual orientations, and they have played a role in Malaysian society. For example, many *mak andams* (persons who are responsible for making up brides at weddings) are *mak nyah*, and they have been somewhat acceptable in Malaysia society. Before the Islamic resurgence, which took place in Malaysia in the 80s, many *pondan* were *perempuan jogets,* or commercial dancers. They worked at nightclubs as dancers and also hired out at weddings to perform *joget,* a popular Malaysian folk-dance. However, this is the traditional way that homosexuality has been expressed in Malaysia. As mentioned earlier, those who do not see themselves as *pondan* may not relate to such activities, and, certainly, the modern manifestations of homosexuality would reject such roles.

None of the couples in this study are confined to the role model that has been portrayed by the *mak nyah* or *pondan* in Malaysia. The fact that they do not know how gays and lesbians should behave, along with the fact that they do not want to identify themselves as *pondan,* suggest that they are actually in search of their own identity.

In the case of Roslan, Lee and Azlan, being gay means one must act like a "straight" man. How they feel and act could be the result of modern manifestations of homosexuality. It appears that there is some amount of fear in all three in being identified as gay or lesbian, as this could result in discrimination. It appears that all of them are afraid of being stigmatized, being looked down upon, and not being respected by others. For that reason, all three couples try as much as possible to portray to the majority of their straight friends that they are not gay or lesbian. This is also a form of denial that is closely related to self-awareness and self-acceptance.

Positive role models appear to be lacking since gays and lesbians are repressed in Malaysia. There is no public figure who is openly gay nor any lesbian with whom young gays and lesbians can identify. Therefore, it is a common perception among Malaysians that to be gay is to be a transvestite or a man who dresses as a woman (Baba, 1995). As for *pondan* or *mak nyah,* even though they have played a role in Malaysian society, they are still not fully accepted. Therefore, even if gay men were to follow their role models, they would still be looked down upon by the society.

The stigma that is attached to homosexuals in Malaysia, whether they are *pondan* or "straight" acting, does not allow for both groups to have a positive image of themselves. The negative pictures of being gay do not help gay men and women to feel comfortable with their sexuality.

Socialization

Everyone needs to be socialized in order to feel fully comfortable with his or her own culture and subcultures. Socialization is a learning process where people develop their own personality and comprehend values, attitudes, norms, and societal expectations of their own cultures or subcultures (Blumenfeld & Raymond, 1993). In order to go through this process, a person needs agents of socialization. In most cases, parents or caretakers act as these agents, particularly at a very early age. Once they enroll in school, their teachers, friends, and other adults also influence the process of socialization.

At present, human sexuality is rarely taught in either high schools or universities in Malaysia. The general view is that sex education should not be introduced because it would condone people in engaging in sexual activities outside of marriage. The misconceptions about sex education also drive parents, teachers, educators, and others further into fear and confusion about sexuality (Baba & Global, 1996; Khoon, 1996).

The cases described here show that all individuals may have been more comfortable with their sexuality had they been given the right information about human sexuality at an earlier stage in their lives (Khoon, 1996). In the case of Rokiah and Ramli, for example, both do not see themselves as being lesbian or gay even though they are in long-term same-sex relationships. Perhaps being identified as gay or lesbian is not as important as loving, respecting, and providing support to one another. No matter the views of society on homosexuality, they continue their relationships and are willing to improve them. However, lack of identification as gay or lesbian creates conflict with their partners.

In the case of Azlan, Roslan, and Lee, their respective families and relatives have been putting pressure on them to get married. Had they learned to be more assertive with their sexuality, they might be able to help their family to accept them instead of finding or creating excuses for not getting married. Culturally, Malaysians are expected to obey their own parents (Mahathir, 1996), and perhaps not wanting to *menderhaka* or betray has made it more difficult for Roslan and Lee to approach their parents about their own sexual identity.

In looking at the individuals in this study, all of them could have been more assertive about their sexual orientation had they been given a strong foundation concerning sexuality. A positive outlook about sexual orientation could have helped them better in dealing with their families' and their straight friends' perception, about gays and lesbians. A strong foundation could also have helped a sense of self-acceptance, and thus could have facilitated the development of the relationships.

IMPLICATIONS

Based on the personal experiences of these couples, there are several approaches which can be taken as to how gays and lesbians in Malaysia can be helped in living more positively with their own sexual orientation. These approaches are certainly not going to eliminate the gay and lesbian community's problems as a whole, but perhaps may help some gays and lesbians and even *mak nyah* to feel comfortable with themselves. These approaches are based on some of the constraints or limitations of the present situation of gays and lesbians in Malaysia.

The Need to Redefine the Role of Pink Triangle

Pink Triangle (PT), which is the only organization to serve the gay and lesbian community, needs to redefine its role by providing more assertive social programs for gays and lesbians (personal communication, 1966). It should introduce social outreach programs for those who are not sure about their sexuality by providing them with information and resources. Gays, lesbians, *mak nyah,* transsexuals, bisexuals, and transgenders need to know that they are different, and they should be informed that it is all right to be different. They need to know that they are not alone. If necessary, they need to be in touch with other individuals, groups, or clubs where they do not feel alone and isolated. At the moment such programs do exist but have not been the major focus of PT. Furthermore, such programs are limited to those who are residing in Kuala Lumpur.

In addition, PT should be actively involved in promoting public understanding about gay and lesbian issues through public forums or seminars. It can play an active role by informing the Malaysian public that homosexuality is not a mental illness, that homosexuals are not more likely to molest children, and that they are not necessarily sexually compulsive.

PT also needs to act as an information and referral service for individuals, groups, and organizations that need to learn more about gay and lesbian related issues. This is the only way that the public can be properly informed rather than misinformed about gays and lesbians.

A self-help group can also be set up for gays and lesbians in order to help them deal with their problems. Examples of these problems are: how to live positively with their own sexual orientation, how to come out to friends and family members, and how to deal with other gay and lesbian related issues.

Setting Up Similar Organizations

Similar organizations also need to be set up in other parts of the country since gays and lesbians do exist in other cities and small towns in Malaysia. According to some members of PT, they had talked of setting up a similar branch of PT in Penang a few years ago, but because the number of gays and lesbians in Penang is relatively small, and because they are not united, the plan was canceled.

Gays and lesbians in other parts of the country need support groups and need to meet other individuals who have similar interests. They also need to be informed with regards to resources such HIV/AIDS updates, gay and lesbian literature, and meeting places for gays and lesbians. With their experience, the Pink Triangle organization can help other groups initiate and set up similar organizations. For example, with the support of its members, PT has been very self-reliant and has conducted fund-raising events with its own theatrical group performing in a gay bar and gay-friendly discotheques. It should, therefore, be possible to start a similar group somewhere, especially when the PT, itself, is willing to help out.

Setting up Meetings and Natural Helping Networks on Gay and Lesbian Issues

PT and other interested individuals can initiate national forums or workshops on gay and lesbian issues. These workshops could be held as private functions in order to encourage more participation from the gay and lesbian community.

Natural helping networks are created by individuals who need each other's support when facing problems of living (Lewis & Suarez, 1995). In the case of Malaysia, a few informal sub-groups and natural helping networks exist among gays and even *mak nyah*. These sub-groups have been very valuable and useful in supporting some individuals in the case of family and relationship problems. However, they are not effective in helping with societal issues such as discrimination, employment, and housing.

On the whole, I believe gays, lesbians, and *mak nyah* in Malaysia are bound to have psychosocial problems, especially when there is very little access to formal help. Setting up natural helping networks can help reduce some of the problems faced by this community. Interested and concerned individuals can act as key persons to identify groups that may benefit from these natural helping networks. These key persons need to be trained on how to set up these groups. Through PT, it would be possible to identify interested individuals from various parts of Malaysia who once trained could set up natural helping networks in their own communities.

CONCLUSION

Gays and lesbians in Malaysia are far from being socially accepted. Socio-cultural and political constraints have made them become quite repressed. This study also indicates that problems of self-acceptance, social isolation, positive role models, and socialization are some major areas that need to be looked into. Nonetheless, the act of love does not stop couples from having long lasting relationships. Despite all of the psychosocial problems faced by them, they have learned to cope with and manage their lives accordingly. Perhaps they could have better lives and more satisfying relationships if they did not feel obliged to hide their sexual identity.

NOTES

The author gratefully acknowledges friends, Dr. Mohd, Amiruddin Fawzi of Universiti Sains Penang, Malaysia, and Ronald MacFarlane of Community AIDS Service Penang, Malaysia, for their comments on an earlier draft of this manuscript. The author also wishes to thank the participants in this study.

REFERENCES

Baba, I. (1995). Social work students' readiness to work with persons with HIV/ AIDS and their families in Malaysia, Singapore, and Thailand (*Doctoral dissertation*, Barry University School of Social Work, 1994).

Baba, I. (1996). Managing Relationships in Young Romance. In *Global Channel 2, Radio & Television Malaysia*. Malaysia.

Blumenfeld, W. J. & Raymond, D. (1993). *Looking at Gay and Lesbian Life*. Boston: Beacon Press.

Cass, V. C. (1979). Homosexual identity formation: A theoretical model. *Journal of Homosexuality*, 4(3), 219-235.

Chasterfield, R. (1994). Parents should accept their gay children. In *Insight*, New Strait Times: Kuala Lumpur.

Coleman, E. (1981-2). Developmental stages of the coming the process. *Journal of Homosexuality*, 7(2/3), New York: The Haworth Press, Inc.

Eichberg, R. (1991). *Coming out: An act of love*. New York: A Plume Book.

Harian Metro (1995). *JAIP siasat kelab homoseks*. In Semasa. Malaysia

Humana, C. (1992). *World human rights guide*. New York: Oxford University Press.

Khan, M. J. (1991). Factors affecting the coming out process for lesbians. *Journal of Homosexuality*, 21(3), 47-70.

Khoon T. Y. (1996). *Rape cases involving children: the importance of sex education*. Paper presented at the Regional Conference on Early Childhood Education, Kuala Lumpur, Malaysia.

Kinsey, A. C., Pomeroy, W., & Martin, C. (1948). *Sexual behavior in the human male*. Philadelphia: W. B. Saunders.

Lamat, N. (1984). *Persatuan Mak Nyah tidak dakwa tidak dapat perhatina kerajaan*. Mingguan Malaysia: Malaysia.

Lewis, E. A. & Suarez, Z. E. (1995). Natural helping networks. In National Association of Social Workers (19th ed.) *Encyclopedia of Social Work* (pp. 1765-1772). NASW Press: Washington DC.

Lewis, L. A. (1984). The coming out-process for lesbians: Integrating a stable identity. *Social Work*, 29, 464-469.

MAC (1996). *Activity report and 5 year plan (1996-2000: Working paper for AIDS/ STD Unit Ministry of Health*. Malaysian AIDS Council.

Mahathir, M (1996). We need our own opinions. In *Views, The Star*, Nov. 27. Malaysia.

MD. Ali, Z. (1996). *Kelab Eksklusif Homoseks* in Harian Metro. Malaysia.

Ministry of Health, (1996). *Klafikasi jangkitan HIV di Malaysia 1985-1996*. Kuala Lumpur: Ministry of Health.

Moses, A. E. & Hawkins, R. O., Jr. (1982). *Counseling lesbian women and gay men: A life-issues approach*. St Louis: C. V. Mosby.

Murray, S. (1992). *Oceanic Homosexuality*. New York: Garland Publishing, Inc.

Nagaraj, S. & Yahya, S. R. (1995). *The sex sector: An unenumerated economy*. Kuala Lumpur: Universiti Pertanian Malaysia.

New Strait Times (1995a). When your spouse is gay. In *People*, NST: Malaysia.

National Opinion Research Center (1989-1992). *General Social Survey*. Chicago: Author.

Personal Communication (1996). With one of senior members of Pink Triangle.

Oxford (1992). *Oxford Advanced Learner's Dictionary.* Oxford: Oxford University Press.

Rogers, P. (1993, February 15). How many gays are there? *Newsweek,* 46.

Rahman, M., Hashim, N., & Ariffin (1984). *Memahami Corak Hidup masyarakat pondan serta implikasinya terhadap masyarakat di Malaysia.* laporan Penyelidikan Kerja Sosial. Pusat Pengajian Sains Kemasyarkatan, Universiti Sains Malaysia.

Safar, R. (1994). *Asrama bebas homoseks.* Nasional, Berita Harian: Malaysia.

Signorile, M. (1994). *Queer in America.* New York: Doubleday.

Let Them Take Ecstasy: Class and Jakarta Lesbians

Alison J. Murray

INTRODUCTION

Through visiting and living in Jakarta since 1983, I have witnessed a basic social division reproduced by propaganda, myth, and mutual incomprehension and by the barbed wire that physically separates elite houses from their alleyside neighbors. Gated communities, guarded shopping malls, and the "beautification" of sections of central Jakarta increasingly distinguish the land of the "haves" from the "have-nots" crushed in between and around them: a dichotomy based on class.

Indonesia's vast wealth is highly concentrated in the hands of the upper class: "upper class" is shorthand for the royal Javanese, Government, bureaucratic, and army elites, and for the expanding business classes to which they are financially linked. The lower classes are formed of the original Betawi people, ex-slaves brought from around the archipelago, and later immigrants, mostly from Central and West Java, who have formed spatially identified urban *kampung* (village) communities. The upper class, looking outward to an internationalized consumer culture, has little connection with the lower class, who look inward to the neighborhood (cf Murray 1991a). Ostentatious displays of wealth and developments such as toll roads and gated complexes that displace the old *kampung* are increasing the alienation and dispossession of lower-class youth growing up to unemployment.

[Haworth co-indexing entry note]: "Let Them Take Ecstasy: Class and Jakarta Lesbians." Murray, Alison J. Co-published simultaneously in *Journal of Homosexuality* (Harrington Park Press, an imprint of The Haworth Press, Inc.) Vol. 40, No. 3/4, 2001, pp. 165-184; and: *Gay and Lesbian Asia: Culture, Identity, Community* (ed: Gerard Sullivan, and Peter A. Jackson) Harrington Park Press, an imprint of The Haworth Press, Inc., 2001, pp. 165-184. Single or multiple copies of this article are available for a fee from The Haworth Document Delivery Service [1-800-342-9678, 9:00 a.m.–5:00 p.m. (EST). E-mail address: getinfo@haworthpressinc.com].

I want to show that class is also the main division between Jakarta's lesbians. A discussion of the dominant ideology of women's sexuality, which invisibilizes and stigmatizes homosexuality, and scenes from everyday urban life will illustrate how lesbian experiences vary according to context. Jakarta's dominance creates contradictions in that it is both the pinnacle of the ideology of "Indonesian culture" (seen as essential to unite the country) and the gateway to Western ideas such as lesbian/gay culture (seen as deviant and de-stabilizing). While Western decadence should be withheld from the masses, the segregation of the elite allows them to play in private. At the same time, Indonesia has its own traditions of homosexuality, which are now overlaid with the globalizing culture, creating various hybrid local scenes.

The relation of the elite to urban subcultures is more complex than "class conflict," but I am using class as a starting point and lesbian as a signifier of non-conforming sexuality. There is no lesbian "community" in Jakarta, since class overdetermines both gender and sexuality. There can be strategic communities and identities: the lesbian label can have strategic uses for those with privileged access to global networks, whereas disclosure in Jakarta or association with lower class lesbians means loss of status. For the lower class without privileges to lose, overt signifiers of "deviance" within a subcultural street milieu suggest a source of resistance to power. However, in order to avoid entrenching individual women in any specific context, I prefer the concept of multiple and shifting identities.[1]

Thus my aim is not only to add to the paucity of work describing or even acknowledging Asian lesbians, but also to develop an understanding of the context of sexual practice and the effects of class differences. While some post-colonial feminists (e.g., Spivak 1987) have criticized the work of Western women in Asia, I feel that it can be useful as long as the author's position is clearly stated. Academic studies from outside and inside Indonesia have tended to reproduce the elite-based view of women and sexuality, or they have only addressed representations of this view (e.g., Parker 1995; Sen 1993; Suryakusuma 1987). Due to the mutually suspicious relationship between classes, which an outsider can sometimes circumvent, I think it is valid to discuss my experiences of Jakarta's subcultures. The author's sexuality and sexual experiences significantly affect the research, and this should no longer be a taboo subject (see Kulick & Wilson 1994).

SEX, CLASS, AND DISCOURSE

Now that there is more openness about what really happens in "the field," I should say that while I may identify, depending on the occasion, as a lesbian or a sex worker or an academic, in Jakarta I have had male and female lovers and clients, Indonesian and non-Indonesian. These experiences often had nothing to do with my research at the time, but they have helped to inform the present analysis of sexuality and class. The people I knew through the 1980s were part of Jakarta's lower-class subcultural milieu, where lesbian sex is more common than the lesbian identity confined to women with short hair and other prescribed "lesbian" signifiers. Meanwhile closeted networks of upper class lesbians are linked to the growing global lesbian and gay movement, but usually maintain a "straight" appearance in Jakarta. Because of the separation of social worlds, it was only through the international circulation of gays and lesbians through Sydney that I met people who later introduced me to their friends in Jakarta in 1993: without personal introductions, it would be difficult to find these women.

Indonesia's all-pervasive state ideology attempts to create an "imaginary community" (Anderson 1987) based on Javanese elite and Dutch petit-bourgeois values combined with the requirements of capitalist expansion. The ideology of the "happy and healthy" nuclear family indoctrinates the idea that marriage to a man is essential to make a woman complete; sexuality and sexual practices are thereby controlled by being subsumed within correct gender roles. Suryakusuma (1987) describes the systematic social pressure on (elite) women to fulfill their "destiny" as housewives and mothers, which is constantly reinforced through the education system, the family welfare program, and official women's organizations. Predominant among these is the civil service wives' organization in which the husband's rank denotes the wife's position.

The faithful housewife model is clearly inappropriate for lower-class women, and, to some extent, the elite construct of the ideal woman aims to protect upper-class women from the uncivilized and promiscuous tendencies of the lower classes, who are constructed en masse as "deviant bodies" (cf Foucault 1978; Groneman 1995). The danger represented by the overwhelming numbers of the "Other" encourages the appearance of conformity, while a concept of the masses as uneducated and dependent justifies unequal status and privilege.[2]

The dominant discourse distinguishes regulated sexuality in the public arena from hidden sexuality, and upper class women who can afford to employ maids to do the housework are left with long hours to amuse themselves within their enclaves. Since appearances are all-important, extra-marital sex is acceptable, even expected, as long as it stays in the hidden realm: it doesn't really matter who the sex is with or if money is exchanged. Behind closed doors, there are model housewives with spare time and rising disposable incomes running escort services, distributing pornography, and having gay affairs. They make arrangements by phone, and, if they leave their gated sanctums, their cars have human or electronic devices to ensure that the gates open and close without their having to set foot on the street (cf Krisna 1978). In contrast, the street life and high density housing of the lower classes does not give the option of hiding, but their behavior has been mostly ignored by both researchers and the authorities.

WESTERN LABELS AND JAKARTA JUICES

While lesbianism is not officially illegal, a Minister for Women's Affairs stated that lesbianism is not part of Indonesian culture or state ideology (*Suara Karya* 6 June 1994), using a common technique of blaming anything undesirable on the decadent West while simultaneously embracing all kinds of clearly inappropriate Western technologies and consumer goods. The Minister's statement is ridiculous since "Indonesian culture" is an imposed construct and since Indonesia has deep-rooted homosocial traditions. Islam is influential in the construction of "Indonesian culture," and given that 90% of Indonesians give their religion as Islam, my impression is that a disproportionate number of Indonesian lesbians come from Christian, Chinese, or other backgrounds. Interpretations of Islam are used to repress sex in general, even extending to pre-Islamic traditions; for instance, an artist friend had a painting depicting a *linga* and *yoni* (Hindu male and female symbols of fertility) censored from her exhibition without notice. Dede Oetomo (1991, 1995) and Gayatri (1995) have researched homosexual and homosocial activities in the Hindu-Buddhist pantheon, Javanese legends, and in other parts of the archipelago.

Covert lesbian activities are thus an adaptation to the ideological context, where the distinction between hidden and exposed sexual behavior allows for fluidity in sexual relations ("everyone could be said to be bisexual" according to Oetomo 1995) as long as the primary presentation is heterosexual/monogamous. It is not lesbian activity that has been imported from the West, but the word *lesbi* used to label the Western concept of individual identity based on a fixed sexuality. I have not found that Indonesian women like to use the label to describe themselves, since it is connected to unpleasant stereotypes and the pathological view of deviance derived from Freudian psychology (cf Foucault 1978).

The concept of butch-femme also has a different meaning in Indonesia from the current Western use which implies a subversion of norms and playful use of roles and styles (cf Nestle 1992). In Indonesia (and other parts of Southeast Asia, such as the Philippines, Thailand's, *tom*-and-*dee*: Chetame 1995) the roles are quite strictly, or restrictively, defined and are related to popular, pseudo-psychological explanations of the "real" lesbian. In the simple terms of popular magazines, the butch (*sentul*) is more than 50% lesbian, or incurably *lesbi*, while the femme (*kantil*) is less than 50% lesbian, or potentially normal. Blackwood's (1994) description of her secretive relationship with a butch-identified woman in Sumatra brings up some cross-cultural differences and difficulties that they experienced and could not speak about publicly. The Sumatran woman adopted masculine signifiers and would not be touched sexually herself; she wanted to be called "pa" by Blackwood, who she expected to behave as a "good wife." Meanwhile, Blackwood's own beliefs, as well as her higher status due to class and ethnicity, made it hard to take on the passive female role.

I want to emphasize here that behavior needs to be conceptually separated from identity, as both are contextually specific and constrained by opportunity. It is common for young women socialized into a rigid heterosexual regime, in Asia or the West, to experience their sexual feelings in terms of gender confusion: "If I am attracted to women, then I must be a man trapped in a woman's body." Women are not socialized to seek out a sexual partner (of any kind), or to be sexual at all, so an internal "feeling" may never be expressed unless there are role models or opportunities available. If the butch-femme stereotype, as presented in the Indonesian popular media, is the only image of lesbians available outside the metropolis (e.g., in Sumatra), then this may affect how women express their feelings. However, urban lower-class lesbians engage in a range of styles and practices: some use butch style consciously to earn peer respect, while others reject the butch as out-dated. The stereotype of all lower-class lesbians whether following butch-femme roles or conforming to one subcultural pattern is far from the case and reflects the media and elite's lack of real knowledge about street life.

The media has an important role in influencing public opinion to accept the ideological construct of heterosexism (cf Oetomo in *Jakarta Jakarta* 22 June 1993; Gayatri 1995; and the clippings collection, *Gays in Indonesia*) through the constant portrayal of any sexual behavior outside marriage as sick and deviant. Articles are reinforced with "expert" psychologists and advice columns, even though Indonesia's official medical guidelines finally stopped classifying homosexuality as abnormal in 1983. On the rare occasions that lesbians have been mentioned, typical reports cover suicides, women forced to go to psychiatrists to be "cured" and forced into marriage, and lesbian pseudo-marriages where one women takes the "man's role." I think the report from the Beijing women's conference that Indonesian lesbians are "declared mad and locked up" (*Sydney Morning Herald* 11 September 1995) is an example of a lesbian rights group pushing their case a bit too far, however. Marriage, for some women, may be a practical solution, which allows greater freedom "behind the scenes."

The imagery of sickness creates powerful stigmatization and internalized homophobia: women may refer to themselves as *sakit* (sick). An ex-lover of mine in Jakarta is quite happy to state a preference for women while at the same time expressing disgust at the word *lesbi* and at the sight of a butch dyke; however, I have generally found that the stigma around lesbian labels and symbols is not translated into discrimination against individuals based on their sexual activities. I have been surprised to discover how many women in Jakarta will either admit to having sex with women or to being interested in it, but again, this is only rarely accompanied by an open lesbian (or bisexual) identity. I have found it hard to avoid the word "lesbian" to refer to female-to-female sexual relations, but it should not be taken to imply a permanent self-identity. It is very important to try and understand the social contexts of behavior, in order to avoid drawing conclusions based on inappropriate Western notions of lesbian identity, community, or "queer" culture.

WHERE ARE THE LESBIANS IN GAY JAKARTA?

As Altman has pointed out (1995), while there is a relationship between copied Western models and hybrid responses to local conditions, we should "interrogate the assumptions of the international lesbian/gay movement about a common global identity which is the basis for a new sort of global political movement." It seems that Indonesians, particularly gay men, are finding a place in the international movement and its political agenda, as well as its cosmopolitan bar scene, but probably to a greater extent than Indonesian gays and lesbians are finding a common identity among themselves.

The growing strength of gay and lesbian voices internationally has helped the rapid expansion of Indonesia's gay movement and magazine *Gaya Nusantara,* headed by Dede Oetomo. Oetomo noted the absence of lesbians in the movement in "Indonesian lesbians: where are you?" (*Gaya Nusantara* #10, 1989), followed by Rosawita's "Where are the Indonesian lesbians?" (*"Di mana para* lesbian Indonesia?" *Gaya Nusantara* #18, 1992). Rosawita points to the ideological suppression of women in all spheres as making lesbians more silent than gay men and as giving them little basis for coalition with gay men. At the Gaya Nusantara national conference of 1995 held in Bandung, only one woman attended who was from Ujung Pandang, and she had only just "come out" as a lesbian. If sexuality is perceived as male and people are defined in relation to men, then it follows that gay men are hypervisible and lesbians are invisible (cf S. Murray 1994).

I suggest that the form of this invisibility varies with class: higher class lesbians choose to hide to retain their power, while the regime chooses not to see lower class subculture at all. To acknowledge lesbians would allow women an active sexuality, which is not part of "women's destiny." Blackwood argues that "In male-dominant cultures . . . it is impossible for women to assume a cross-gender role because such a behavior poses a threat to the gender system and the very definitions of maleness and femaleness"(1986), but this seems to apply specifically to the upper class in Indonesia, and perhaps moreso than in other Southeast Asian societies (for instance, in Thailand, there are a number of butch *toms* in senior business positions).

Various authors have commented on the relatively strong position of lower-class Javanese and Balinese women (e.g., Stoler 1977), and women in Jakarta can identify strategically with the subversive potential of the street milieu which is not specifically focused on "gay and lesbian solidarity." The lower-class male equivalent of the gender crossing butch dyke, the *banci/waria* (transvestite or transgender), has been popularized and ascribed a "traditional" place in Indonesian culture, with organizations enjoying government patronage (Oetomo 1995; Murray 1991b). Again, the overt *banci* are only a small percentage of men who have sex with men without necessarily identifying as gay. Gay male style in Jakarta has become more open and trendy since at least the mid-1980s (Murray 1991b, *"Gay makin gaya,"* Jakarta *Jakarta* 22 May 1993), but its focus on socializing around a bar scene at night is not considered appropriate for unmarried women and is unaffordable for lower class women unless they are bar girls.

In Bali, the long history of Western gay male presence is now being revived, and, with the growth of gay tourism and the power of pink dollars it is even being encouraged and advertised in Sydney's gay press (*Sydney Star Observer, Capital Q*). Hinduism and tourism have influenced the state to allow greater sexual freedom, but it should be emphasized that Bali's cruising spots and bars are oriented to the tourist, with some bars not allowing entrance to locals without accompanying tourists. Western lesbians have also started going to Bali, usually in pairs, and there is no equivalent cruising scene. A resident wrote to Sydney's *Lesbians on the Loose* that "Bali is hell for lesbians," although she subsequently "came out" in America and then met a Western woman back in Bali.[3]

Indonesia can appear to Westerners as a very tolerant culture, as segregation of the sexes is accompanied by very physical public homosocial behavior; however, in discussions with women, they repeat how confusing it is to feel sexually attracted to women without feeling deviant, how difficult it is to meet other lesbians, and how hard it is even to recognize them. As an outsider, it is easier for me to ask people straight questions about their sex lives, and many Indonesian lesbians have seemed to me to be much more open in the company of non-Indonesians and away from the rules of conventional behavior. Women from rural areas often move to the nearest city and then to Jakarta to find other lesbians and greater anonymity.

I met an upper class woman from Semarang who had just arrived in Jakarta hoping to meet lesbians; she said she was not brave enough to venture out at night, and then asked whether a woman with short hair must seek a partner with long hair, whether lesbians are sick or sinful, and what they do in bed. She wanted to know the signs to identify lesbians, but there are no definite signs or "secret handshakes" that I am aware of, except for slang expressions for lesbian such as Lisa Bonet/Lisbon, which may be used to sound someone out. In the next sections, I will first discuss the world of upper-class lesbians, closeted at home but "out" overseas, and second, the hybrid milieu of lower-class lesbians, with a gulf of mutual incomprehension between the two.

GLOBAL GAY STYLE AND MUTUAL INCOMPREHENSION

The international lesbian/gay movement which Altman analyzes is an urban phenomenon only accessible to the upper classes in Jakarta, who also have more opportunity to meet overseas lesbians, have greater awareness of role models such as k. d. lang, and have access to gossip about the sex lives of Indonesian film stars and ministers. Thus, in spite of being hidden inside Indonesia, in the early 1990s, upper-class lesbians were coming out overseas and enjoying the international gay lifestyle with its meccas in Amsterdam, San Francisco, and Sydney; they could use a lesbian identity strategically to tap into the funding available to fly "representatives" from "Third World" countries to conferences and festivals; and Indonesian lesbians were also involved in the Asian Lesbian Network (ALN).

ALN was formed in 1986 and holds regular conferences around the region promoting networking and human rights and identifying "sources of pleasure as well as oppression" in an Asian identity (Fung 1995, 128). ALN has lately been split by controversy, such as the problem of differentiating lesbians living in Asia and those living outside in the diaspora. The ALN network can offer interesting comparisons around the region, although I have only had brief contacts with them; for instance, the upper-class networks in Singapore and Kuala Lumpur are as secretive as those in Jakarta, while only in the Philippines did I find women debating class issues (from a Marxist perspective). Women living in the West have been more explicit in aiming to strengthen Asian lesbian visibility–for instance Sydney Asian Lesbians won a best-float award for the Sydney Gay and Lesbian Mardi Gras Parade in 1995.

Occasionally, upper-class Indonesian women have tried to form lesbian organizations, informed by feminist ideas (feminism is also un-Indonesian according to the women's minister) and excluding non-intellectuals. The link with feminism is another barrier to coalition with gay men, and some feminist lesbians have stated that they are responding against "patriarchy" rather than being propelled by desire. There is little consensus over whether homosexuals are born, made, or curable, although essentialism ("I was born like this so I can't help it") may be used strategically in the pursuit of particular agendas (see also Wieringa's critique of constructionism, 1989). My perspective of multiple and shifting identities attempts to avoid any simplistic binary division of the population (cf Valentine 1993).

Feminist critiques of butch-femme roles as reproductions of the patriarchy alienate some women, while feminist non-government organizations that do not openly support lesbian rights often have lesbians among the staff who feel unable to be open about their sexuality. The prevailing ideology of the real or butch lesbian means that women who are prepared to organize and identify as lesbians are expected to be butch and, therefore, are stigmatized (cf Gayatri 1995, who founded the lesbian network Chandra Kirana). Gayatri has described the "sort of" upper class network in Jakarta, with its "active rumor and gossip circuit" (1995, 6), consisting of cosmopolitan, well-read and well-traveled women. These women often "came out" or had their first lesbian experience overseas and tend to compare Indonesia unfavorably with the "freedom" of the West. They come out to each other through private dinner parties and so on but not to their families or wider society, stressing that family pressure is the main reason for silence. According to Gayatri, strategies like sham marriages and silence are a form of resistance.

I would argue that rather than being a form of resistance, this silence is a conservative response because these women have a stake in the status quo and a primary identification with the immediate family as part of the ruling elite. Maintaining the hierarchies of power means making sure the family does not "lose face." Ostracism from the family would mean losing their position, and crossing the class divide by associating with lower-class women would also be a path to "social exile." It is probably necessary to grow up in Indonesia to appreciate the difficulty of taking such a step, not least because of the distrust and suspicion with which the poor treat the elite. No one is likely to come out of the closet if it offers no advantage, nor if they can afford to live a "double life" with one foot in the busy lesbian scenes of the West.

Lower-class lesbians are excluded from the global movement by the lack of two essentials: money and the English language (cf Altman 1995); I have also suggested various ways in which class divides Jakarta lesbians. The hidden elite networks are closed to lower-class women, and the upper-class women with "good" reputations and "good" jobs have little desire and less opportunity to understand or try to meet lower class women. The gulf of mutual incomprehension is reinforced by spatial segregation and assumptions which associate lower class lesbians with butch-femme roles, promiscuity, and insalubrious nightlife. Elite women are at pains to avoid these associations, and to sanitize the image of lesbians, which could also be seen as being insensitive to women who are part of streetlife and who do sex work for reasons such as poverty.

When I took an upper-class woman to a bar in the nightlife area of Blok M, Jakarta she called her girlfriend to come down and join us; when that women arrived, she called her friend by mobile phone from her car outside to check that it was really safe to come into such a place. Similarly, when I was in Bali, I talked to a lesbian from Jakarta about favorite places to check out women (*cuci mata*); she responded that she would never go to places like Blok M at night, as she only liked educated girls, not bar girls. When I have taken lower-class friends to upper-class women's houses, they have said later that they were made to feel uncomfortable. One woman said, "I felt like a servant," but I felt she had also slipped into deferential behavior. These examples illustrate that while divisive attitudes may be unintentional, they are certainly entrenched.

STYLE AND SUBCULTURE: SEX, DRUGS, AND HIV

The subcultures of the urban poor reclaim the spaces between power and powerlessness by constructing an alternative style (Hebdige 1978), although subcultural styles tend to be dismissed by both intellectuals and the authoritarian state unless they can be commercialized and appropriated (for instance, *banci* or transgender style: Murray 1991b). Jakarta's subcultural styles are not coherent or easily categorized, but rather a bricolage of local elements, reinterpretations of imported concepts, transient sub-groups, and spaces; visible lesbian style such as a butch-femme aesthetic is part of a range of sexualities and sex-for-trade.

State control in Jakarta reaches down to the household level, with intrusive family planning programs regulating sexuality, and identity cards being essential for people's claim to citizenship and their right to move around. Laws are unclear and inconsistently applied, with the security forces having seemingly unlimited powers of extortion and violence. In order to adapt and survive, the lower class exploits the contradictions between what is said and what is done; they are inclined to take risks, live for the moment, and worry about consequences when they happen (for instance, the neighborhood in Manggarai where I lived in 1984-5 has been threatened with demolition for over ten years, but when I visited in 1995, the people were still there making the most of their everyday lives, having nowhere else to go).

With limited access to communications technology or long distance travel, people still rely on face-to-face interaction and their own networks, which are identified with a small spatial location and over which there can be no sense of ownership or permanence, and also discrete local scenes which exist away from the main thoroughfares of urban life. As central Jakarta is incrementally "tidied up" and street life forcibly discouraged, I have found that many subcultural elements have relocated to the outskirts. For instance, a number of my friends now live in Depok, south of the city, which has rapidly grown into a heterogeneous urban sprawl. A particular street stall, run by a strong and extroverted woman who provides cheap beer and food until the early hours, has been adopted as an informal meeting place. In my experience, this kind of highly spatially localized arrangement, depending on personal acquaintance, is typical of the lower-class scene.

As well as informal or temporary night stalls, subcultural or "queer" spaces include bars, prostitution locations, shopping malls, and alienated land. As none of the people within the milieu conform to social norms, it is preferable to reject them altogether and to establish status among one's immediate peers. While different groups may have conflicting or competing interests, this does not amount to discrimination, so that women who do choose to identify as butch are able to take pride in creating a good "act" (similar to other adopted styles, such as *banci*/transvestites, *perek*/"experimental girls" and *jago*/street toughs). Butches have been characterized in the manner of baboons fighting over femmes for supremacy, but this is far from the reality. It is true that, as in other subcultures, there is a loose hierarchy of small groups and local leaders who are generally butch women.

Street butch style, with its signifiers including short slick hair, men's clothes, smoking, drinking, sharp pool playing, and pimping of girlfriends, can be compared with the demimonde of American bars in the 1950s: "It was here in this sexual and social underworld that lesbians developed distinctive styles of dress, forms of romantic inter-action and character types, all of which were rooted in working class subculture" (S. Murray 1994, 351; cf Kennedy & Davis 1993 on lesbians and class). These bars were places where lesbians were ac-cepted rather than specifically lesbian spaces. Similarly, in Jakarta, a typical subcultural scene such as a *jaipongan* (popular lower-class dancing) venue under an expressway flyover is popular with lesbians but also attracts transvestites, under-age prostitutes, local godfathers in safari suits, street toughs, and so on.

While taking pride in the butch style is some women's choice, it is not the only option. Contemporary Jakarta is a world away from 1950s America, with a hybrid urban subculture that also draws on and paro-dies the discourse of 1990s technology and official jargon and images such as Madonna and lipstick lesbians, that sometimes appear on the non-satellite TV channels. While it exists, I don't think that butch-femme is as evident, as numerically large, or as stylistically marked as in the Philippines, for instance. And because the butch lesbian is the "real" lesbian, women who do sex work or otherwise sleep with men, or who are in relationships where neither they nor their girlfriend is butch, do not need to equate sexual behavior with a sexual identity; they have the freedom to play without closing off their options.

I first met lower-class lesbians in the Blok M bar scene. In fact, my first experience of lesbian sex was when a Western man paid to watch me with an Indonesian woman. While some of the bar workers are emphatically not interested in women, many of them are, and there is a strong link between lesbian and prostitute bar/street genres. Bar work-ers who are living in a "contract wife" situation (living together for the period of a work contract) with an expatriate are relatively well off, and, in periods when their boyfriends are out of town, they may pay for sex with women. Australian workers would call these "boy-friends" regular clients, while the Jakarta women suggest a level of emotional attachment linked to longer-term aspirations of marriage and/or emigration, as is common in expatriate bar scenes throughout Southeast Asia. Greater sexual freedom and notions of romantic love are integrated with economic pragmatism and necessity.

It is common knowledge in Jakarta that the "Ladies Nights" at various discos giving free admission to women are frequented by "women-loving-women." Some other places, such as a bar in Menteng (Sunindyo and Sabaroedin 1989) may become known as somewhere to meet or pick up lesbian prostitutes, but are usually very transient. At "Ladies' Nights," there are butch-femme couples, where the femme may also be a sex worker, and a range of other women whose sexuality is too fluid to pin down with a label; they have no strategic use for "lesbian" but also no need to appear "straight." Those who have moved to Jakarta avoid family pressure, but lower-class "families" and households are also less likely to conform to the bourgeois norm and include a variety of disparate people, such as individuals renting rooms for themselves, and transient and non-monogamous relationships. Early marriage is often rapidly followed by divorce, thereby avoiding the taboo on pre-marital sex, and two women living together are not usually remarked on.

Western organizations may influence some upper-class lesbian groups to construct their situation in terms of "human rights," but their lesbian practice is not the source of oppression for most lower-class women. Indonesian opposition groups have tended to dismiss issues of sexuality as upper class concerns, which are tangential to the main political struggle for social justice. Recently the potential of HIV/AIDS to decimate the urban poor has suggested the need to prioritize sexuality; however, AIDS needs to be seen in the context of Indonesia's pre-existing urban health problems, such as high levels of infant mortality, which remain unaddressed.

This overview of lower-class lesbian life in Jakarta has indicated the dangers of the long-standing assumption that lesbians are at low risk for HIV/AIDS. While women may prefer women, they also have sex with men, commercially and for pleasure, and are involved in intravenous drug use (IDU), which has recently increased in preference to previous methods of slashing the skin or smoking drugs (IDU is another taboo subject in Indonesia, and I have found that the stigma is still too great to be able to write about it). This has serious implications for HIV, as well as showing the urgent need for more research on female-to-female transmission. The reasons for avoiding a lesbian identity mean that an HIV/AIDS campaign targeting lesbians is unlikely to succeed, and a best practice strategy would need to cover women's sexuality in a range of scenarios that are appropriate for lower-class women.

NEWLY EMERGING SEXUALITIES AND THE ISLAMIC BACKLASH

Apparently conflicting but probably related trends in 1990s Jakarta are the subversion of dominant discourse by the New Emerging Sexualities (see Murray, forthcoming) flaunted by upper-class youth and the increasing repression based on Islamic morality and conservatism. Neither offers anything for the urban lower classes who continue to be seen as disposable and as getting in the way of development. The new openness about sexuality, which has come with the era of AIDS, and the Government's inability to control people's awareness of overseas trends, such as the international gay and lesbian movement–through overseas travel and information superhighways–seems to have made gays and lesbians more acceptable. Young urban women are aware of more options than the butch-femme stereotype, and I have heard of a female-to-male sex change in Jakarta (described as a "teapot with a permanent erection").

Increasing commodification of everything, including the body, and rising disposable incomes have also been linked to the phenomenon of upper-class *perek* ("experimental girls") selling sex to businessmen in shopping malls. While these experimental girls were exposed as a scandal in the late 1980s (e.g., *Tempo,* 3 September 1988 *"Oh Remaja, Oh Jakarta*/Oh Youth, Oh Jakarta,"* and *Jakarta Jakarta* 21 May 1989 *"Pelajar? Pelacur?*/Schoolgirl? Prostitute?), the term *perek* is now in common usage to imply promiscuity, bisexuality, etc. If alternative sexualities are seen as trendy and cosmopolitan by the upper classes, perhaps the hypocrisy of regulated/hidden sex will start to decline. There has also been a great proliferation in the types and availability of drugs, including designer drugs such as ecstasy, and an explosion in use among the upper classes, including "scandals" involving pop stars

(Suryakusuma 1995, *Forum Keadilan,* 4 December 1995, *"Hobi Baru*: Ecstasy/New Hobby: Ecstasy*"*). A clampdown on nightlife has reduced the nightclub trade without affecting the distribution of ecstasy throughout "young executive" society (*Review Indonesia* 24 July, 1996).

The counter trend of Islamic conservatism has lead to a backlash against sex, drugs, and prostitution. Legal forms of oppression are being strengthened, and AIDS education efforts have met stiff opposition from religious leaders demanding that people who want to buy condoms should have to produce a marriage certificate. Suryakusuma's analysis points to an authoritarian regime under threat: "In the midst of the spate of social, economic and political crises, the clampdown on the sex industry is the easiest, the most sensational and the most hypocritical as it does not touch the fundamental root of social unrest: violence, manipulation and injustice, all of which are condoned, even carried out, by the state" (1994, 18).

The clampdown is not only hypocritically based but has class-differentiated effects. Rich people whose behavior seems to have stepped beyond current limits are observed by the cynical to avoid censure by embarking on a haj pilgrimage to Mecca. The sex industry is a big money spinner for the government, army, and businessmen, and most moves are symbolic but ineffective. It is mainly street and bar prostitutes who are arrested, thereby disrupting the survival strategies of the street milieu in which they work. Commercial sex is an important economic support for alternative subcultures, for lesbians more than any others, since they have fewer economic opportunities or options for male support.

The crackdown on drugs and alcohol has led to the crushing of late-night informal drinking stalls and street entertainment places. Cheap alcohol, known as AO, and backyard-production pills, such as "BK," are denigrated as gutter rubbish and are increasingly hard to find, at the same time as $100 pills of ecstasy, well beyond the means of the urban poor, are flooding Jakarta. The new consumers are the children of the elite, whose own pockets are lined with the profits of drugs and corruption (Forum Keadilan op cit): even if these consumers knew about it they would not see a problem in the disappearance of local street drugs ("let them take ecstasy").

POWER AND MULTIPLE IDENTITIES

The University of Sydney's conference in September 1995 on emerging Asian lesbian and gay communities acknowledged the rapid development of alternative sexual discourses, influenced by the strength of the Western lesbian and gay movement, in countries like Indonesia. However, when thinking about Jakarta's lesbians, I see the Western-Indonesian dualism as too simplistic, as is the homo-heterosexual distinction which is impossible to quantify or apply in a fixed way to either behavior or identity in Indonesia. I have argued that class is the central divisive factor preventing the development of an Indonesian lesbian community, but the general distinctions I have made between lower- and upper-class women should not be taken as setting up another binary opposition.

In the hybrid urban lower-class milieu, people marginalized in various ways develop survival strategies and subcultures where a range of sexual behaviors are accepted and sex work is an important source of earnings. Lesbians, even if they identify with this imported label, are unlikely to want to segregate themselves from this supportive milieu. The performance of identity and experience of the body varies with time and place–an obvious example being the lesbian sex worker–meaning that it is more appropriate to use a concept of multiple and shifting identities in the context of local specificity's of power.

Lower-class women's relative powerlessness due to lack of money, education, and connections, ironically, leaves them freer to create their own subcultures; in order to retain their power, the upper class has had to hide behind a wall of "socially correct roles." A general observation could be made that a lack of understanding of "how the other half lives" has made people more likely to believe Government propaganda and media stereotypes. The ideological basis of power would be undermined if people from different backgrounds in Jakarta were more willing to communicate with each other straightforwardly. This is obviously the reason why some of them do not, but I have found most that Jakartans are quite accepting of a range of sexual behaviors by people they actually know and are even impressed by women who manage to have a wild time and get away with it.

The struggles of feminist lesbians and butch-femme street scenes are largely unknown to under-20-year-old urban women growing up with a barrage of global signifiers that are no more or less meaningful than the repressive ideology of Javanese elitism, and who labor under the general impression that with money you can do anything. Sex work offers quick money, but it is also changing. The butch pimp/femme worker is in decline: younger women are more likely to play with butch signifiers than to aim to "do" butch best among their peers. Despite, or because of, the government's efforts, sexuality in Jakarta is becoming "post-modern"–multiple, fluid, and experimental.

I have described diverse sexual practices and identities to show how women may adapt or perform according to local structures of power, arguing that power in Jakarta is experienced and strategically deployed through class. I have glossed the range of urban social constructions into a dialectical pairing of "upper" and "lower" class as a snapshot, taken through the lens of lesbian sexuality, of a rapidly developing and complex picture. The inherent contradictions in Jakarta's superculture, which allow the elite to spend their wealth in the global supermarket while imposing a national moral standard on a poor, largely agricultural country of nearly 200 million, create spiraling hypocrisy which the taboo on mentioning class conflict cannot hide indefinitely. Challenges to the existing hierarchy and its barbed wire walls come from the possibilities of communication in virtual space and the overt sexuality of both elite youth and lower-class subcultures, which bring people together in the same physical space of the street.

NOTES

1. I develop the concept of multiple and shifting sexual identities further in Murray (forthcoming). The ideas about lesbians and class in this chapter have been presented at the forum on Alternative Sexualities at the Asia-Pacific Congress on HIV/AIDS at Chaing Mai, 17-21 September 1995, and at the conference, Emerging Asian/Australian Lesbian and Gay Communities, The University of Sydney, 29-30 September 1995. Finally, I am grateful to the International Institute for Asian Studies, Leiden, for a visiting exchange fellowship which allowed me to complete this writing.

2. *Wong cilik*, or little people, used to refer to the lower classes, implies that people have lower requirements for space and resources; scaling-down reduced individual characteristics and thus claims to individual human rights. Indonesian political cartoons generally depict lower class people as very small, while the elite and security forces are so big that often only a hand or foot fits in the frame.

3. More recently, she has written, "living *in* a lesbian relationship in Bali is heaven. Living *without* one, is hell" (personal communication 1 July 1998). By 1998/99, there was a lesbian group established in Singaraya and lesbian tours to an "exclusive resort" advertised in *Lesbians on the Loose*.

REFERENCES

Altman, D. (1995). The globalisation of gay identities, paper at the conference, *Emerging Lesbian and Gay Communities*, The University of Sydney, 29-30 September.

Anderson, B. (1987). *Imagined Communities: Reflections on the Origins and Spread of Nationalism*. London: Verso.

Blackwood, E. (1986). Breaking the mirror: the construction of lesbianism and the anthropological discourse on homosexuality. In *Journal of Homosexuality*, Vol. 11, No. 3/4, 1-18.

Blackwood, E. (1994). Falling in love with an-other lesbian: reflections on identity in fieldwork, in D. Kulick & M. Wilson (Eds.), *Taboo: Sex, Identity and Erotic Subjectivity in Anthropological Fieldwork*, New York: Routledge, 51-75.

Chetame, M. (1995). Lesbian lifestyles and concepts of the family, paper presented at the conference, *Thai Sexuality*, The Australian National University, 11-12 July.

Foucault, M. (1978). *The History of Sexuality, Vol 1: An introduction*, London: Penguin.

Fung, R. (1995). The trouble with Asians in M. Dorenkamp and R. Henke (Eds.), *Negotiating Lesbian and Gay Subjects*, New York: Routledge, 123-130.

Gays in Indonesia. (1984). Selected articles from the print media, Fitzroy: Sybylla Press.

Gayatri, B. J. D. (1995). Coming out but remaining oppressed. Lesbian in Indonesia: a report for human rights. Paper for *International Gay & Lesbian Human Rights Commission Global Lesbian Rights Report*, San Francisco.

Groneman, C. (1995). Nymphomania: The historical construction of female sexuality." In J. Terry & J. Urla (Eds.), *Deviant Bodies*. Bloomington: Indiana University Press, 219-250.

Hebdige, D. (1978). *Subculture: The Meaning of Style*. London: Methuen.

Kennedy, E. & M. Davis. (1993). *Boots of Leather, Slippers of Gold*. New York: Routledge.

Krisna, Y. (1978). *Menyusuri Remang-remang Jakarta*. Jakarta

Kulick, D. & Wilson, M. (Eds.). *Taboo: Sex, Identity and Erotic Subjectivity in Anthropological Fieldwork*. New York: Routledge.

Murray, A. (1991a). *No Money No Honey: A Study of Street Traders and Prostitutes in Jakarta*. Singapore: Oxford University Press.

Murray, A. (1991b). Kampung culture and radical chic. *Review of Indonesian and Malayan Affairs*.

Murray, A. (forthcoming). *On Bondage, Peers and Queers: Sexual Subculture, Sex Work and AIDS Discourses in the Asia-Pacific*.

Murray, S. (1994). Dragon ladies, draggin' men: Some reflections on gender, drag and homosexual communities, *Public Culture*, 6, 343-363.

Nestle, J. (1992). *The Persistent Desire: A Femme-butch Reader*. Boston: Alyson.

Oetomo, D. (1991). Homoseksualitas di Indonesia. In *Prisma*, 7 July, 84-96.

Oetomo, D. (1995). The dynamics of transgendered and gay identities in Indonesian societies, paper at the conference, *Emerging Lesbian and Gay Communities*, The University of Sydney, 29-30 September.

Parker, L. (1995). Conceptions of femininity in Bali, paper at the *Third International Bali Studies Workshop,* Sydney University, 3-7 July.

Sen, K. (1993). Repression and resistance: Interpretations of the feminine in New Order Cinema, in V. Hooker (Ed.), *Culture and Society in New Order Indonesia,* Singapore, OUP, 116-133.

Spivak, G. (1987). *In Other Worlds.* New York: Routledge.

Stoler, A. (1977). Class structure and female autonomy in rural Java, *Signs,* Vol 3, No. 1, 74-89.

Sunindyo, S. & Sabaroedin, S. (1989). Notes on prostitution in Indonesia, in G. Pheterson (Ed.), *A Vindication of the Rights of Whores.* Seattle: Seal Press.

Suryakusuma, J. (1987). *State Ibuism: The Social Construction of Womanhood in the Indonesian New Order,* Den Haag, MA thesis.

Suryakusuma, J. (1994). The clampdown on Indonesia's sex industry, *Indonesia Business Weekly,* 16 September, p. 18.

Suryakusuma, J. (1995). Only the good die young, *Indonesia Business Weekly,* 24 April, pp. 30-31.

Valentine, G. (1993). Negotiating and managing multiple sexual identities: Lesbian time-space strategies, *Transactions of the Institute of British Geographers,* NS 18, 237-248.

Wieringa, S. (1989). An Anthropological Critique of Constructionism: Berdaches and Butches. In D. Altman et al. (Eds.), *Homosexuality, Which Homosexuality?* London: GMP Publishers, 215-238.

Drink, Stories, Penis, and Breasts: Lesbian Tomboys in Taiwan from the 1960s to the 1990s

Y. Antonia Chao

INTRODUCTION

The terms "*T*" and "*Po*," which refer to the two lesbian sexual roles, have been widely used by Taiwanese lesbians over the past thirty years and are now frequently posited by the mass media as representative of female homosexuality.[1] Originally derived from the English word "tomboy," *T* refers to the "masculine" part in the *T-Po* relationship. Literally meaning "wife," and "*T*'s wife" in this case, *Po* refers to the "feminine" counterpart to *T*.[2] In addition, "the *T*'s body" has in recent years conjured up social fantasies at once of lesbian eroticism and of gender transgression. It has become a favorite topic both in grass-roots lesbian periodicals and in mass media, such as films and pulp fiction.

While invented in the sixties, *T* and *Po* (as the sex-gender identity categories alternative to heterosexual normality) did not come fully into formation until the first *T*-bar was opened in 1985–that is, at a time when Martial Law was soon to be abrogated along with the lifting of police force's regulation of unconventional social space. Commonly understood as "lesbian bars," since the outset, the *T*-bars have provided a performative setting for individuals to associate with each other and to act out their sexual roles. The setting is performative not

[Haworth co-indexing entry note]: "Drink, Stories, Penis, and Breasts: Lesbian Tomboys in Taiwan from the 1960s to the 1990s." Chao, Y. Antonia. Co-published simultaneously in *Journal of Homosexuality* (Harrington Park Press, an imprint of The Haworth Press, Inc.) Vol. 40, No. 3/4, 2001, pp. 185-209; and: *Gay and Lesbian Asia: Culture, Identity, Community* (ed: Gerard Sullivan, and Peter A. Jackson) Harrington Park Press, an imprint of The Haworth Press, Inc., 2001, pp. 185-209. Single or multiple copies of this article are available for a fee from The Haworth Document Delivery Service [1-800-342-9678, 9:00 a.m. - 5:00 p.m. (EST). E-mail address: getinfo@haworthpressinc.com].

only because the practices lesbians engage in at the bar are often fairly theatrical, but also because the symbols and strategies they employ in producing and reproducing their sexual identities are both cultural and improvisational.

In this article, I demonstrate a specific way of forming lesbian identities from the following angles. To begin with, I highlight the difference between earlier lesbians and *T*-bar-oriented ones to show the fact that the latter have established a sex-gender identity distinct from the former. Then I demonstrate the specific ways by which present lesbians construct their identities and sexual roles in the context of the bar. Finally, I argue that internal to such a form of identity-formation is a particular way of producing a sexual body that cannot be articulated through normative–namely, heterosexualized–means.

THE TOMBOYS BEFORE T-BAR

The term *"T"* was invented in the sixties Taipei by, interestingly, gay men at gay bars as an abbreviation for "tomboys." *T*s at the time wore masculine outfits, including ties, tuxedos, pants, male underwear, and short hair, as well as conducted "non-feminine" acts, such as smoking, consuming alcohol, yelling swearwords, and gesturing and speaking in a "mannish" manner in both public and private domains. Before 1985, the only sociocultural site where "tomboys" could freely hang out together and show off their girl friends was the gay bar, which characteristically provided drag shows and heartedly welcomed "tomboys," who, to a large extent, considered themselves "men" as well. A 49-year-old "tomboy" recalled in the spring of 1994:[3]

> We were seen as *real* men back then, and we were certainly respected and acknowledged as such there. In fact, at one point the owner of *Yuanzhuo* [*Round Table*-a most popular gay bar from the 1960s to the 1970s] half-jokingly announced to his patrons that the bar was not for gay men anymore but rather for tomboys. This is how the term *T* was created.

During the decade prior to the gay-tomboy-mixed period, "tomboys" hung out at the dancing halls in grant hotels, such as Central Plaza (*Zhongyang ziudian*) at the Hilton–one of the few Westernized locales at the time. The previously noted "tomboy" recalled:

Most of the people there belonged to an older generation. Most rich people back then were elderly ones, anyway. Remember it was in the fifties and the sixties when the majority of Taiwanese were still fairly poor. Hence only really wealthy people, or socially desperate ones like us, could and would afford grant hotels. We tomboys had nice time there despite the fact that people around us treated us as kids instead of adults. That was the penalty we had to suffer.

Being considered "as" kids was certainly not pleasant for "tomboys"–obviously, what they wanted was be considered "real men." However, it might be exactly this *childlike* front forced on them that explained away their unconventional outward appearance. That is, being paralleled to "kids," which connotes "socially immature," they were tolerated by people–who were correspondingly labeled "adults"–while acting out an unorthodox sexuality. This tolerance, I argue, was derived from a societal recognition and even encouragement of childhood gender-crossing and/or a-genderedness–for girls in particular. Indeed, adults relatively tolerated female juvenile disobedience at the time. In her analysis of Taiwanese womanhood in the same historical period, Wolf (1972: 65) points out this relatively unrestricted attitude toward little girls:

> Taiwanese parents assume that children cannot really "understand" until they are around six years old. They claim that until then they do not try to teach them anything and expect little in the way of obedience.

In outwardly "juvenilizing" tomboys, the "adults" in grant hotels obviously drew on familial strategies, as noted by Wolf, to conventionalize the unconventional–"When children are little you should praise them, and they will be happy and do what you want" (Wolf, 1972: 68)–and to legitimize their noncommital attitude toward (adult) gender transgression. "Tomboys" did not overlook the cynicism inherent in such an intentional mis-recognition. This is why the previously noted "tomboy" referred to others' noncommital attitude at grant hotels as a "penalty."

Nonetheless, this does not at all mean that "tomboyishness" was completely tolerated or unacknowledged at the time: while it might have been tolerated in "Westernized"–that is, more or less "alternative"–locales like grant hotels, it was definitely not the case in the society at large. In many respects, "tomboys" were thought of as transgressing sex-gender codes, including dressing and acting "properly." This was at the time when a legal act against *qi zhuang yi fu* (wearing odd or inappropriate outfits, in particular gender-crossing ones) was strictly in force under Martial Law. At a time when any offenders of the given social order would be demonized in political terms (usually by being labelled as *fei die* [the Communist spy]), tomboys were frequently charged by the police on the count of treason. What follows is a typical press account of a "politically suspicious tomboy":

Yang Qiangyu, a female dressed as male [*nu ban nan zhuang*], was arrested this morning on the count of treason. Aged thirty, Yang is a resident of Feng-yuan City in Taichung Prefecture, with only an elementary school degree, no previous police record. She, *nu ban nan zhuang,* met Lin *X* Yin (aged twenty-one) in Taichung, November 1982. Later Lin took a hairdressing job in San-chung. Yang stalked Lin there and beguiled Lin into living together with her. Lin told the police that they had lived together for eight months, yet during sex they only caressed each other because Yang claimed to have contracted gonorrhea. Yang told Lin that she held a bachelor degree in medical science from Taiwan University[4] and was appointed a secret agent by *mou fang mian* [a certain (unidentified) force or aspect. In Martial-Law Taiwan it was a euphemism for politically insidious groups like Communist China and the Taiwanese Independence Movement] while studying in the United States. Yang also said she came back to Taiwan together with an agent dispatched by "a certain illegal organization" to carry out "a certain secret mission." In addition, she claimed to hold a passport with a diplomat's visa, have a mailing address with "a certain organization" in Japan, and be a correspondent to "a certain news agency." As a result, Lin never suspected her.

Because of Yang's odd and mysterious manners, people gradually developed suspicion about her identity. They finally made a report to the police. At three this morning the police arrested Yang at her residence (*"'Nuwang mishi' lai tai? 'Taiwan renyao' zuo guai."* ("'A foreign secret agent' posted in Taiwan? 'A human prodigy' is playing tricks."). *Zhongquo Shibao* 7 July 1983

This was a typical report on lesbianism in Martial-Law Taiwan: that the "truth" of female homosexuality should be, on the one hand, revealed (through sex acts), and, on the other hand, concealed (by being affiliated with *mou fan mian,* an equally unidentified political force). Note also that there is an *X* put in the middle of Lin's name. For "privacy's sake," both mass media and government reports use *X*-euphemistically meaning "crossing out"-to substitute for the middle character of a name in cases like juvenile delinquents, victims of sexual assault, and, more recently, people who are living with AIDS. In this vein, mass media's presumably considerate ways of treating Lin's name entailed a divergence in understanding lesbian roles. At the time, a *Po*'s sexual misconduct was largely blamed on her tomboy with the presumption that a *Po* is not an inborn lesbian, rather, she acquires a wrong sexuality through tomboys. That is, tomboy's homosexuality was thought to be both biological and contagious. This logic is manifested circuitously in the report that Lin's modesty was verified by Yang's "gonorrhea"-a sexually transmitted disease.

It was also the time when women's roles and obligation were conceptualized and regulated primarily with reference to conventional Confucian ideology. An ideal woman, on this premise, is expected to be subservient to her father, husband, and son, respectively, each embodying the form of patriarchal power in the three ideally consecutive stages of her life: the natal, the marital, and the genealogical. In addition, female and male genders were understood to be mutually exclusive. In short, there was literally no gender category provided by the given society for those who renounced, transgressed, and/or appropriated their gender positions assigned at birth.

Tomboys' anti-feminine acts at that time would normally cause the following effects. First, in public space, they wittingly or unwittingly passed as men. Many tomboys growing up during this period of time related to me "passing" stories, such as being asked out of women's rest rooms or using men's rooms without being harassed and being called "sir" at stores. Second, in the private domain, however, they were under stringent family pressure to marry the opposite sex. In part, to evade such a daughter's obligation, many tomboys considered seriously the possibility of conducting transsexual surgery so as to be "the right sex." A 50ish tomboy recalled, in the summer of 1994, such a strong concern with sex change in the 1960s:

> Back home my mother complained to me all the time: "What is the *nie* [sin] I conducted in the past life that makes me having a kid like you?" I managed to comprehend my peculiarities as well. Once I read a Japanese magazine article featuring the fact that homosexuality is caused by maternal sex-glandular mis-excretion during pregnancy. That is, it is an inborn trait rather than anything else. I thus concluded that my misfortune would be called off after conducting a sex-change operation. In a fit of excitement, I showed my mom the article. She, however, got very upset, "It's already too much that you are wearing men's clothes and underwear, and now you are even thinking about changing your sex! How will I have the face to see our relatives and ancestors [after you do it]?" I said to her that since most of our relatives were on Penghu [an isle distant from the island of Taiwan] there was no way they would hear about it.[5] At this point, even my younger sister, who was always sympathetic to me, took my mom's sides. She yelled at me: "It's enough! How dare you humiliate Mother like this!" I later gave up on the idea of sex change because of my poor financial situation. Otherwise I would fly to America[6] to take up the surgery anytime. I always think that it would be wonderful having a penis, this way I would become a complete man–even just for one single day.

A secular Buddhist notion, *nie* refers to the moral debt, which is built up through misconducts, one shall recompense either later in this life or in the next life. In addition, Taiwanese commonly think that this form of debt will be repaid, at least partially, through one's descendants. According to conventional Chinese patrilineal ideology, one and one's descendants are forever linked in the name of the patriline. Therefore, what happens to the latter is symbolically equivalent to that of the former, and vice versa. The *nie* in this tomboy's case seems to be attributed retrospectively in the sense that the discovery of the daughter's mis-fit/fortune sufficiently renders the mother culpable, not the other way around. However, "What is the *nie* I have conducted?" is also a common assertion Taiwanese parents make while disciplining children by reminding the latter of their patrilineal obligation and debt to the former. This is why the tomboy's sister reprimanded her from the perspective of their patriline: even though the mother is considered by the patrilineal ideology an outsider forever and an unnamable other (Seaman, 1981), without her contribution to making the genealogy biologically connected, the patriline will vanish as well (Sangren, 1996). At the same time, women's power is virtually redeemed through her offspring, in particular sons. It is, therefore, interesting to note that in this case, a sexually transgressive daughter's conduct is linked to the mother's reputation–both are considered "outsiders" to the patriline.

A striking distinction can be drawn between earlier tomboys and contemporary *T*s in terms of a desire to be "a complete man" via sex change. It is not to say that the latter are not interested in *bian xing* (sex change), though. Quite the contrary, this issue is frequently brought up, especially in exclusively *T*-context. However, very few of them would go through the whole process of sex change. In my following analysis, I argue that sex-change surgery is merely one step to reinforcing one's "*T*-ness," rather than being a completion of "manhood." In short, earlier tomboys considered themselves real men despite a lack of something congenitally "essential" in gender terms. By contrast, present *T*s largely consider themselves only "*T*s." Toilet use is one way of differentiating between these two groups of lesbians. As noted before, tomboys could pass as men in the men's room. By contrast, while many *T*s use the men's room (especially in the *T*-bar), this is more a performative act to highlight to others their *T*-ness. As a thirty-two-year-old *T* stated in the fall of 1993:

> Chen Xin [a 50ish tomboy] shocked me the first time we met. A mutual friend introduced me to her on the basis that we both are *T*s. However, our friendship had a difficult start. We met at a restaurant and had dinner together. We talked about our *Po*s, which was fine. Then I left for the restroom. She followed me there and stopped me in front of the women's room. She knocked on my shoulder and shouted at me: "I'm so disappointed with you! Are you a *T* or not? Why are you using women's room? Remember: we are men, real men. So now go use men's rooms! You stupid coward!" I was shocked! I'm a *T* all right, but not a man! Finally I still went in the women's room, leaving her furious outside. After that she refused to talk to me for half a year. Sometimes it's very difficult making friends with older *T*s. They

have completely different conceptions of this *T-Po* thing from mine.

In the following section, I will show the formation of the present *T*-ness along with an analysis of the *T*-bar as a performative site for lesbians to act out their sexual identities.

THE PERFORMATIVE CONTEXT OF THE T-BAR

Wang You Gu (Forget-sadness valley), the first *T*-bar, was opened by a *T-Po* couple in a red-light district of Taipei in 1985. Since then, more than thirty *T*-bars have been opened in Taipei, Taichung, and Kaohsung, the three major cities of Taiwan–also the three newest and most "Westernized" ones. All the owners of these bars are lesbians, and most of them used to be frequent patrons of earlier *T*-bars. As a result, the style of management and the types of patrons have remained fairly consistent since the outset. Most nightclubs since the early twentieth century have retained strong Japanese flavor in terms of providing hostesses, encouraging heavy drinking, and, over the past two decades, singing karaoke (a synchonized singing machine originally produced in Japan). These features were adopted by Wang You Gu and have been followed by the majority of the later *T*-bars as well.

A typical *T*-Bar usually occupies a suite or the basement of a business building. It is set up with a dim light, a karaoke podium in front (which serves as a dance stand after midnight), several TV screens hanging from the ceiling (which show a music video of each song ordered by the karaoke singer), and ten to twenty tables occupying the remainder of the bar. On top of which is a karaoke song-list, as well as a bar counter at which *shaoye* (young lord; meaning the *T*-attendant) serve drinks. Like regular nightclubs, most *T*-bars provide *gongzhu* (princess) or *gongguan* (popular relations)–that is, *Po*-hostesses, drinking, playing *hua ziuquan* (drinking games involving two players showing varying numbers of fingers in response to commands given by each other), and flirting with *T*-patrons.

Performing karaoke is very important to establishing one's reputation and sexual role with other lesbians. The karaoke audiences include all the people present at the bar, and joining in karaoke performance erases social boundaries between those who previously were strangers to each other. Sitting on the stool in front of the karaoke machine, the singer sings in sync with the rhythm and the lyrics shown on a TV screen, which are simultaneously displayed in the same music tape shown on the TV screens facing the audience. The audience interacts intimately with the singer by commenting on, physically reacting to, and even joining with her. Anyone, either the patron or the employee, feels free to participate in this collective performance. It follows that the quality of the singer's voice does not really matter as long as she is willing to allow for such a collective participation. In the case of an unbearably bad performance, which takes place frequently owing to heavy drinking, the audience will mount the karaoke podium to "help her out," to use their words. By contrast, people always hiss loudly at those who either act too straight or fail to abide by the participation rule.

Most songs ordered at the *T*-bar are heterosexual love songs already popular in the society at large. While every once in a while, frequent patrons will choose among them a *guoge* (national anthem)–usually the most ordered song–that represents the whole *quan* (circle; the circle made of all *T*-bar-oriented lesbians). The term *guoge* is derived from picking up a connotation of the Taiwanese national anthem which is supposed to represent the whole nation and is very likely the most often heard song in Taiwan. It is replayed *ad nauseam* in school, in theater before the showing of each film, and on TV before and after the daily program. From late 1993 to early 1995, the *T*-bar *guoge* is *Shangxin ziudian* (the bar of sorrow), a fairly popular *taiyu* (the major dialect in Taiwan) song originally produced by the female singer Jiang Hue. Its music video tape alludes to a past heterosexual love, in part, by putting Jiang and Shi Wenbin, a popular *taiyu* male singer, singing together. Its heterosexual theme, however, does not at all disturb *T*-bar patrons' identification with the song. For its lyric characteristically depicts one's despair with lost love *at a bar:*

> Pour me one more shot
> If you do understand
> Please don't ask me where I am from
> Will not speak out
> The sorrow in my mind
> Subject to my lost love
> Waiting persistently
> But my love never comes

In a world full of amour
I am yet to discover a true heart
My sorrow then overflows
It's good to be in love
Now without love
But so what
Tonight only solitude accompanies my heart

This song highlights quintessential bar scenes that the patrons find natural to identity: heavy drinking, solitude, mourning over lost love, and the possibility of having spontaneous but apathetic carnal encounters with total strangers at the *T*-bar.

I should note that songs with either explicit or implicit lesbian themes are *not* welcomed at the *T*-bar. *Ku hai nu shen long* (A female dragon deity in a bitter sea), a *taiyu* song by the woman singer Li Yijun, was very popular from mid-1993 to early 1994 and was celebrated by both popular culture critics and feminist intellectuals as the first mainstream lesbian song of Taiwan. The part to invoke lesbianism goes as follows:

Not interested in men
Love to make girl friends
Feminine elegance unfound
Masculine charm pronounced
No one is like me
With a disturbed mind
Drinking non-stop
Why non-stop
End up only with a sorrowful heart

For whom do I get drunk
For whom am I disturbed
A female dragon deity lost in a foreign bitter sea
Hate to be a woman
Still dressed as woman
Drunk and disturbed
What a pitiful woman
Should never have wandered around
Could have made a normal woman
But the cruel world has pushed me down

A vamp in a confused world
Nobody would take her as wife
Let out a heavy sigh
A beauty with an ugly fate

The presumed theme of lesbianism or gender-crossing was not at all appreciated by *T*-bar lesbians. During my fieldwork from mid-1993 to mid-1994, I heard it ordered only once at *T*-bars. It was sung by a burly *T* in a typically *T*-husky voice, and the audience was completely silent and non-responsive, which is very unusual at the *T*-bar. This was probably owing to this too "literal" rendition of the song–in particular regarding the part:

A vamp in a confused world
Nobody would take her as wife
 Let out a heavy sigh
A beauty with an ugly fate

If there exists any "text" or "scenario" for *T*-bar lesbians to identi-ty with and to act out their sexuality, it is definitely not the one understood as "gender transgression" by the wider society. Similarly, neither the term "homosexuality" nor "lesbian" is ever used by them as an identifying label nor is ever referred to either at the bar or in practices of daily life. In the case of a burly *T* singing *Ku hai nu shen long,* the singer violated the rule of karaoke identification that what is crucial is an appropriate sentiment-provoking setting (such as a for-lorn drinking bar) rather than a supposedly sexually correct theme.

Immediately after the patron is seated, either a *shaoye* or a *gong-guan* will come to serve her–the former catering to *Po,* whereas the latter to *T.* The typical *shaoye* outfits include a shirt, a tie, pants, and sometimes a tuxedo as well; whereas a *gongguan* (or *gongzhu*) wears heavy make-up, long hair, sexy outfits, such as mini-skirts revealing arms, breasts, and legs. Like her counterpart in heterosexual hostess clubs, a *gongguan* will sit on the *T*-patron's laps, play with her ties, lean on her shoulders, and *sajiao* all the time. *Sajiao* refers to exagger-ated feminine acts characterized by playful submissiveness in flirta-tious undertones and by the idea of "female infantalization" (Allison, 1994).[7] It is also a performative act in the sense that at least one audience member is required, and that it often alludes to TV actreses like Lin Meizhao, a *taiyu* soap opera actress who many *T*s argue to be the most *jiao* woman–that is, the best one at *sajiao*.

The attendant's service begins with the following greeting, "By what name may I call you?" Which implies that an invented name is expected rather than the real one: the former allows for performance at one's own command, whereas the latter is a product of the given patriline given at one's birth. After names are exchanged, the attendant will converse, in a generally casual tone, with the patron about recent events related to the bar. The following account about a former *shaoye* is a typical one:

The *guonguan:* We used to have a *shaoye* whose name is Xiaowei,[8] do you know her?

I: Is she originally from Chia-I?

She: That's right. She was back to Chia-I half a year ago. She has a quick temper, remember? She even picked fistfights with other employees.
She is not used to living in Chia-I anymore and complains to me about it on the phone once in a while. "Big sister [*jiejie*]," she would say, "I want to go back to Taipei!" She had her fortune told there and the fortune-teller saild to her that her temper will always have a bad effect on her love life. Indeed, there were many *Po* found her charming but they soon would be put off by her bad temper. They all dumped her sooner or later.

I: She told me once that she used to own a tea shop in Chia-I with her *Po*.

She: That was long, long time ago, though. That *Po* is her first wife.

I: Did she have other *Po* after that?

She: Oh, yes, but she is single most of the time. You see, her temper is too bad.

I: Are fortune-tellers able to see if one is a *T*?

She: Of course. They would tell you much more than that if they feel like it. If you are born with this destiny, you will never be able to change it. My father always says to me that everyone's destiny is given at birth, and he is certainly right about that.

Conversations like this one are "functional" in the sense that they provide updated knowledge about other *T*-bar lesbians, either present or not, with reference to whom the two conversing people can build up a closer, more intimate relationship between themselves. Note the title "big sister" mentioned in the previous case. It is a conventional *T*-bar-oriented term for a younger *T* to greet an older *Po;* in response, the latter would call the former "little brother" (*didi*). The use of these kinship terms suggests an appropriation of orthodox kinship regulation in governing non-sexual *T-Po* relationships. For example, since one is prohibited by incest taboo to conduct amorous practices with one's siblings, one should equally refrain from taking on sexual relations with one's *T*-bar "sisters" and "brothers." Like biological older sister and younger brother in Chinese society, an emotionally intimate relationship is expected between their *T*-bar counterparts. In this regard, *T*-bar little brothers normally would confide in their big sisters about their personal affairs and emotions–like Xiaowei to the *guonguan. Po*, by contrast, usually do not greet each other by kinship terms, but prefer nicknames instead. Such a radical difference thus reveals the very erotic tension between *T* and *Po*–a tension that sometimes has to be displaced through building up a *de facto* kinship relationship. Otherwise, other forms of connections (such as *T-T* brotherhoods) cannot be successfully formed. In any case, during the previously noted conversation, the *guonguan* mentioned the term "big sister" in part to build up a friendly atmosphere with me–by sharing with me her age (early thirties), a story about a "little brother" (in her early twenties) and thus making me another "big sister" to Xiaowei, thereby her cohort.

Another type of conversation takes the form of story-telling and is equally "functional" in establishing proper *T*-bar relationships. It normally takes place after drinks are ordered by the patron. Drinking serves a fairly important social function at the *T*-bar and involves rigidly defined rituals like proposing toasts. In Taiwan, alcohol is supposed to be consumed and shared with friends at social functions and failure to continue exchanging toasts with others is symbolically equivalent with a refusal to join in the collective drinking ritual–at the *T*-bar this thus either means determined offense or results in undermining of one's sexual reputation and *T*-bar identity. Once a *Po* stopped by my table several times proposing toasts to a *Po* friend of mine. Each time, however, the latter ignored her by various strategies, such as turning around to join in conversation with patrons at the neighboring table, and leaving for the restroom. Finally, the former *Po* left the bar in obvious disappointment and even hatred. Later, I found out that they had a bitter argument two weeks before over a joint investment in a restaurant. The first *Po* took the strategy of proposing toasts in an attempt to reconcile with her friend; the other, however, took the counter-strategy of displaying her unwillingness to reconcile and accused, in public, the former of her disloyalty. Since many of their mutual friends were present that night, the latter's accusation was meant to be serious–no wonder the first *Po* left in dismay.

After a more casual relationship is built through exchanging toasts, previous strangers–either employees or other patrons–may now converse in more intimate tones. For two *T*, a brotherly-like bonding may be formed after their years of birth are revealed by the typical greeting: "What's your year-range?" The "year-range" here means one's position in the Republic calendar which dates from 1912. For example, if one was born in 1964 (that is, the year fifty-three by the Republic calendar), her year-range is then "the fifties," the short for which is "five-headed." One normally finds her cohort within the same year-range, and would call others either "big brother" (*dage*) or "little brother" (*xiaodi*), according to her relative positional in the year-range. For a *T* and a *Po,* normally, a love story, which is almost always a failed one, is presented by the former after the initial toasts have been exchanged. The type of story-telling, in this case, represents a typical *T*-bar way for the *T*-story-teller and the *Po*-story-listener to negotiate their sexual roles. Erotic tension is implicit in such an exchange, and failure to abide by the rule of the game results in disruption of one's appropriate sexual role. The following case highlights the pleasure and danger of telling stories in this regard.

During my preliminary PhD fieldwork in the winter of 1991, once at a *T*-bar a much younger *T* came to me and proposed a toast. Immediately afterwards, she told me the following personal story:

> Before I came to Taipei this past summer, I had lived in Taichung for all my life. Back then I had a *Po* for three years who was as pretty and as sweet as you are. Last winter I began to carry out my husband's duty of making money for my wife. You know, *we men* are always into business; it's just part of *our* nature. So I opened up a tea house and then invested much of my time and money in the business. You know, *we men* are always like this. Since I did not have as much time for my wife as before, she got very upset. You know, *she is a woman.* And of course you know

how *these women* are. She refused to understand that I was doing it for her and started to picked fights with me. I tried to show her reason, but she did not want to listen about it at all. Oh, *women!* We had lots of fights. Finally she left me for somebody else. My heaven, I was heartbroken! So I closed down my business and came to work here. Now every night I meet many pretty women but I just am not that interested in them. I still love my wife. . . . But can't you see how lonely I am?

The genre of this *T*'s story recalls popular *taiyu* masculine love songs in which the male protagonist swears everlasting love for his ex-lover, who failed to recognize his true heart and then deserted him. Usually "he" has recently moved from his hometown in rural Taiwan to an urban area to seek a more profitable future and to heal his love wounds. In other words, "he" has experienced two forms of disorientation–a geographical one and an economic one in terms of social mobility–which are condensed into a lost love embodied by a woman unresponsive to his life-pursuit. First released in 1982 and a popular song of this genre, *Xinshi shei ren zhi* (Who would know of my heart) exemplifies these features of heterosexual masculinity:

> If I am not to speak out my heart
> Nobody will ever know of it
> Once in a while I do think about divulging
> The sorrow overflowing my stomach
> That I once walked into the underground world
> Was all my fault
> Now I regret it so hard
> Yet nobody would believe me
> Oh my love
> If you had spared me a little understanding
> You would have known
> Please be patient
> Men are not without tears
> Yet dare not to let them down

By the time I came to comprehend the significance of such a *T*-story-telling act, I had heard the same type of story five times at the *T*-bar. I was thus flustered and put off by its, what I thought at the time owing to my study of lesbian feminism in the United States, chauvinist undertone and its possible inauthenticity–in fact, I had been wondering if all the *T*-bars in Taipei had conspired to circulate such a form of stories. As a result, I decided to challenge the *T* this time. We then had the following dialogue after her story was finished:

I: You said your wife left you for somebody else.
She: So I did.
I: Then tell me: Is that somebody else a man or a woman?
        [She looked at me blank, then I repeated the question once again.]
She: Well, it's a man [reluctantly and making out an uneasy smile].
I: A man? Are you talking about a *real* man?
She: Well, yes. You know how women are [more uneasily].
I: Oh, yes, women are like that.They always go for men–is that what you are saying [in a sarcastic tone]?

She immediately changed the subject, and we toasted each other one more time. Shortly afterwards, she left my table and never came back that night. Later, I realized that, in calling her *T*-ness (note: not her heterosexual masculinity) into question, I had jeopardized my already-tenuous *Po*-position in the *T*-bar context. The problem of my identity at the time derived from the following two reasons: first, I did not quite fit with an ideal, accessible *Po*-type because of my relative elderliness (late twenties) at most *T*-bars, which are geared to younger lesbians and which register a strong flavor of youth culture–a recently emerging life style commensurate with the development of commodity culture after the lifting of Martial Law; and, second, my "advanced" educational background (doing post-college study in the West) contrasted strikingly with most *T*-bar patrons who have either a secondary school or a professional school degree–both are considered "backward" by a Chinese society that emphasizes the necessity of intellectual elitism.[9] These problems were not solved until much later when I had learned to take on proper "big sister" manners and was then regarded by most of my informants as such. In other words, what makes one properly *quan nei* is more her capability of abiding by *T*-bar rules than her "right" sexuality.

In the previous case, what I failed to acknowledge at the time is the fact that story-telling is one of the performative acts a *T* takes on in the bar so as to produce a *T*-ness. Likewise, it is a performative act for a

Po-listener to display her *Po*-ness by acting as a patient, understanding, and responsive listener. Heterosexual pronouns are among the culturally available codes a *T* draws on to make her performance theatrical and to claim her male gender identity. Another code is the male sex organ, many *T* which evoke either at social functions with both *T* and *Po* or during sex. For the former, there are always certain particularly bold *T* displaying their "penises" by, for example, imitating an ejaculation by uncorking a bottle of champagne held in the crotch. This act never fails to bring the tempo of the gathering to its climax–the audiences, both *T* and *Po*, unanimously respond to the "drag show" with great joy and excitement.

The following story highlights the necessary theatricality of such a performance and the arbitrary relationship between sex organ and sexual identity. Many frequent *T*-bar patrons related to me the story of a former *T* who wanted to be more *T*. As a result, she underwent complete sex-change surgery. After she came back to the bar informing people of the surgery, people hesitated to take her as a *real T* anymore. According to my informants, she would sit on the corner the whole evening; no *Po* ever approached her. Finally, she disappeared from the bar scene. The story has a surprising ending: she ended up working at a regular hostess club and became popular among "old farts" (*laoto*), to use their words.

Quite a few *T*s are claimed by others to have carried out sex-change surgery, as a matter of fact. Yet they rarely go through its whole process–that is, by winding up with a "penis." Instead, they take up the surgery to re-position physical signs on their bodies, such as breast-removal and inducing the growth of facial hair by hormone injection. In order to make oneself *look* more *T*–significantly, not more *male*–certain "make-up" may be put on, including dressing properly, cutting hair short, growing body hair, and, in extreme cases, undergoing sex-change surgery. The surgery is not to change one's sex or gender but rather to further stress one's original gender–that is, *T*. In addition, the male genitalia functions as a powerful symbol in conjuring up both the tempo of social gatherings and eroticism in sex only when it remains invisible–otherwise, one's identity will be called into question. The ending of the previous story–be the story authentic or not–demonstrates this point, for giving sexual service to "old farts" is definitely the most humiliating job one can ever imagine for a *real T* to take on. A similarly pathetic story was told to me and four other *T*-bar lesbians in the winter of 1993 by a *T* in her early twenties. Her "big brother" had undertaken a complete sex-change surgery which transplanted a pig's tail into her crotch. Afterwards, her *Po* had to tap her thighs, which presumably would stimulate the nerve system at command of the new sex organ, in order to "flip the thing up and down." This story was, by and large, meant to be ludicrous because of terms like "pig's tail" and "flip up and down"–and, indeed, the audience burst into immediate laughter. The fun part of the story also comes from the fact that the agency of the "penis" is not at all assumed by the big brother; instead, she can only *imitate* an erection by a *Po* tapping her thighs. What, then, is the point of having an artificial body part that is so artificial that it cannot even be used at one's free will–especially since a *real T* should be the initiator of sex acts with her *Po?* The young *T* added that often she felt like tapping her big brother's thighs for taking a peep at the flipping of the "pig's tail." However, "my big brother is too embarrassed to let me do so," the *T* said. Her embarrassment, I suggest, is derived from the fact that the proposed act would show her sex organ to be, indeed, not at all under her control–since everyone, including a little brother, can now get access to it. I finally asked the young *T* if I would ever meet with the big brother at the *T*-bar. "She does not come to the bar anymore," the *T* replied in a matter-of-fact way. "Remember? With a pig's tail she is not a *T* anymore. Now she is a man."

Another body organ with a similarly theatrical characteristic for *T*s is the kidney. I first heard of a *T*-kidney during my preliminary research in the spring of 1992. Once I chatted and drank *shaoxing*, a sweet Chinese rice wine, with a fairly eloquent *T* at a bar. She kept proposing toasts to me until finally she put down her glass in an exaggerated *T*-manner and claimed to me, "I cannot go on drinking like this anymore because *shaoxing* deteriorates my kidney." Later I discovered that the statement regarding one's kidney is frequently made by *T*. The function of the kidney is central to many Taiwanese men's concern about efficient sexual faculty for, according to Daoist medicinal philosophy, the organ embodies masculine sexuality. In fact, *shenkui* (kidney deterioration) is a cultural euphemism for "incapability of being man," meaning "unable to get an erection." Advertisements for medicines that are argued to improve kidney function appear in all forms of mass media, including fliers on the street. A typical advertisement of this genre goes as follows:

> *Shenkui* can result from the following conditions: working too
> hard, heavy engagement in social functions, insomnia, sitting up
> overnight, incontinent drinking, over-indulgent sex, and mas-
> turbation. These improper acts weaken the kidney and leads to
> depletion of one's yang components. Finally the following symp-
> toms of sexual impotence would occur: failure of erections, sore
> waist and aching back, lack of semen, nocturnal emissions,
> opaquely colored urine, vertigo, fatigue, infirmity in feet, and
> week ankles. Taking appropriate medicine will complement the
> kidney, strengthen the semen, and erect the yang. As long as the
> faculty of your kidney is improved, your shenkui will be cured.
> ("Zhongguo yixue baodao" (A report on Chinese medicine) Di-
> yisho Baodao 1988 (22 May–4 June):53)

In the *T*'s case, "theoretically" she does not have "this" kind of
kidney–one determines erection and production of semen–yet nobody
showed discomfort with her statement. Her statement was meant–to
everyone's knowledge–to show off her *T*-ness (in particular to a *Po*
like me). There exists a crucial difference between an ordinary masculine discourse and a *T*-one regarding the kidney. The former revolves
mainly around the most effective ways to *bu* (tonicize), namely to
invigorate, its function rather than a speculation about the cause of its
deterioration, for the cause is not only common knowledge but also
everywhere. By contrast, there is colorful language concerning what
kinds of food and acts may affect the *T*-kidney, among these are
smoking Menthols and drinking *shaoxing,* which thus strengthen
one's sexual charm. Similarly, thick and dark body hair is frequently
associated with a lively sex life for *Ts*. Some claim that salt induces
hair thickening and thus add large quantities of soy sauce to the side
dishes ordered at the bar. Some argue for tea leaves and apply used
ones to arms, legs, and upper lips. Different from the kidney, body hair
is a more visible sign of one's sexual availability. *Ts* frequently roll up
sleeves to others–in particular to other *T*–to show their thick arm hair.
"See how thick it is? This means superb sexual faculty. This means
your *Po* will be satisfied in bed," they say.
    Different from all the aforementioned body parts are *T*'s breasts:
they have to be concealed from *Po* by all means. Some tape their
breasts, and others bind them with a piece of cloth. In fact, *T*'s need to
conceal their breasts is so urgent and so popular that a form of bra

called "breast-binding underwear" has been advertised over the past three years at many *T*-bars and in major grass-roots lesbian newsletters. A twenty-two-year-old *T,* Shaode, in the spring of 1994, recalled to me her breast-taping history:

Shaode: I began to tape my breasts at fourteen. In summertime when I tore off the tapes, there would pour a basin full of sweat [from my armpits]. I was waitressing at a restaurant at the time and was required by the boss to hold plates overhead while catering to customers. After a while, my armpits would hurt like hell. Sometimes it bled as I tore off the tapes in showers. Next morning before it was healed up I taped my breasts again. As a result, it was never healed over. My mom was so amused by my (flat) chest that she touched my back (to feel the tapes) all the time.

I: Who told you to do this?

Shaode: Xiao Meiguo [a nickname literally meaning "little America"] from Yung-Ho,[10] a *T* I first met at Pan-Ch'iao's *Xiang Ji Cheng.*[11] Then I passed this knowledge on to my (*T*) brothers in Pan-Ch'iao, such as Acheng. At that time all of us smoke amphetamine[12] heavily. Whenever Acheng got high, she did a lousy job of taping her breasts. One day she showed up with a protruding breast and a flat one. We all burst into big laughter. Then I took her to the restroom and redid it for her. Even though I got high all the time as well, I was still the best (at taping) [looked proud of herself]. You must understand that breast-binding requires skills: you have to make your breasts small, but not completely flat–otherwise they would look like man's chest, very *biantai* [abnormal; sickening]. Hei, it's a very difficult job to do especially with tapes. I don't know why, but *T* tend to have large breasts: mine are 36 inches, which is called "ordinary," and some of my (*T*) brothers are 38. 38! That would make taping difficult indeed.

Bianbian [a nickname literally meaning "flat-flat"]: Today my co-workers teased my name: they said it should be *Bobo* [a slang word literally meaning "wave-wave" and usually referring to "large boobs"] instead of *Bian-bian.* I felt out of place. I felt so awkward that I wished I had been somewhere else. Oh, how much I envy Awen [a *T*-friend]! Hers are only 32!

I (to Shaode): So you have seen Acheng's naked breasts?

Shaode: Of course, lots of times.

I: So it's not a problem for *T* to look at each other's breasts.

Shaode: What are you talking about? I don't get your question.

I: How long did you tape your breasts?

Shaode: About half a year. At that point Acheng and I took a *shaoye* job at a *T*-bar. The first time we went there people asked us how we did with our breasts. So we said tapes. They just laughed and laughed non-stop. Then they showed us girdles. Since then I have been using girdles.

I: Do people know of that in your workplace?

Shaode: Speaking of workplace, hei, that really gives me problems. You know, it's very difficult for *T* to work with *quan wai ren* [those who are outside of the circle; meaning "straights" in this case]. With them I'm always conscious of my breasts. I'm afraid that, after taking a look at them, my co-workers would realize my *quan nei* identity. Whenever I do job interviews, I have to constantly tell myself to push my (bound) chest outward toward the interviewer. That makes me feel very cheap. Sometimes I even wear lipsticks (at interviews). Can you believe that?

Xiaoyi (another *T*): Your job really is not that bad compared with mine. My boss even requires all female employees to wear make-up. At first I thought about quitting even though the job is paid well. Finally my *Po* got a natural-color lipstick for me, which solved my problem.

I (to Shaode): Has anyone there recognized your *quan nei* identity? Anyone harassed you because you are a *T*?

Shaode: I don't know. You wouldn't believe this: there always are some guys pursuing me! For example, we have this sissy guy in my team asking me all the time to give him a scooter ride home. *Biantai!* Once I called in sick and later he called me up at my parents' house, telling me how much he was missing me. *Biantai!* He even said to me once that I look like his ex-girl friend. So I said, "What? She looks like me? How terrible!" He is blind!

The "sissy guy" is *biantai* (meaning: a freak) in part because asking for or giving a scooter ride to an opposite sex has flirtatious connotations due to close physical contact on the bike. It is usually a man giving a woman a scooter ride, rarely vice versa–or, the guy became "sissy" to Shaode by asking her for a ride. Shaode thus meant to say: "What does a sissy guy want from a (masculine) *T?*" Shaode was one of the most "*T*" "little brothers" of mine, meaning neither her looks nor her body language could possibily be associated with conventional femininity by Taiwanese standards. This is why she teased the "sissy guy" by saying that it was "terrible" that she looks like his ex-girl friend: the ex-girl friend is either a *T* (who, therefore, broke up with him) or "ugly" (that is, "unfeminine"). This is why he "is blind."

Several important features about a proper *T*'s body and her interactions with both other *T* and straights are manifest in the previous account. To begin with, a *T*'s breasts shall be concealed–by means of either taping, binding with girdles, or putting on "breast-binding underwear"–from the heterosexual gaze. I argue that this is an act to de-femininize one's body by making the socially defined feminine sexual body parts–the breasts in particular–both invisible and numb. The breasts shall be invisible because in the given society they are understood to provoke man's amorous desire and attention and to position one's sexual availability relative to other (straight) women. This concern becomes increasingly urgent in contemporary Taiwan because of a societal obsession with enlarging woman's breasts so as to verify her correct femininity. Advertisements for products reputed to aide in either bust-enlargement or breast-beautification are now ubiquitous and prominent in all media forms. One, by featuring a voluptuous White woman, says to its customers:

She Is a Woman. She Is the Woman of All Women! Don't You Wish to Be a Real One? Let *Sai Mei Su* [the product's brand name] Fulfill Your Dream!

On the other hand, the act of de-feminizing one's breasts is also to make them numb (from heterosexual sensations). As Shaode said, tearing off the tapes sometimes would result in bleeding, which, however, did not at all stop her from doing it–as if that body part was completely numb.

The need to de-feminize one's body, significantly, is not to make it masculine, or male. As Shaode pointed out, "You have to make your breasts small, but not completely flat–otherwise they would look like man's chest, very *biantai*." The non-*biantai* chest, obviously, can be looked at by other *T*s because they are not sexual. However, they definitely cannot be seen by *Po*. In the fall of 1991, a thirty-year-old *T* recalled "a most mortifying moment" in her sexual history:

She: Five years ago I was with a *Po* who constantly asked me to take off my clothes in sex. Even though at the time I would do just about anything to please her, I still said No. Period. She was not a *quan nei ren*, you see. I was the first *T* she had been with. So she did not know of *the rule*.

I: Why, then, didn't you teach her about the rule?

She: Well, since she never asked me directly so why should I bother?

I: Why was she this way?

She: Hei, how could I know? Remember? She was a *quan wai ren*, right? Once I was about to make love to her, you know what she did to me? She jumped from the bed and tore open my shirt down to the waist. I was so stunned that I was totally frozen. Unlucky for me, that day I was wearing a white, lacy bra decorated with shining beads–you know, at the time I was living with my mom and she just bought all these cute bras and ordered me to wear them. . . . How would I know why my mom did that? I guess she just hated seeing me going around as a *T*. In any case, no sooner had my *Po* seen the bra than this stupid woman yelled, "Gee, how cute they are!" Shit! That really turned me off! I was so conscious of the fucking bra that I simply could not do it. Right away she saw my embarrassment and said, "Oh, I'm sorry." Shit! That was even worse! Anyway, that was it. We broke up right after that.

Obviously, in order to make one's body sexual to a *Po*, a *T* refrains from showing her naked breasts–this, to use the *T*'s words, is called "the rule." Failure to abide by it would then result in a *Po* appearing asexual to the *T*.

CONCLUSION

While the terms *T* and *Po* were invented thirty years ago, *T* as a gender category distinct from "man" did not come into being until a collective, performative space–the *T*-bar–was constituted and allowed for lesbians' practices of sexual identities. A radical distinction between earlier tomboys and recent *T*s can be drawn in terms of one's conceptualization of her sexual body. In the article, I approach the issue by showing the significance of certain body parts, including kidney, body hair, penis, and breasts, in forming a *T*'s self-identity.

NOTES

1. This paper is taken from my PhD dissertation, which was partially funded by the SSRC and the ACLS. I would like to thank the following people for their constructive criticism and advice: P. Steven Sangren and John Borneman at Cornell University, Gerard Sullivan, and two anonymous reviewers. I am also grateful to my girl friend, Hsiao Wen-tsai, who participated in the whole process of my fieldwork.

2. All the transliterations from the Chinese adopt the Pinyin system except official names in Taiwan, which follow the Wade-Giles system.

3. This article is based on ethnographic fieldwork (conducted for my PhD) in Taiwan's lesbian community from June 1993 to July 1994 and December 1996 to May 1997. During these two sessions of fieldwork, I carried out interviews with 43 lesbians and participated in their everyday practices, including work, socializing, dating, religious activities, and family relationships. By "lesbian community," I follow Kennedy and Davis's (1994) notion of bar-oriented, working-class individuals. Nearly all of my informants were working class or had limited access to cultural capital, in contrast with lesbians who have participated in Taiwan's gay rights movement since the early 1990s. These women are exclusively students or graduates of prestigious colleges and universities, and are familiar with North American notions of gay rights and queer theory.

4. To many Taiwanese, this is the most prestigious degree in Taiwan.

5. Penghu has been Taiwan's top military base since 1949 and was prohibited, under Martial Law, from tourist visits until the early 1990s.

6. "America," meaning the United States, has been imagined by most Taiwanese gay people as a dreamland in which unrestrained homosexuality can still be acted out.

7. I am grateful to Michael Wittmer for his suggestion of the term and of the linkages between Taiwanese and Japanese nightclubs.

8. In order to protect their identities, all informants in this article have been given pseudonyms.

9. It is beyond the scope of this article to analyze the on-going conflict between *T*-bar-oriented *quan nei ren* and "intellectual" lesbians. Suffice it to note that the former, by and large, suspect the integrity of the latter, while the latter, as inspired by feminism and queer theory from college study, consider the former to be "reproducing heterosexual hegemony," but see them, nevertheless, as exotic.

10. A sattelite city of Taipei.

11. Pan-Ch'iao is a neighboring city of Yung-Ho. Xiang Ji Cheng (Fragrant Chicken Town) is a local counterpart to McDonald's and sells roast chicken and other Chinese fast foods. Chain fast-food stores in Taipei are, by and large, hang-outs for youths.

12. From the mid-1980s to the early 1990s, amphetamine addiction was a rampant social problem throughout both rural and urban areas in Taiwan, and in particular among teenagers.

REFERENCES

Allison, Anne (1994). *Nightwork: Sexuality, pleasure, and corporate masculinity in a Tokyo hostess club.* Chicago: University of Chicago Press.

Sangren, P. Steven (1996). "Value transformation/appropriation and gender in Chinese local ritual organization and practices." Paper given at the annual meeting of the Association for Asian Studies, Honolulu, 11-14 April.

Seaman, Gary (1981). "The sexual politics of Karmic retribution." In Ahern, Emily Martin and Gates, Hill (Eds.). *The Anthropology of Taiwanese Society.* Stanford: Stanford University Press. pp. 381-396.

Wolf, Margery (1972). *Women and Family in Rural Taiwan.* Stanford: Stanford University Press.

Asian Values, Family Values:
Film, Video, and Lesbian
and Gay Identities

Chris Berry

INTRODUCTION

In a recent essay about gay life in Asia, Dennis Altman (1995: 125) noted that "the past decade has seen the growth of a commercial gay world beyond its few existing bastions such as Bangkok and Tokyo to cover most of the countries of Asia." As I have pointed out in an earlier article focussing on East Asia[1] (Berry, 1998a), this development is being complemented by increased film and video representation of gay men and, to a lesser extent, lesbians and other queer characters and communities.

This article examines some of those East Asian film and video representations. Its purpose is not to discover how people live. It does not assume that films are or should be a mirror reflecting reality. For example, as Altman (1995: 131) notes in reference to *The Wedding Banquet,* the representation of these emergent Asian gay communities is itself notably lacking in these films. But where Altman sees this lack of representative depiction as a failing, this article operates from a different basic understanding of the nature and function of cultural representation. It sees these films as registering and expressing some

[Haworth co-indexing entry note]: "Asian Values, Family Values: Film, Video, and Lesbian and Gay Identities." Berry, Chris. Co-published simultaneously in *Journal of Homosexuality* (Harrington Park Press, an imprint of The Haworth Press, Inc.) Vol. 40, No. 3/4, 2001, pp. 211-231; and: *Gay and Lesbian Asia: Culture, Identity, Community* (ed: Gerard Sullivan, and Peter A. Jackson) Harrington Park Press, an imprint of The Haworth Press, Inc., 2001, pp. 211-231. Single or multiple copies of this article are available for a fee from The Haworth Document Delivery Service [1-800-342-9678, 9:00 a.m. - 5:00 p.m. (EST). E-mail address: getinfo@haworthpressinc.com].

of the ways in which being gay (or sometimes one of the various other queer identities) is imagined both by self-identified gay men and by others. In other words, these films do not necessarily tell us about the empirical realities of gay lives in East Asian communities, but they do tell us something of what it means to be gay in East Asian cultures.

As Altman points out in his article, the Asian gay worlds he writes about are hybrid formations. They are distinct from older locally specific queer communities, such as the transgendered Indonesian *waria* or *banci* or the Thai *kathoeys*. Gay in the worlds he writes about is not only the basis for a social identity as well as a form of behaviour, but also concerns sexual object choice without involving a change of gender identity from masculine. As Altman points out, this gay identity is something adopted from Western culture but necessarily hybridized in its transplantation into various local Asian cultures.

What this article sets out to examine is how this hybridization is occurring on the level of representation and self-representation. I argue that hybridization through appropriation by local East Asian gay men precludes conceiving of these representations in terms of the classic Self/Other binary divisions of colonialist and orientalist thinking (Said, 1978). They cannot and should not be understood as setting up a fixed and naturalized Asian gay identity versus a Western gay identity. Instead, a subtle conceptual framework is required to accommodate these multivalent and sometimes contradictory articulations.

José Muñoz has recently examined the videos of Canadian gay filmmaker Richard Fung. Muñoz (1995) borrows Homi Bhabha's concept of "colonial mimicry" (Bhabha, 1984). Here, a colonial subject mimicking the colonialist can be seen as an act of resistance in certain circumstances, for at a minimum it provides a position of agency and subjectivity for those denied both in the Self/Other constructions of pure colonialist discourse. In Muñoz's focus on Fung, this mimicry involves both re-writing the discourses of colonialism in the Caribbean to instate the otherwise excluded agency of the colonial subject, and the discourses of North American gay male porn videos to instate the otherwise excluded agency of the Asian gay man.

This article argues that while the films in question can be seen similarly as instances of mimicry and re-writing, they cannot be seen simply and solely as instances of colonial mimicry. Rather, their hybridization consists in their simultaneous appropriation of the Western model of gay identity and its re-writing into established local (and possibly already hybrid rather than pure or authentic) narrative patterns. In this way they counter both local and neo-colonial forces and discourses that objectify, oppress, or are simply blind to the existence and specificity of East Asian gay identities and cultures.

This article examines that process in regard to one particular issue, namely the social mapping of gay identity in relation to family and kinship. I argue that gay identity is defined and socially positioned in relation to family in these texts in two dominant ways. First, it appears as a problem within the networks of kinship obligations that constitute the family and bind the individual into it, and this trope constitutes a site of cultural hybridity and contradiction in which both selfhood as psychology or personality and selfhood as family role are rewritten. Second, it appears as something lived in marginal spaces. For the most part, these spaces are not alternative communities, or at least they are free of the structure and hierarchy of the family culture, and this is signified by the narrative patterns and structures of the films as well as their content. These marginal spaces are normally invisible to the larger society, but in representing them, these texts write them into culture and make them visible.

Furthermore, as I have argued elsewhere (Berry, 1994), the limited but nonetheless international circulation of cinema and video from East Asia enables these emergent gay and other queer identities to participate in the constitution of an increasingly globalized gay culture. However much they might borrow from existing Anglo-American models of gay identity, as Bhabha's concept of "colonial mimicry" suggests, their very existence means that those Anglo-American models can no longer be perceived as universal. Certain historical and social specificities of those Anglo-American models, therefore, can be made apparent against this new and more culturally diverse backdrop, and there is the possibility of challenge, review, renegotiation, and renewal for all of us.

Therefore, these images of gay identity are somewhat different from the dominant Anglo-Saxon post-Stonewall tropes that construct gay identity as something that involves "coming out" of the blood family and joining other, alternative communities. Finally, I argue that these differences not only demonstrate how gay identity is being hybridized in its adoption and adaptation into Asian cultures, but also constitute a challenge to the blindness of Anglo-American models of gay identity to the issue of relationships to blood family.

THICKER THAN WATER

In my earlier work (Berry, 1994), I found representations of gay and other queer characters had increased in East Asian cinemas from the very occasional focussing on the topic and scattered minor characters to the point where they had become relatively regular. However, at the time, this tendency seemed confined to certain territories only. For example, I knew of no significant films produced in either the People's Republic of China or South Korea, with the possible exception of *Farewell My Concubine,* a film set safely in the past and also involving considerable overseas post-production investment.

Since then, as well as continuing production in other territories, the first South Korean gay feature film, *Broken Branches,* has appeared. A mainland Chinese film, *The Postman,* has featured gay characters in minor roles, and the first gay film, *East Palace, West Palace,* has recently been completed (Berry, 1998a). This indicates that this is a continuing and growing phenomenon.

These films and videos from East Asia, which centre on gay and other queer characters, can be broken into three categories. First, there are feature films aimed at a mainstream market and the general culture in which they are produced. *Wedding Banquet* and *Farewell, My Concubine* are probably the best-known examples, and, like most of the films in this category, both were directed by straight men. Second, there are a considerable number of independent short films and videos shot by gay Asian men (and one or two lesbians). These are mostly aimed at a specialized market, and a significant proportion of them have come from diasporic filmmakers. Possibly, Hamid Naficy's term "transnational filmmakers" might apply equally well or better in these latter cases. Oki Hiroyuki in Japan, Richard Fung in Canada, and Quentin Lee, born in Hong Kong and now based in North America, are all good examples of the independent gay filmmaker shooting primarily for gay audiences. Third, there is a crossover category of features that could be said to be festival or art house films, with a niche market. A good example might be Tsai Ming-Liang's film about three lonely people and an empty apartment in Taipei called *Vive L'Amour.* Despite winning various awards, including Best Film at the Singapore International Film Festival, it has unfortunately had limited international distribution. Another example would be the film which won Best Director at Cannes 1997 for Wong Karwai, *Happy Together.* This film is about a doomed gay relationship being conducted on the road by two Hong Kong tourists in Argentina. Or Tsai's follow-up to *Vive L'Amour, The River,* in which a father and son bump into each other in the darkness of a gay sauna and incest ensues.

In the first type of film, whose production values and budget alone indicate an aim for a general audience, a dominant trope is the representation of gayness as a family problem. The genre of the family melodrama and/or comedy is usually adopted for this purpose. The Japanese films *Okoge* and *Twinkle,* the Taiwanese film *The Wedding Banquet,* and the South Korean *Broken Branches* are all good examples. Both *Okoge* and *Broken Branches* feature closeted gay couples. In each case, the older partner is married. The younger partner is not, but he has not come out to his family. *The Wedding Banquet* and *Twinkle* also focus on gay sons who have not come out to their families.

Of course, hiding sexual behaviour is not necessarily a problem for the maintenance of the family unit. Indeed, one might suggest that in many cases it is essential. What is a problem for the family in these films is not sexual behaviour in itself but an exclusive sexual orientation whose development into an exclusive sexual and social identity in turn interferes with the ability to perform one's role in the family.

In *Broken Branches,* the married partner has compartmentalized his life and thus avoided the move from homosexual behaviour to exclusive preference and identity with its attendant difficulties. In the gay bar and with his partner, the married man Sung Gul lives a gay life hidden from his family and colleagues. Outside the bar, he performs the standard family roles of husband and father like most other men. However, there is a price to be paid for this. For instance, it is only possible for him to spend the whole night together with his unmarried lover Jung Min in the most exceptional of circumstances. And while Jung Min complains that he always puts Sung Gul first, Sung Gul bluntly tells him that seventy percent of his love is for the family, and thirty percent for Jung Min.

In *Okoge,* on the other hand, it is when the married partner is forced by his understandably jealous wife to choose between her and being gay that he begins to make the move from compartmentalized behaviour to an exclusive identity. However, this is more than just a matter of personal choice. It also affects Tochi's work as a salaryman. Partly, this is because his wife is the boss's daughter. It is also because his colleagues are homophobic, as is shown in one scene where they express their fear and loathing of gays over lunch, expecting him to join in.

Outed at work soon after, Tochi explains to his gay friends that he has lost all respect and is obliged to resign. But he goes out with a bang, not a whimper. Acting as a colleague's best man at a large wedding ceremony, he performs the role but rewrites it to make a space for his gay identity. Instead of his real wife, he brings a plump drag queen friend done up in full make-up and kimono. Together, they sing a child's song, which has come to function as a gay theme in the film, and then exit, leaving the groom angry and the bride in tears.

However, in all four films, the difficulty of reconciling family obligations and gay sexual orientation is focussed more on the unmarried men with already formed exclusive sexual identities. It comes to a head around the expectation that a son will get married and produce children to continue the patriarchal family line, as is expected in societies and cultures whose values have been informed by Confucianism (Hall and Ames, 1987, 1995). In *The Wedding Banquet* and *Okoge,* both the sons have gone to considerable lengths to avoid conflicts between their family roles and their sexual identities.

Taiwanese Wai Tung in *The Wedding Banquet* has been able to fulfil both roles by moving to New York, living the post-Stonewall gay lifestyle with an American lover and simultaneously being a good son by managing the family's property investments in the city. In *Okoge,* the unmarried lover Goh has chosen to be a self-employed craftsman precisely in order to avoid all the heterosexual expectations that we see go with Tochi's salaryman job.

However, it is not up to either Wai Tung or Goh alone to decide when or whether or not to seek out a wife, and this inevitably brings the latent contradiction between family role and sexual identity to the surface as family members play matchmaker. Indeed, *The Wedding Banquet* opens with a scene in that Mecca of Anglo-American gay culture, the gym, where Wai Tung listens to a cassette tape letter from his mother about the latest possible bride on his Walkman while he does his routine on the machines. The scene seems to suggest that the old adage "out of sight, out of mind" may not be so easily realized.

In many ways, the narratives in these films play out a conflict between two different models of selfhood, producing gayness in East Asia in these films as a trope signifying ongoing cultural hybridity and contradiction. One model of selfhood is signified in the films as more local, the other as a western import. In the former, self is defined relationally according to one's role in a group, in this case the family. In the latter, selfhood is defined as a set of psychological traits.

This notion of a divide between a local relational self and a foreign-originated psychological self is widespread in academic as well as popular discourse. To take Chinese culture as an example, research on the concept of the self is extensive, ranging from the interpretation of ancient philosophical texts to contemporary social science studies. A wide variety of different opinions exists, but most commentators seem to agree that social relations have played a large role in the definition of self in Chinese culture since Confucian times and that this persists today. Where researchers differ is in their value judgements of the Chinese social and relational self and how absolute they believe it to be.

In studies of contemporary Chinese societies in the social sciences, Francis L. K. Hsu (1971, 1985) stands as a critic of the Eurocentric values underpinning much western work on China. He argues instead that the western approach to self in terms of individualized psychology is inadequate and truncated, failing to take into account the fundamental role of human social relations in defining self. Hong Kong critic Lung-kee Sun (a.k.a. Sun Longji, 1983), on the other hand, agrees on the importance of the collective, anti-individualist character in Chinese culture, but believes it is detrimental to the development of Chinese society.[2] The shared belief in the importance of the social and relational definition of the self by scholars of contemporary Chinese culture has also carried through into empirical social science studies that attempt to verify or measure aspects of this quality (Yang, 1986: Bond and Hwang, 1986).

In research on Confucian thought about the self, although Munro (1969, pp. 23-9) stresses that Confucians believe in natural equality, he acknowledges that they also believe in a hierarchical social order. This social order defines the self according to the position taken up in the hierarchy and the traits attached to that position. It also prescribes appropriate behaviour (*li*) towards both those above and below one in the hierarchy as motivated by the traits attached to and reciprocal relationships between positions in the hierarchy.[3]

In work on pre-modern Chinese narrative, Andrew Plaks (1977) has also noted the relative importance of social relations in defining character; characters are differentiated less by psychological traits than by the particular combination of social roles they embody. Interestingly, he observes in classical narrative that characters are not psychologi-cally essentialized as is often the case in Western fiction. But that they tend to change their behaviour according to the circumstances they find themselves in, and that, furthermore, this changeability is not seen as a weakness of character but as adaptability. This is in accord with Munro's analysis of Confucian values: he concludes that Confucians both value conformity to the requirements of one's position in the social order and education and self-improvement as a road to privilege (Munro, pp. 23-5, 90-9). From this perspective, a successful person is one who can transcend any individualized or psychological character-istics she or he may have to assume. As well as the behaviour ap-propriate to a change in her or his position in the social order and the question of whether or not a particular person can do this may provide the driving hermeneutic for a narrative, as appears to be the case for these films.

To what extent these findings are generalizable to non-Chinese East Asian cultures is as debatable as the various ideological frameworks they are processed through. However, the four films under consider-ation here all seem cognate with these findings. In representing gay-ness as a family problem dramatizing the ongoing conflict between different models of selfhood, these films do not represent a desire for sexual relations with members of the same sex as something intrinsi-cally foreign that is threatening so-called Asian family values from the outside. Rather, they represent the model of selfhood built on that desire as a challenge that is already within the family and must be worked through. It is in this sense that gayness as a family problem is a trope of ongoing hybridity and contradiction, rather than simply some foreign thing that can be resisted.

Furthermore, the drive of the films is towards a reconciliation of contradictions and conflict, however strained this reconciliation may appear, as is so often the case in melodrama aimed at mainstream audiences. In *Broken Branches,* for example, the film ends with the unmarried Jung Min fantasizing a scene in which he is finally able to bring his lover home to his family, presenting him to the elders much as he would present a bride. In this re-writing of a more traditional narrative trope, he both fulfils his family obligations and simulta-neously produces a space for his gay identity within the family.

In *The Wedding Banquet, Okoge,* and *Twinkle,* the reconciliation of the contradiction takes the form of simultaneously producing a son and making gayness visible to the family or broader community. In order to achieve this, of course, a potential mother is needed. And this brings me to my next point about the way in which gayness is represented in these films. Rather than the main opposition being between homosexuality and heterosexuality, it is represented as being between those who are willing and able to play traditional family roles and those who are not. In each of these films, as well as the gay characters, there are also a number of women who fail to conform to the standard role for a daughter.

In *The Wedding Banquet,* there is a young mainland Chinese woman who needs a green card to stay in the United States and whose prime devotion is to her artwork rather than to playing the role of dutiful daughter-in-law and wife. Wei Wei marries Wai Tung to solve both their problems, seduces him on the wedding night, and gets pregnant. She, Wai Tung, and his American lover then form a sort of family unit, with two fathers to help look after the child while she gets on with her career.

Okoge focuses on the "fag hag" of the title, an orphan whose background includes being brought up in a mixed Japanese-American family and being sexually abused by the father in a second foster family. Made pregnant by an equally abusive former soldier, who then abandons her, Sayako is rescued by Goh, and together with her baby son, the three of them form a sort of family unit at the close of the film.

In *Twinkle,* the drama concerns two families. One has the gay son, the other a daughter with an alcohol problem. The gay son has a college student boyfriend, and again the three of them become a sort of family unit, with her even expressing her desire for artificial insemination with a mixture of both men's sperm.

Although *Broken Branches* does not follow this structure, it covers all the children, including daughters, in a complex traditional family in which the father has had four wives. None of the children fulfil traditional obligations, but all of them also find their personal desire frustrated by family obligations and interference. The contortions the other three films put themselves through to find plausible young women characters to be willing wives is a testament both to the power of the ideology of the family and their determination to find a place for gayness within it. Furthermore, although each of the women gets something from her participation in these arrangements, this should not blind us to the fact that none of the films even attempts to address the question of how their sexual desires are to be satisfied.[4]

SOULS ON THE ROAD

Although the narratives of the melodramas discussed so far suggest that the family is almost ubiquitous and inescapable in East Asian cultures, some of the other films, and in particular the independent and experimental films or the festival films, do find other spaces within which to represent gayness. However, this space is rarely that of the emergent gay community. Indeed, it may well be that of all the films under consideration here, only *Okoge* suggests the gay community as an alternative, structured community for the individual who takes up a gay identity.

In Chinese culture, the world of the opera troupes is another such marginal community where homosexuality appears consistently in the cinema. As well as *Farewell My Concubine*, there is also a Taiwanese film about a contemporary troupe of female opera singers called *The Silent Thrush*. However, like the gay community in *Okoge*, there is ambivalence about this space, as opera singers were itinerant entertainers who were traditionally on the lower rungs of society.

Ellen Pau's experimental video, *Song of the Goddess*, also evokes the world of the opera, but it does not exactly signify it as an alternative marginal community. Instead, gossip and legends about female opera singers from the past intersect on the soundtrack with the noises of contemporary Hong Kong, while the images include women bathing together and caressing each other, or shadowy opera singer figures superimposed ghost-like over everyday scenes of contemporary Hong Kong life.

What makes Pau's video different from *Farewell My Concubine* and *Silent Thrush* is the absence of a sense of a structured community, with hierarchy and established roles and relationships to define identity. Instead, this other space is marked as marginal, elusive, tacit, and even invisible to outsiders. In this, it is similar to the space of the outcast in other contexts, that of the "soul on the road" in Japanese culture, or the "rivers and lakes" that the heroes of Chinese martial arts legends float down. Seekam Tan (1993, 1994) has explored the way in which Hong Kong queer culture and homoeroticism intersect with these spaces in both martial arts films and the contemporary generic equivalent, the Hong Kong action movie.

One director in particular foregrounds the way in which this space is defined against the space of the family and the hierarchical, ordered, relational networks of which it stands at the centre. This is Tsai Ming-Liang, with his trilogy composed of *Rebels of the Neon God, Vive L'Amour,* and *The River.* After seeing *The River,* it becomes clear that the young man played by the same actor in all three films is also the same character, as his parents from the first film reappear in the third. Here, I would like to focus in particular on *Vive L'Amour,* although it should be noted that many of the remarks I make could also apply to the other two films. The title of the film is highly ironic, as it is very much about loneliness, melancholia, and grieving (Berry 1998b). The focus is on three isolated characters and an empty apartment. For most of the film, there is no dialogue, and so we never really find out what they are called, and while there are many incidents and chance meetings, there is none of the tight structure and cause and effect patterning found in the melodrama genre.

One of the characters is a woman real estate agent. About thirty years old, she lives alone and spends most of her life in empty houses waiting for prospective buyers. The Mandarin Chinese word for house is *jia,* which is also the word for family. So these are *jia* without *jia,* spaces which call attention to the absence of family.

As well as the woman, there is a young man of about twenty who steals a key left hanging in the front door lock of one the apartments the woman handles. He works as a salesman for columbaria, or niches for funeral urns. Various scenes emphasize the ironic relation of this work to family. For example, as he walks up and down the rows of columbaria, another salesman is talking to a group of prospective buyers. He tells them how there are niches for couples and families, and how some people bring their friends to buy a niche close to theirs so they can visit easily and play mahjong in the afterlife. The young man also walks into a room where his colleagues are playing a sort of variant on musical chairs. Everybody takes on a family-defined role for the game, for example, as oldest brother, but the young man looks on from the sidelines, not taking up one of these family roles and participating.

A second man, somewhat older than the first, is a street hawker. At night in Taipei, sellers lay out their wares on sheets on the sidewalk, a practice known as "rolling out a carpet" (*bai ditan*). This allows them to roll them up and hide them should the police come by, as this is an illegal activity. Apart from his sheet, he has a car, two mobile spaces that signify his itinerant status, his lack of a fixed abode or family. He also comes by a key to the empty apartment.

There is no doubt that *Vive L'Amour* is a film about loneliness and melancholy. It ends with the woman sitting alone in a park, crying through an excruciatingly long take. However, we should not forget that these three people have chosen their lifestyles and work. There is nothing in the film to suggest that poverty or anything else has forced them. Furthermore, the empty apartment they all use becomes a space in which they work through certain unspoken needs. For the estate agent, it becomes the place she takes the carpet seller back to after she picks him up one night, the place they use for their one-night stands. This immediately marks both of them, but particularly her, as defectors from the conventional patriarchal family by virtue of their sexual practices.

For the young columbarium seller, the apartment is also a space for him to work through needs that could not be realized within the family. He first attempts suicide. Then he goes through a series of roleplays. First, he buys a watermelon, mimes kissing it, and then uses it as a bowling ball. Later, after he and the street hawker discover each other in the apartment, they begin to use the apartment together, functioning as a sort of household, cooking for each other, washing clothes and so on. When the columbarium seller discovers that his new flatmate sells women's clothes, he tries some of them on.

The scenes in the apartment end with one in which all three of the main characters are brought together. The young man is masturbating absent-mindedly when the street hawker comes back with the real estate agent. He hides under the bed, and they proceed to have sex on top of it. As their passion rises, he starts masturbating again, constituting a sort of threesome with one invisible partner. The next morning, the real estate agent leaves the street hawker sleeping on the bed. The columbarium seller comes out from under the bed, lies on it, and, careful not to disturb him, kisses the street hawker before leaving. This seems to retrospectively signify that just as they have been using the apartment to express their sexuality, so he has been using it to come to terms with his.

Vive L'Amour and many of the other films, which locate homosexuality in a marginal space of isolation and lack of community, are at best ambivalent about this space. However, the films of Japanese independent experimental filmmaker Oki Hiroyuki do not seem tinged with melancholy. Instead, they could be said to celebrate the space of the margin as a free space for exploration and enjoyment of gay sexuality. Oki's early films are mostly short and not so short diary-like films shot on super-8, such as *Colour Eyes, Melody for Buddy Matsumae,* and *Swimming Prohibited.* They combine apparently random and banal shots of street scenes, buildings, trains, seafronts with the occasional flash of a young man who has taken the filmmaker's fantasy, somebody masturbating in an apartment, and so on.

Most recently, Oki has combined these elements into a documentary tribute to his hometown, Kochi, commissioned by the Kochi Art Museum, and a short feature film. The documentary *Heaven 6 Box* is a city film in the manner of Ruttman's *Berlin, Symphony of a City* and Vertov's *Man with a Movie Camera,* and its 6-part structure is edited to 6 pieces of music. Again, various figures appear, some of whom may be local personalities, others of whom appear to be gay friends. The feature, *I Like You, I Like You Very Much,* strings similar elements around a narrative of a crisis that occurs in a couple's relationship when one partner takes a fancy to a man he sees on the train. Greater emphasis is placed not only on narrative but also on more drawn-out sex scenes, and there is a sense of a loose network of friends and acquaintances. But there is little evidence of a community with social institutions and commercial activities.

TAKING IT HOME

The films discussed above are presumably made primarily for the local cultures in which they are produced. However, film circulates globally through networks that include the theatrical distribution of features like *The Wedding Banquet,* festival and television screenings of films like *Vive L'Amour,* and niche market direct-mail video sales of films like *I Like You, I Like You Very Much.* As such, they add to a repertoire of representations of gayness that has hitherto been very much dominated by the post-Stonewall Anglo-American model.

With these East Asian films available as a basis for comparison, that model appears more culturally and historically specific. Like them, gayness is represented with reference to the family, and there are two models, one more mainstream with blood family present, and one more tending to be made by and for members of the queer communities without blood family. But there are also significant differences. In the East Asian mainstream films, there is an effort (however strained) to integrate gayness with the obligations of traditional family roles. In the Anglo-American equivalents, gayness has tended to mean leaving the space of the blood family. In the East Asian films by and for members of the queer communities, gayness is located in and defined by the hazy amorphous spaces of marginality, but the Anglo-American equivalents have tended towards locating gayness in and defined by alternative communities.

Taken together, the two dominant Anglo-American patterns assume a clear and radical separation between homosexuality and the family. Kath Weston has written a book about the recent emergence into cultural visibility of the "chosen family" in queer cultures. However, she heads her chapter on attitudes that pre-date the emergence of the chosen family "Exiles from Kinship" and divides it into sections with titles like "Is Straight to Gay as Family Is to No Family?" (Weston, 1991, pp. 21-42)

In pre-Stonewall cultural representations, as Vito Russo (1987) has documented so amply, this separation between family and gayness meant that the great bulk of queer characters on the screen were without blood family, and, for the most part, loners without kinship ties of any sort. Often, they were also monstrous. With the social changes marked by the gay and lesbian liberation movements, mainstream Anglo-American culture started to attempt to put gay identity into the picture in a more positive way, but this basic separation remained largely unquestioned.

Hollywood's first big effort in this direction was *Making Love*. It centres on three characters: Claire; her husband, Zack; and Bart, the gay man he gets involved with. For Zack, coming to terms with his sexuality not only means coming out to his wife, but also means divorce and leaving Los Angeles for New York. "I don't want a double life," he tells her, and the final shot of the film shows him driving away from the family home into the distance. Much the same pattern is found in the earlier British film, *Victim*, in which a lawyer comes out to his wife. She says she will stand by him, but there is no suggestion that a new family unit along the lines of the threesomes in *Okoge*, *The Wedding Banquet*, and *Twinkle* is about to the established.

Even the independent feature, *Desert Hearts,* directed by a lesbian and aimed at a lesbian audience but fashioned on mainstream models, followed this sort of pattern. The film opens with Vivian arriving in Reno from New York, having left her husband to get a divorce. During the film, she develops a relationship with Cay, who is living with her mother and brother. The film ends with Cay leaving her mother and the two of them leaving Reno. Again, there is no suggestion of resolving the issue by finding a space for gayness within the family.

I would argue that this pattern constitutes a rewriting of the narrative patterns that surround the anomic, psychologized model of selfhood discussed as "western" in the debates around selfhood in Chinese culture detailed above. "Coming out" suggests not only openness, but also a movement, a journey outwards towards the realization of full subjecthood. Whereas a relational and role-determined model of selfhood permeates the East Asian family melodramas examined here, here it is a psychological, personality-based model. What is at stake is not so much duties, hence the absence of any great concern with parents and filial obligations in the British and American films mentioned. Rather it is a matter of self-expression. And the deeper narrative pattern to which this is wedded is that of the hero who sets out on the quest. Like finding the Golden Fleece, finding oneself means leaving home.

This kind of selfhood is often discussed as oedipal. As the stereotypical Hollywood happy ending with the formation or confirmation of the couple indicates, the ideal narrative of the quest ends with the establishment of a new and separate family unit (de Lauretis, 1984). Not surprisingly, then, both *Making Love* and *Desert Hearts* also adapt this model. The same is often true of the post-Stonewall films by and for members of the queer communities. But these tend to represent gay and other queer characters as already established and operating not necessarily in the space of a family unit but within an alternative community marked out by the absence of blood family. The AIDS film *Longtime Companion,* for example, features an entire network of friends functioning as a chosen family, and at no point do members of the various characters' blood families make any significant appearance. The same is true of the recent lesbian film, *Go Fish,* in which there is a network of friends functioning as an extended family with an older lesbian couple as mother figures and again no evidence whatsoever of blood family.

Of course, it may be that as emergent gay and other queer communities become more established in Asia, the space of the margin noted in the second type of film above will become the space of the alternative community in the manner of these films. Whether this pattern gets appropriated into these cultures along with that of gay identity itself remains to be seen.

As far as global gay culture is concerned, there is apparent pressure to face and deal with the nexus of the gay subject and the blood family in some of the East Asian films. This makes me question some of the assumptions that underlie the dominant Anglo-American models of gay identity outlined here. I do not mean to suggest by this that these films present new models that we should learn from. Indeed, I doubt very much whether many people inside or outside East Asian cultures will feel drawn to the rather unlikely and strained scenarios depicted at the conclusions of some of those films. Rather, I hope that my discussion of the films has presented them as dynamic sites of ongoing contestation and hybridization around models of selfhood, and it is in this way that I believe that they participate in broader ongoing debates.

Just as Wai Tung, in *The Wedding Banquet*, is chased around the world by his mother's voice, so I doubt that many of us in post-Stonewall Anglo-American culture are as devoid of any thoughts about our blood family as the dominant cultural patterns would suggest. However, the oedipal model of the complete and autonomous subject that seems to underlie these Anglo-American representations requires a supposedly complete resolution of ongoing dynamic interactions as a sign of psychological health and well-being. These assumptions have been under question in various fields of debate for some time now and particularly by certain feminist theorists, such as Mathew (1991), who wish to advance a more relational model of subjectivity. They question the repressions and oppressions involved in maintaining the fiction of the fully autonomous subject, both in terms of the price paid by those whose agency is denied and who are constructed as objectified Others to confirm the autonomous subject, and also in terms of the autonomous subject itself.

Perhaps, therefore, it would be good to end this paper with reference to one of the most hybrid films of all: a video piece by Hong Kong-born, North American based Quentin Lee. In many ways, *The Anxiety of Inexpression* is the home movie from hell. Lee documents his college life, his sex life, acting in a pornographic film, and so on, all the while relentlessly analysing and discussing these experiences and his status as a gay man and an Asian American. He is out to his parents and his family but his sexuality seems invisible and unacknowledged within his family life. However, by showing us a compartmentalized life all on the one tape, he is insisting on putting them together. And indeed, this impulse develops as the film continues, when Lee uses video editing techniques to overlay elements from one area of his life on top of the other.[5]

Finally, the video presents the family Christmas scene, itself a signifier of cultural hybridity. It begins with the title from *A Christmas Carol,* complete with holly and the song "Deck the Halls" playing on the soundtrack. Scrooge performs on one part of a split screen while shots of Lee's family appear in the other. The soundtrack oscillates between the two, one in English, the other in Cantonese. As Tiny Tim looks forlornly through the window at all the things he cannot get for Christmas, an overlay shows the Lee family cleaning out a department store. Then a thoroughly racist comedy (about Christmas dinner in a Chinese restaurant) shares one side of the split screen with cooking in the Lee home. Then an overlay of someone urinating into a toilet is placed over family scenes, and finally shots of Lee having sex with his lover are overlaid, too. As "Silent Night" plays on the soundtrack, Lee begins to speak about his own silence and invisibility:

> You know, again it's Christmas Eve and again even with my family celebrating Christmas, I feel very much like the Other, for a couple of reasons. My family and me . . . My whole subjectivity is constructed to feel that I am not part of the whole normalized crowd who's supposed to celebrate Christmas because I'm not white, I'm not heterosexual on top of that, and even within my whole family, I feel very . . . I'm always holding this fucking camera! Trying to get things, trying to shoot things, you know. And look, you know, of course I construct myself as this otherness machine and I piss everybody off and my sister got pissed off at me. But it seems that this otherness is my only protection, the only protection from feeling delegitimized, because I delegitimize myself first, from being constructed as the other, because I construct myself as the other first . . .

Indeed, the great irony and delight of watching this episode is to see how in videoing and editing together all the things that seem to oppress him, make him invisible and divide his Asianness from his gayness, Lee is already counteracting them. In opting for fragmentedness on the verge of incoherence, Lee manages to invoke all the various narrative patterns and spaces I have discussed here, putting them together into one dynamic, contested hybrid space. The result may not be harmonious, but it is certainly something more than the standard Anglo-American post-Stonewall model of gay identity, and more than any allegedly traditional idea of what Asian family values are or should be.

NOTES

1. For the purposes of this article, I define East Asia as those territories and cultures in which Confucianism has had a powerful influence, including diasporic communities. This is in no way intended to imply homogeneity across these cultures and territories.

2. Sun develops some of his ideas further and moderates some of his criticisms in a more recent article (1991). Sun's attitude is echoed in recent books by popular pundits advocating greater individualism as one of the answers to China's problems, such as *The Ugly Chinese* by the Taiwanese author Bo Yang (1986). The author acknowledges on page 15 of the Taiwanese edition that this study is based on *The Ugly American* and other similar books already written in other countries.

3. Ning Ma (1992, pp. 74-148) also devotes considerable space to this point and many of those in the following discussion in his outline of what he terms the "correlative" Chinese self and its roots in the Confucian "habitus" of Chinese culture as a feature of Chinese melodramtic film.

4. In my travels around the East Asian lesbian and gay scene, I have encountered considerable numbers of young heterosexual men and women who happily proclaim themselves to be "queer straights." Perhaps this indicates that "queer" is also being hybridized into these cultures in a way that specifically refers to this coalition of various people who are not conforming to the sexual and gender expectations that would traditionally go with their place in family hierarchies.

5. If the family is the primary site in which Asianness can be experienced as a positive identity rather than a form of otherness in American culture, yet at the same time the space in which gay identity is most invisible, it might be legitimate to speculate that the division between family and gay identity is particularly keenly felt among gay, lesbian, and other queer Asian Americans. For further discussion of some of these issues, see Takagi (1994).

FILMOGRAPHY

The Anxiety of Inexpression, Hong Kong/USA, dir: Quentin Lee, 1992.

Berlin, Symphony of a City (Berlin, Die Symphonie Der Grossstadt), Germany, dir: Walter Ruttman, 1927.

Broken Branches (Naeil ui Hyahae Hununun Kang), South Korea, dir: Park Jae-Ho, 1995.

Colour Eyes (Irome), Japan, dir: Oki Hiroyuki, 1992.
Desert Hearts, USA, dir: Donna Deitch, 1986.
East Palace, West Palace (Donggong, Xigong), China, dir: Zhang Yuan, 1996.
Go Fish, USA, dir: Rose Troche, 1994.
Farewell, My Concubine (Bawang Bie Ji), China, dir: Chen Kaige, 1993.
Happy Together (Chunguang Zhaxie), Hong Kong, dir: Wong Karwai, 1997.
Heaven 6 Box (Tengoku no Muttsu no Hako), Japan, dir: Oki Hiroyuki, 1995.
I Like You, I Like You Very Much (Anata-Ga Suki Desu, Dai Suki Des'), Japan, dir:
    Oki Hiroyuki, 1994.
Longtime Companion, USA, dir: Rene Norman, 1990.
Making Love, USA, dir: Arthur Hiller, 1981.
Man With a Movie Camera (Chelovek s Kinoapparatom), USSR, dir: Dziga Vertov,
    1929.
Melody for Buddy Matsumae (Matsumae-Kun No Senritsu), Japan, dir: Oki Hiroyuki,
    1989.
Okoge, Japan, dir: Nakajima Takehiro, 1992.
The Postman (Youchai), China, dir: He Jianjun, 1994.
Rebels of the Neon God (Qingshaonian Nazha), Taiwan, dir: Tsai Ming-Liang, 1992.
The River (Heliu), Taiwan, dir: Tsai Ming-Liang, 1996.
The Silent Thrush (Wusheng Huamen), Taiwan, dir: Sheng-fu Cheng, 1991.
Song of the Goddess, Hong Kong, dir: Ellen Pau, 1993.
Swimming Prohibited (Yuei Kinshi), Japan, dir: Oki Hiroyuki, 1989.
Twinkle (Kira Kira Hikaru), Japan, dir: George Matsuoka, 1992.
Victim, UK, dir: Basil Dearden, 1961.
Vive L'Amour (Aiqing Wansui), Taiwan, dir: Tsai Ming-Liang (Cai Mingliang), 1994.
Wedding Banquet (Xiyan), Taiwan, dir: Ang Lee (Li An), 1992.

REFERENCES

Altman, D. (1995). The new world of "gay asia." In S. Perera (Ed.), *Asian and Pacific Inscriptions: Identities, Ethnicities, Nationalities*. Melbourne: Meridian. 121-138.

Berry, C. (1998a). Staging gay life in china: Zhang Yuan and *East Palace, West Palace*. *Jump Cut*. Forthcoming.

Berry, C. (1998b). Where is the love? the paradox of performing loneliness in *Vive L'Amour*. In L. Stern and G. Kouvaris (Eds.), *Caught in the Act: Performance in the Cinema*. Sydney: Power Institute Press. Forthcoming.

Berry, C. (1994). Sexual DisOrientations, or, Are Homosexual Rights a Western Issue? In C. Berry, *A Bit on the Side: East-West Topographies of Desire* (69-104). Sydney: EMPress, 1994. Reprinted in a revised form as Sexual DisOrientations: Homosexual Rights, East Asian Films, and Postmodern Post-nationalism. In X. Tang and S. Snyder (Eds.), *Cultural Politics in East Asia*. Boulder, CO: Westview Press, 1996, 157-183.

Bhabha, H. K. (1984). Of Mimicry and Man: The Ambivalence of Colonial Discourse. *October 28*, 125-33. Republished in H. K. Bhabha (1994). *The Location of Culture*. London: Routledge. 85-92.

Bo, Y. (1986). *Choulou de Zhongguoren (The Ugly Chinaman)*. Taibei: *Lin Bai Chubanshe*. A pirated mainland edition was published the same year: Guangzhou: *Huacheng Chubanshe* (Huacheng Publishers). English edition: D. J. Cohn and Jing Qing (Trans.). Allen and Unwin: Sydney, 1992. This is based on the translation that appeared as "The Ugly Chinaman"–a speech given at Iowa University, *Renditions* 23 (Spring 1985).

Bond, M. H. and K. Hwang. (1986). The Social Psychology of Chinese People. In M. H. Bond (Ed.), *The Psychology of the Chinese People* (pp. 213-264). Hong Kong: Oxford University Press.

de Lauretis, T. (1984). Desire in Narrative. In T. de Lauretis, *Alice Doesn't: Feminism, Semiotics, Cinema*. Bloomington: Indiana University Press. 103-157.

Hall, D. & R. Ames. (1995). *Anticipating China: Thinking Through the Narratives of Chinese and Western Culture*. New York: SUNY Press.

Hall, D. & R. Ames. (1987). *Thinking Through Confucius*. New York: SUNY Press.

Hsu, F. L. K. (1971). Psychological homeostasis and *jen*: Conceptual tools for advancing psychological anthropology. *American Anthropologist*, 73, 23-44.

Hsu, F. L. K. (1985). The Self in Cross-cultural Perspective. In A. J. Marsella, G. De Vos, Francis L. K. Hsu (Eds). *Culture and Self: Asian and Western Perspectives*. New York: Tavistock Publications. 24-55.

Ma, N. (1992). *Culture and Politics in Chinese Film Melodrama: Traditional Sacred, Moral Economy and the Xie Jin Mode*. Unpublished doctoral dissertation, Monash University, Melbourne.

Mathew, F. (1991). *The Ecological Self*. London: Routledge.

Muñoz, J. (1995). The autoethnographic performance: Reading Richard Fung's queer hybridity. *Screen 36*(2), 83-99.

Munro, D.J. (1969). *The Concept of Man in Early China*. Stanford: Stanford University Press.

Naficy, H. (1994). Phobic Spaces and Liminal Panics: Independent Transnational Film Genre. *East-West Film Journal 8*(2), 1-30.

Plaks, A. (1977). Towards a Critical Theory of Chinese Narrative. In A. H. Plaks, (Ed.), *Chinese Narrative: Critical and Theoretical Essays*. Princeton: Princeton University Press. 339-48.

Russo, V. (1987). *The Celluloid Closet: Homosexuality in the Movies* (rev. ed.). New York: Harper and Row.

Said, E. (1978). *Orientalism*. New York: Pantheon.

Sun, L. (1983). *Zhongguo Wenhua de "Shenceng Jiegou"* (*The "Deep Structure" of Chinese Culture*). Hong Kong: Jixian Publishers, 1983. Extracts from this study are translated and included in G. Barme & J. Binford (Eds.), *Seeds of Fire*. Hong Kong: Far Eastern Economic Review Ltd., 1986. (30-6, 136, 163-5, 226-32, 250, 311.)

Sun, L. (1991). Contemporary Chinese Culture: Structure and Emotionality. *Australian Journal of Chinese Affairs* 26, 1-41.

Takagi, D. (1994). Maiden Voyage: Excursion into Sexuality and Identity Politics in Asian America. *Amerasia Journal 20*(1), 1-18.

Tan, S. (1993). Delirious Native Chaos and Perfidy: A Postcolonial Reading of John Woo's *The Killer*. *Antithesis 6*(2).

Tan, S. (1994). From Fairies to Queer Dong. Unpublished manuscript.
Weston, K. (1991). *Families We Choose: Lesbians, Gays, Kinship*. New York: Columbia University Press.
Yang, K. (1986). Chinese Personality and its Change. In M. H. Bond (Ed.), *The Psychology of the Chinese People*. Hong Kong: Oxford University Press. 106-170.

Homosexual Rights as Human Rights
in Indonesia and Australia

Baden Offord
Leon Cantrell

INTRODUCTION

At the World Human Rights Conference in Vienna in 1993, the Singaporean Foreign Minister Wong Kan Seng stated: "Homosexual rights are a Western issue, and are not relevant at this conference" (Berry, 1994: 73). This statement was made to counter the introduction at the conference of homosexual rights by Australian gay activist Rodney Croome (Berry, 1994). In 1992, the Malaysian Prime Minister "claimed that enhancing democratic rights would actually *lead* to homosexuality" (La Violette & Whitworth, n.d.: 582). The purpose of this paper is to examine an important area made explicit by the above. In the last few years, the issue of homosexual rights has become a controversial feature in the general international human rights debate (Amnesty International, 1994; La Violette & Whitworth, n.d.; Heinze, 1995; Hendricks et al., 1993; Altman, 1994; Wintemute, 1995). This debate is increasingly articulated in the West but notably absent in relation to Asian cultures and nations where it is no less relevant.

The intention of this paper is to discuss some of the crucial issues that arise as concepts such as homosexual rights become situated in Asia. In other words, how are emerging gay and lesbian communities in Asia articulating homosexual rights? Are such rights meaningful in

[Haworth co-indexing entry note]: "Homosexual Rights as Human Rights in Indonesia and Australia." Offord, Baden, and Leon Cantrell. Co-published simultaneously in *Journal of Homosexuality* (Harrington Park Press, an imprint of The Haworth Press, Inc.) Vol. 40, No. 3/4, 2001, pp. 233-252; and: *Gay and Lesbian Asia: Culture, Identity, Community* (ed: Gerard Sullivan, and Peter A. Jackson) Harrington Park Press, an imprint of The Haworth Press, Inc., 2001, pp. 233-252. Single or multiple copies of this article are available for a fee from The Haworth Document Delivery Service [1-800-342-9678, 9:00 a.m.–5:00 p.m. (EST). E-mail address: getinfo@haworthpressinc.com].

233

Asia? The concept of homosexual rights problematizes several areas, such as definitions of sexuality and identity, cultural relativism versus the universalism of human rights, the individual and community, cultural imperialism, cultural convergence, globalization and international relations, to name a few. As the implications of such an analysis as this are many, it is important to take an approach that involves the legal, social, cultural, and political standpoints. Our aim, however, is to give an introduction to this subject and to identify basic conceptual problems and develop a conceptual framework.

In order to focus on these issues, this paper will examine homosexual rights as human rights in the two distinct nations of Australia and Indonesia. These two countries have been chosen because of their contrasting cultural, social, legal, and political values and attitudes. They are neighbors yet represent totally different perspectives on human rights, and concepts of homosexuality are complex and difficult to define in both cultures. Indonesia is a Muslim nation with a strong communitarian philosophy, while Australia is a liberal democracy with a strong individualist base. Using the window of human rights, this paper attempts to locate gay and lesbian rights. The juxtaposition of how these rights are situated in Indonesia and Australia helps the gay and lesbian theorist understand the problems associated with formulating the concept of homosexual rights in a cross-cultural context.

It is not the purpose of this paper to deliver a categorical representation of homosexual rights as human rights in Indonesia and Australia. Rather, the purpose of the authors is to tease out some of the salient issues outlined above in order to further a theoretical appreciation of the homosexual rights discourse as it impinges on the margins of Asia. It is our contention that an analysis of the Australian/Indonesian interface in relation to homosexual and human rights is one of the most precise ways in which the emerging gay and lesbian communities in Asia can be understood. A relational understanding through socio-cultural studies offers potential insights into how gay and lesbian life is articulated in the globalized world of the 1990s.

ISSUES OF DEFINITION

In this paper, the term homosexual is being used to denote "a sexual orientation (exclusively or predominantly, but also, for some purposes, fleetingly) directed towards persons of the same sex" (Heinze, 1995:

47). The term includes gays and lesbians as well as bisexuals, transvestites, and transsexuals.

Problems of definition exist in attempting to situate the concept of homosexual rights in the human rights context. This is a subject that has a resonance with legal, cultural, and postmodern discourses. From the legal perspective, "'Sexual orientation' and 'sexual minorities' are anything but obvious terms, in non-Western cultures, but also in the Western cultures that produced them" (Heinze, 1995: 31). This derives from the fact that sexuality and identity are highly contentious areas which are under immense debate within most schools of thought (Fuss, 1989; Stein, 1990). For a formulation of homosexual rights to be substantive, the whole question of identity is crucial in terms of organizing a gay and lesbian presence in law and politics. In the West this issue has been discussed by Eve Sedgwick (1990), who has demonstrated the fundamentals of a homo/hetero binary construction that pervades Western culture. Wayne Morgan (1995) has fused the legal implications of this dichotomy with queer insights and has situated the position of homosexual rights in the tension between the necessity of a fixed identity and the implicitly pluralist subject which cannot be fixed. Morgan addresses the use of queer as a response to resisting definition of identity into hetero and homo sexual polars. More than that, he notes that while debates on gay and lesbian signifiers are nothing new, the concept of "identity" itself "has perhaps, never been under such sustained attack" (Morgan, 1995: 31). Thus, defining homosexuality in Western culture is problematic and complex. Is one essentially homosexual or constructed to be so?

Asian concepts of homosexuality are also complex and problematic. Various scholars have pointed out that the construction of homosexuality in Asia is as multifaceted as anywhere else (Altman, n.d.; Caplan, 1987; Fung, 1995). In Indonesia there has been a long tradition of homosexuality which has been "recognized, accepted and institutionalized" by Indonesian societies (Oetomo & Emond, 1991). As well, the *banci* and *waria* forms of homosexuality are different from the modern gay Indonesian, but the fluidity of sexual identity is being confused and altered as the situation changes in Indonesia because of the media and the influence of Western models of gay identity (Oetomo & Emond, 1991: 15-16).

It is clear that definitions of homosexuality are problematic in Australia and Indonesia. In Australia, this is because of the perceived fixed nature of the lesbian and gay entity entrenched in the legal and political discourse. (However, the contemporary challenge of queer theory (Jagose, 1996) to fixed identities reveals a continuum of uncertainty with regard to non-fluid, static sexualities.) In Indonesia also, the fluidity of sexuality that exists is further complicated by the globalization of the gay fixed/essentialist stance and contemporary gay and lesbian representations. But perhaps all this forms a cogent theory for understanding homosexual rights in the human rights context. Morgan (1995: 31) states that: "Queer seeks to destabilize boundaries, hence categories, and hence the system (including law) which is based on these categories. Queer is fluidity." Out of this is possibly where the concept of sexuality in its rawness coalesces with Asian sexuality in its actuality. It challenges the notion of a gay monolithic identity in Indonesia or Australia and transforms the whole problem of identity into the *burden of identity*. This *burden of identity* refers to the inconsistency between formulating a recognizable political, gay identity and the deconstruction of sexual identity.

What is certain from all this is that there is a common link between Australian and Indonesian concepts of homosexuality and that there is a common *burden of identity* which has arisen in both cultures in response to legal, cultural, political, civil, and economic pressures. The whole question of definition is thus integral to understanding homosexual rights in either society. Organizing around an identity gives power and community and thus makes explicit a credible constituency. This was the catalyst for gay and lesbian activists in Western societies which has produced organizations such as the International Gay and Lesbian Human Rights Commission. This is the catalyst that is influencing educated, urban Indonesians. The emergences of gay and lesbian publications and organizations in Indonesia since 1982 have occurred because of this catalyst (Oetomo & Emond, 1991: 18).

It must not be ignored, however, that there do exist differences of perception in relation to the homosexual experience in Australia and Indonesia simply because of different localized complexities. One example is the Indonesian attitude towards family and community that is often held in contrast to the Australian attitude towards the importance of the individual. Negotiating homosexuality (in all its various forms) depends entirely on the cultural and social context. For this, Australia has a well-developed, visible gay and lesbian rights lobby while in Indonesia the gay and lesbian rights movement is situated where Australia was about 30 years ago.

HOMOSEXUALITY AS A MARGIN
BETWEEN EAST AND WEST

One very significant feature which becomes clear from the above is that as gay and lesbian theorists begin to research homosexual behavior in specific cultures and societies, it becomes easier to understand the homosexual experience in a global context. The implications of a comparative approach to homosexual rights using Australia and Indonesia underscore the confluence of margins between different cultures.

Homosexuality has recently become a cultural tool that is being used to substantiate certain notions of cultural purity. This sentiment is discussed by Chris Berry at some length in his book *A Bit On The Side* (1994:73). He notes that in the present postcolonial, postmodern, globalized world of the 1990s, Asian nations such as Singapore, Malaysia and China make sure that the: "specter of homosexuality is couched in terms of geography and cultural difference." Joseph Chan (1995: 35) maintains that "few Asians would defend . . . the right of homosexuals." This gives the impression that homosexuality does not exist in Asian nations, as put forward by the Singaporean Foreign Minister at the beginning of this paper. It is an assertion that homosexuality is not visible in Asia and, therefore, requires no status.

There is immense irony in this position because the moment homosexuality is asserted to be irrelevant, it gains a status in the margins; in a global world of technology, the *margins speak*. Denis Altman talks about the pan lesbian/gay master identity that is prevalent in the world today, derived from the West. He acknowledges the effects of the "global explosion of communications" (Altman, n.d.: 5). What appears significant in this is that the margins of the West are drawing closer to the margins of the East. An example of this is the communication between AIDS organizations. The AIDS Council of New South Wales in Sydney holds a file of Indonesian AIDS organization contacts and frequently has enquiries from Indonesian activists.

Furthermore, as gay and lesbian theorists ponder on the anxieties of identity and shifting definitions of sexuality, other factors are transforming the issue of homosexual rights. AIDS has consolidated efforts of community resulting in greater cultural awareness of homosexuality. In Indonesia, AIDS groups were formed by gay networks. Every major urban center in Indonesia has an AIDS organization. Such organizations have brought visibility. They have also contributed to a nascent struggle for human rights (Altman, 1994).

Economics and inter-cultural communication are having enormous ramifications for homosexual sensibilities. With a rising mass middle class on a global scale, the margins are beginning to fuse. Some even see this fusion creating an international gay and lesbian emergence from out of the closet. "And, more interesting still, they are doing it in more or less the whole world at once" ("It's not normal to be queer" *The Economist* 6 January 1996: 79).

"ALL HUMAN RIGHTS FOR ALL PEOPLE"[1]

If it is useful to look at homosexual rights through the window of the human rights context as maintained in this paper, then it is necessary to explicate the reasons why. It is important to clarify the situation regarding human rights because there are different perspectives on human rights and their scope.

In Asia the concept of human rights is complex. Asian perspectives on human rights have been described as "ambivalent, tenuous and transient" (Milner, 1993: 27). For many Asian cultures there has not been a ready translation of the term "human rights" into their language, and it often means something entirely different from the dominant paradigm in the world today. In response to the necessity of having to participate in the international human rights discourse, many Asian nations have tried to articulate their own indigenous form of human rights perceptions.[2]

Asian and other non-Western nations have responded in this way because the human rights discourse is conspicuously Western in origin (Heinze, 1995; Freeman, 1995). The human rights debate has been informed in contemporary times by a dichotomy of the perceived universalist or Western approach to human rights and the cultural relativist approach which emphasizes cultural difference.[3] This dichotomy is really unworkable and too simplistic. Current scholarship on this subject is further intensified because it raises the question of whether the universality of human rights is an example of cultural imperialism (Freeman, 1995). This has direct implications for homosexual rights and the global construction of a gay identity. Michael Freeman (1995: 23), however, argues that:

> The human rights doctrine is not imperialistic, because it seeks to protect the vulnerable from the powerful, whereas imperialism

constitutes the domination of the weak by the powerful. There may be conflict between the doctrine and some elements of some cultures, but only when those cultures endorse oppression of some members of society by others.

The most prevalent and convincing argument for the universal nature of human rights is the fact that "however Western its origins," the basis of human rights "is the universality of statist regimes . . ." (Heinze, 1995: 68). The human rights debate thus articulates the tension between the modern state and the "sphere of individual freedom" (Kunhardt, 1987, quoted by Heinze, 1995: 69). It is important to note here the observation of Eric Heinze, who states that as "the frontiers of human rights advance, prospects for cultural disagreement increase" (Heinze, 1995: 70). Homosexuality is thus impacted and changed by these frontiers. Questions regarding individual freedom become sharpened–hence, Asian discomfort at the thought of visible homosexuality in their societies. This explains the Asian construction of cultural difference on this subject, in effect, recreating an inverse case of "orientalism" (Said, 1978).

Imperialism, it must also be noted, has been replaced in contemporary times by globalization, a concept which suggests "interconnection and interdependency of all global areas" (Tomlinson, 1991: 175). Moreover, and not without irony, "the effects of globalization are to weaken the cultural coherence of all individual nation-states" (Tomlinson, 1991: 175). The rhetoric of cultural relativists is breaking apart in the face of a globalized, postmodern, postcolonial configuration.

INDONESIAN PERSPECTIVES ON HUMAN RIGHTS

Perhaps the most important point to make with regard to Indonesia's approach to human rights is that it is circumscribed by its need to maintain a stable and harmonious society, particularly so when its social, religious, and cultural character is taken into account. However, just like other Asian nations, Indonesia has been forced to participate in the human rights discourse because of increased international scrutiny of human rights abuses. The world of the 1990s is a watched world. Non Government Organizations, such as Asiawatch and Amnesty International, are the guardians of international human rights today. Indonesia has been and continues to be stung by accusations and evidence of human rights violations. In the *World Human Rights Guide* in 1992, for example, Indonesia had one of the lowest human rights ratings of just 37% (Humana, 1992: 41). The problems of East Timor, Irian Jaya and Aceh still present major challenges to Indonesia's approach to human rights, as do the problems of media freedom and constraints on the wider intellectual life (Schwarz, 1994: 236-7).

It was the world-wide condemnation of the Dili Massacre in 1991 which brought Indonesia finally to acknowledge the importance of the human rights discourse. Indonesia's response since 1991 has involved the establishment of a National Commission of Human Rights and a general (though monitored) debate on human rights perceptions in both the government and the community. The former Indonesian Ambassador to Australia, Mr. Sabam Siagian, noted in 1994, "A predictable consequence of improved levels of prosperity, better access to information sources and increased physical mobility, is the heightened awareness of Indonesians of their rights as citizens of an independent state" (Siagian, 1994: 66). Of course, for many observers, although this statement of Siagian's might point to some qualitative change, nonetheless, debate in Indonesian society is carefully constrained by a highly monitored press, which, according to Adam Schwarz (1994: 242), "has left Indonesians woefully under informed about the most pressing matters of state and society."

Indonesia's perspectives on human rights are nascent and vague and clearly express a cultural relativist stance.[4] Indeed, there is a further complexity in Indonesia's approach to human rights because for some Indonesian legal experts the concepts of rule of law and human rights do not even exist in Indonesia. They maintain that the state ideology of Pancasila[5] quite sufficiently covers all the demands for justice and human rights protection. They point out those western theories and paradigms are discordant with the Indonesian approach. According to the legal expert Professor H. Azhary of the University of Indonesia, "we don't recognize the concept of legal certainty. What we have, instead, is a quest for justice. Seen in this light, even the concept of power takes on a different meaning. Power is a mandate from God" (*The Jakarta Post* 27 July 1995). He was reported also saying:

> concepts of "rule of law" and human rights as they are known in the western world do not exist in Indonesia, because the 1945 Constitution does not recognize them.

This particular stance adds to the complexity of the Indonesian state. There is a fundamental tension here between religion, law, and secularism (Schwarz, 1994; Adnan, 1990; Pranowo, 1990).

The present-day Indonesian human rights activist Todung Mulya Lubis has characterized Indonesian perspectives on human rights as having the qualities of: "ambiguity, vagueness and inconsistency" (Lubis, 1993). He points out that while the Indonesian government's constraints remain, there cannot be a sustained promotion and protection of human rights. Nevertheless, Lubis (1993: 51) too recognizes the interconnectedness of economic, social, and cultural mechanisms in the 1990s and notes with a cautious optimism: "The possibility of a *human rights peaceful evolution* in this era of globalization is daily growing stronger." This is the context in which homosexual rights in Indonesia have to be viewed.

It may be inferred from the above that homosexual rights in Indonesia might have to be approached from within the framework of Pancasila. This is the mechanism already present in Indonesia's rather convoluted human rights discourse.[6] But it is hard to see how homosexual rights will figure in an ideology that embraces the concept that to maintain order, unity, and social justice, the limitation of rights is justifiable. Minorities are easy to dismiss in favor of unity and order. Of course, underlying this dilemma is the eclipse of the individual by the community. Homosexuality is perceived to be a problem in the West because of the implication of individual freedom and the liberalism it comes from. Pancasila is opposed to liberalism (Darmaputera, 1988). These are some of the complexities that must be taken into account when discussing the human rights context. They form the window through which to examine the concept of homosexual rights in relation to Indonesia.

HOMOSEXUALITY IN INDONESIA

According to the *Third Pink Book*, homosexuality in Indonesia is not illegal, but is treated, when explicit, with hostility by the Islamic majority. A minority of the population is in favor of homosexual rights (Hendricks, 1995). Even though there is apparently no mention of homosexuality in Indonesian law, the Indonesian government's official stand is that homosexuality is illegal. In fact, "It is also against all religious teachings in Indonesia which is what their constitution [*sic*] is based upon" (Yudhi, 1996).

Paradoxically, because closeted homosexuality is tolerated in Indonesia, there has not been the same urgency of legal and political lobbying associated with Western gay and lesbian politics and hence not the same social hostility that is experienced in Western societies. At least, such hostility is not widely documented (Amnesty International, 1994a). The Western paradigm of gay and lesbian activism has helped to inspire Indonesian gay and lesbian organizations, but the characteristics of Indonesian activism are entirely differently situated. As one scholar puts it: "Indonesian values . . . social harmony, peacefulness and the national motto 'unity in diversity'–seem to protect gays from mistreatment more completely than western notions of individual rights" (Williams, quoted by Altman, n.d.: 6) It could be argued, however, that, just like the greater history of homosexuality in the West, homosexuality in Indonesia has been implicit but unexplicated in social, cultural, political, and legal discourses except where permitted by traditional presence–on the margins. Homosexual activism in Indonesia has to negotiate a political and social terrain that is characterized by those imperatives discussed above which are different to countries like Australia. The presence of homosexual activism in Indonesia is notably less virulent, vocal, and demonstrative.

There is, however, a growing, dynamic gay presence in Indonesia. Visiting any of the large urban cities of Indonesia such as Jakarta, Surabaya, Yogyakarta, or Denpasar will reveal gay activities. In Surabaya, for example, malls are popular cruising spaces, particularly after 10 p.m.

In terms of activism Gaya Nusantara is the largest gay and lesbian organization in Southeast Asia and has groups in over 11 cities in Indonesia. It assists in AIDS prevention efforts and is very much involved in supporting and recognizing traditional forms of homosexuality as well as embracing the global gay culture. Gaya Nusantara publishes a journal by the same name that is for sale in general bookshops in Surubaya and widely distributed in Indonesia ("News from Indonesia" *Internal Bulletin* 4. 1996). The journal and the organization serve as meeting points for gay and lesbian activists. Another example is the Yogyakarta chapter of Lentera, an AIDS prevention project of International Planned Parenthood. Idik Prihasawan, the Project Manager, describes their main activities as "workshop, training and outreach . . . we work with the female sex workers, transvestites and also (the) gay group in Yogyakarta" (personal correspondence,

1996). Subjects such as AIDS, STDs, and safer sex are discussed. The subject of homosexual rights has not come up.

Alison Murray has noted that Indonesian lesbians are less than visible for various social and cultural reasons. They appear to be a closed community. There is, however, a lesbian network called Chandra Kirana. Certainly, lesbianism is not represented well in the Indonesian media. As Murray puts it: " . . . while gay men are increasingly out and proud, lesbians have a much lower profile" (Murray, 1995: 22). This brings up one of the problems with regard to organizing around sexuality. In Indonesia, it is obvious that the male homosexual is visible and present. Indonesian lesbians, on the other hand, "have come out to each other, but remain hidden" (Murray, 1995: 23) from mainstream society. This invisibility is universal and reflected in the fact that most people seeking asylum in the world because of their sexual orientation are gay men. As Nicole LaViolette and Sandra Whitworth (n.d.: 581) state:

> The issues faced by lesbians are often concerned with invisibility, isolation and resisting forced marriage. These experiences are much more difficult to document within a traditional legal discourse.

This points once again to the difficulty in definitions of sexuality. The term lesbian as it is known in the West does not mean the same thing in Asia. It means that the conceptual framework that is used to understand the Indonesian lesbian experience fails if it relies on the notion of a fixed lesbian identity. The subject resides in a "silent culture . . . leaving only slight or light footprints in the culture" (Gayatri, quoted in Murray, 1995: 22). This silent and hidden culture of the Indonesian lesbian confronts the concept of the *burden of identity* with little or no impact on the state or society.

As mentioned earlier, there are various forms of gay identity in Indonesian society. There are the transgendered males known as *banci* and *waria* as well as the less visible gay man. The former is part of an indigenous expression of Indonesian homosexuality while the latter is a part of the emerging modern gay (Oetomo, 1996). The expansion of the Indonesian middle class is impinging on all the modes of homosexual interaction and changing the landscape of Indonesian homosexuality. The state and civil society are beginning to show this change through the coverage of gay issues in the media. For example, *The*

Jakarta Post has regular items on such issues. Recently, the opening of the Gay Games in New York was featured, as was the Gay Pride Parade in New York in which a large photograph of a participant was displayed. Part of the photo caption stated: "... only 8% of the French people consider homosexuality a sin" (*The Jakarta Post*, 2 July 1995). An example of a kind of gay release happened when Indonesian newspapers reported the American diver Greg Louganis's self-outing. Two AIDS organizations, MITRA and Kusuma Buan Foundation, received hundreds of phone calls from gay inquirers (*The Jakarta Post*, 14 May 1995). In January 1995, *The Jakarta Post* featured a large article "Homosexual Men Strive to Fight AIDS," accompanied by a photograph of two happy Indonesian gay men. The article talked about homosexuality as a lifestyle as well as addressing AIDS. Below this article appeared a story on the "First Ever Gay Marriages in Sweden" (*The Jakarta Post*, 4 January 1995). It is evident from the number of articles appearing in Indonesian newspapers that there is concern about AIDS. Many of them deal with the problems it presents in a Muslim society (e.g., "NGO targets young people in anti-AIDS drive," *The Jakarta Post*, 11 July 1995). Nonetheless, the media has given homosexuality an increasing visibility. It appears that the middle class and regular media exposure are creating a more politically and socially aware homosexual. New global gay identities are being forged while traditional homosexual identities are being implicated in changing perceptions of sexuality (Oetomo, 1995).

Other representations of homosexuality are frequent on television, MTV, in movies, and in the pop world of teen magazines. A recent example of the latter is in the pop magazine *Mode Indonesia* in an interview with English pop group *Take That*. Not only is there a frank discussion on being perceived as gay (Mark–"*Ah, masa sih gue gay. Baru tau . . . Bagus deh kalo gitu.*" "Well, you think I am gay. That's news . . . that's good then" *Mode Indonesia* 14: 26-29, 28 July 1995), but it is also noteworthy that the word used is *gay* and not *homoseksuil* or *banci*. This underscores the dynamics of inter-cultural communication and the influence of globalization on Indonesian society.

Homosexual rights in Indonesia are articulated by the lesbian and gay community, as can be seen in the journal *Gaya Nusantara*. This articulation, however, has more to do with cultural and social concerns and barely breaks the legal and political silence (Hooker & Dick,

1993). The representation of homosexual rights in Indonesia is known by their omission in both the legal and political discourse.

HOMOSEXUAL RIGHTS IN INDONESIA

Thus, Indonesian perceptions of human rights are determined by cultural, religious, legal, and political complexities. Implicit in these perceptions is the notion that communitarian values eclipse individual freedoms. It is hard to see how homosexual rights can be perceived to be human rights in this context. Despite the opening up of Indonesian society to western influences, a growing middle class, and also despite the growing and popular gay organization Gaya Nusantara, lesbian and gay rights are not at that stage in which they can be recognized and articulated as essentially human rights (Oetomo & Emond, 1991; Hendricks et al., 1993; "Discreetly Gay in Indonesia," *OG* 10. Spring 1992).

As discussed earlier, the concept of human rights itself is problematic in Indonesia, so the evolution of the rights of homosexuals in Indonesia would be meaningless in this context. It may be that as homosexuality becomes more visible there will be a legal and political response. It all depends on the dynamics of Indonesian society as it responds to globalization and economic development and their coeval and consequential features, inter-cultural communication and individual autonomy. The Indonesian homosexual in all this is negotiating the *burden of identity* in a nation that prizes discretion.

AUSTRALIA AND HOMOSEXUAL RIGHTS

Australia, unlike Indonesia, has a well-developed lesbian and gay rights lobby, even though there are certain conservative and reactionary sections of the community which would deny outright that lesbian and gay rights are human rights (Hendricks et al., 1993). For example, homosexuality is still illegal in Tasmania. The difference between Australia and Indonesia, however, is that articulated Australian perspectives on human rights include lesbian and gay rights. It can be said that Australia is on its way to affirming in legal and legislative terms, that lesbian and gay rights are human rights (Chetuci, 1996). That discourse exists, as can be seen in the recent Toonen case[7] that is well presented in Miranda Morris' book *Pink Triangle* (1995). Justice Michael Kirby (who now has a seat on the High Court of Australia) comments in the foreword to this book that violations of homosexuals is contrary to human rights:

> A person's sexual orientation is like their gender or skin color. It is wrong to discriminate upon the ground of sexual orientation as on any other ground of immutable characteristics. (quoted by Morris, 1995: xi)

This comment by an eminent Australian jurist is just one instance of the growing and forthright articulation of lesbian and gay rights in Australia. Despite disparate views on homosexuality in Australia, the discourse on homosexual rights is present and maturing.[8] And it is located in the human rights field. Even though there are clearly defined representations of lesbian and gay identity in Australian society, the *burden of identity* is just as present in Australia as it is in Indonesia.[9] Queer theory challenges the notion of a fixed identity and so appears to threaten gay and lesbian politics. But this threat is largely imagined because queer theory is simply an attempt to deepen the understanding and dynamism of sexual orientation.

FORMULATING A CONCEPTUAL FRAMEWORK FOR MAPPING HOMOSEXUAL RIGHTS

The problem of homosexual rights as human rights, from an Indonesian perspective, is tied up with notions of individuality and community as well as religious attitudes and Pancasila. Homosexual rights represent first and foremost the right of an individual to express his or her sexuality with freedom and dignity, and to do so protected by the law of the State. Herein is the central difficulty. While Asian values remain at odds with western notions of individualism, liberal democracy, human rights, equality, and the rule of law, there is little reason to believe that homosexual rights will be regarded as anything but a part of the degenerate western lifestyle. As in Indonesia, Singapore, and much of East Asia, the values that give primacy to the family institution, deference to authority, and that are promoted by strong, resilient communitarian beliefs will continue to place homosexual rights at the far reaches of any credible political or legal articulation.

For countries like Indonesia, the perception is that the western emphasis on individuality is a destabilizing influence. They are critical of the way in which strong individual freedom gives rise to a state crippled by interest groups and vocal minorities. As H. J. C. Princen (1992: 10) states: "Human rights are dangerous because they aim to defend individualistic freedoms." At a time when Asia is forging ahead as the economic powerbase of the next century, notions of individual freedom appear to remain subservient to economic and political imperatives.[10]

Paradoxically, however, there is a visible homosexuality in Indonesia, and the global culture is impacting and changing indigenous forms of sexual identity. The present situation is being enhanced by cross-cultural communication, bringing with it a sense of gay solidarity across the margins as well as challenging the traditional Western construct of homo and hetero.

The articulation of human rights this century has been the explication of rights which were formerly unacknowledged (and perhaps formerly implicit), including the rights of life, dignity, freedom of expression, and so forth, leading to the affirmation of the individual and protection of the human being (Forsythe, 1983). Since the inception of the Universal Declaration of Human Rights in 1948, there has been a process of clarification and explication of rights where deemed necessary and important to do so. Thus, the creation of the Convention on the Rights of the Child, the Convention on the Political Rights of Women, the Convention Against Torture and Other Cruel, Inhuman or Degrading Forms of Punishment, and so forth are examples of this process of human rights articulation and evolution. Understandings of these rights underscore the dynamic nature of human rights. They have been understood as the world has changed (Heinze, 1995: 87). Without this process of making rights explicit, human beings are at the mercy of all kinds of tyrannies and injustices. That is why it is important in the maturing lesbian and gay Australian community and in the emerging lesbian and gay communities in Asia to consistently articulate and make explicit the fact that "all human rights are for all human beings."

We have argued that the concept of human rights and the extension of those rights to specifically include homosexuals are a contentious subject in both Australia and Indonesia. There are several significant difficulties for homosexual activists in organizing through the human rights context. There is the problem that the international human rights discourse is Western in origin. As we pointed out, however, the fact that this discourse originated in the West does not summarily dismiss its universal application. The world of the 1990s is a configuration of interconnected and interdependent states. The modern state, also of Western origin, is the dominant organizational paradigm in the world today. The overwhelming globalization of the world through the "reality of a capitalist world market" and communication adds complexity to this configuration (Field & Narr, 1992: 16). Australia and Indonesia are both within this configuration, and, as neighbors, the margins of difficulty are at their greatest in terms of their respective perspectives on human rights.

Introducing homosexuality into this context brings the margins of difficulty to the foreground. Homosexuality, as we have argued, remains, by and large, a controversial issue. Formulating a conceptual framework for homosexual rights is thus problematic. In Australia there is the tendency to believe that there is a homogenous gay or lesbian identity. The theorist has to be careful not to assume that the homosexual experience is the same everywhere and that the same type of activism is required. Our discussion of Indonesia shows the failure of such an assumption. If this is not taken into account, the gay or lesbian theorist or human rights scholar may well be imposing an acultural stance on the Asian homosexual.

The human rights discourse is an important and valid way in which to situate homosexuality, just as women have been situated this century and slaves in the last one. It allows us to view the meaning of being a homosexual, a woman, or a slave. It has been put forward in this paper that queer and other postmodern theories can help considerably in understanding homosexual identity. It was suggested that the homo/hetero dichotomy of the West, which is entrenched in state and society, is in need of a revision. Queer theory, aided by insights into Indonesian and other forms of homosexuality, helps to bring about an understanding of the total ambiance of homosexuality (Inada, 1990). Such an ambiance deepens the nature of any discussion on the concept of homosexual rights. As international human rights evolve amidst the confluence or conflict of cultures, contextualized by the global, postmodern, post colonial environment, this conceptual framework will help to bring us closer to a cross-cultural appreciation of how homosexuality is to be regarded. Thus, any discussion about homosexual rights can only be meaningful if the deconstruction of homosexual identity is taken into account (Johnson, 1993). In the end, homosexual rights depend on coherent political unity, informed by pluralist, heterogeneous, shifting characteristics, not by conformity, a monolithic gay entity, or by cultural reproduction. The evolution of homosexual rights in Asia may borrow from Western models of lesbian and gay activism and identity, but their development will take place amidst a landscape of local complexity. The emergence of lesbian and gay communities in Asia brings this whole subject into focus.

NOTES

1. This slogan was used at the World Conference on Human Rights held in Vienna in 1993 (Amnesty International, 1994: 2).

2. China is a good example of this. In 1991, as a response to the international community's post-Tiananmen concerns, China published, A White Paper on Human Rights in China, which outlines its own indigenous human rights (Offord, 1994).

3. However, Turner (1994: 15) argues that the principle of universal human rights rests on the fact that human beings are "ontologically members of a social community of suffering which they cannot escape."

4. While visiting Australia in 1995, before he became president, B. J. Habibe commented, "The value of human rights is not an absolute thing, it's relative to your country" (*The Australian,* 31 May 1995).

5. The five tenets of Pancasila are faith toward one God, humanitarianism, national unity, democracy through consensus, and social justice (Darmaputera, 1988).

6. H. J. C. Princen (1992: 10) notes that the values upheld in Pancasila correspond to those in the Universal declaration of Human Rights: "One should also not forget that the Universal Declaration is very much a summing up of the 'duties' of a government towards its people. The difference of course lies in the fact that the Universal Declaration is very clear in its thirty articles about those rights and the Pancasila is not."

7. Nick Toonen lodged a complaint with the United Nations Human Rights Committee in 1991 asserting that the Tasmanian Criminal Code of 1924 (ss 122 and 123) unfairly discriminated against homosexuals. The Committee found in favor of Toonen in 1994 (Joseph, 1994; Selvanera, 1994; Morris, 1995).

8. For a recent poll on attitudes towards homosexuals, see "Mardi Gras is here, but is it okay to be gay?" *Sydney Morning Herald* 1 March 1995: 15.

9. Consider Heinze's (1995: 55) comment: ". . . in Western societies, which today have the most clearly defined, consciously self-proclaimed sexual minorities and subcultures, the constituent individuals and groups form anything but a coherent whole."

10. The debate about individualism and Asian values has been recently tackled by the Forum of Democratic Leaders in the Asia-Pacific. According to them, "Moral decay is not a 'Western disease' triggered by democracy and freedom but a symptom of industrial development in any society" (*Sydney Morning Herald,* 27 June 1995). For a conservative Asian approach, see Pongsudhirak (1995).

REFERENCES

Adnan, Zifirdaus (1990). "Islamic religion: Yes, Islamic ideology: No! Islam and the state." In Budiman, Arief (Ed.), *State and civil society in Indonesia,* Clayton: Centre for Southeast Asian Studies, Monash University.

Altman, Dennis (1995). *Power and community.* London: Taylor & Francis

Altman, Dennis (no date). "The invention of 'gay' as a global category." Unpublished manuscript. Melbourne: La Trobe University.

Amnesty International (1991). *Violations of the human rights of homosexuals: Extracts form Amnesty International Action Materials.* New York: Amnesty USA

Amnesty International (1994). *Breaking the silence: Human rights violations based on sexual orientation* New York: Amnesty USA.

Berry, Chris (1994). *A bit on the side: East-West topographies of desire.* Sydney: EM Press

Caplan, Patricia (Ed.) (1987). *The cultural construction of sexuality.* London: Tavistock Publications

Chan, Joseph (1995). "The Asian challenge to universal human rights." in Tang, James T. H. (Ed.). *Human rights and international relations in the Asia-Pacific region* London: Pinter.

Chetuci, Joseph (1996). "The moving boundaries: Sources of human rights for homosexuals, legislatures, domestic courts and international law." in Wotherspoon, Garry (Ed.). *Gay and lesbian perspective III.* Sydney: Department of Economic History, The University of Sydney.

Darmaputera, Eka (1998). *Pancasila and the search for identity and modernity in Indonesia society.* Leiden: E. J. Brill.

Field, A. Belden & Narr, Wolf-Dietar (1992) "Human rights as a holistic concept." *Human Rights Quarterly* 14.

Forsythe, David (1983). *Human rights and world politics* Lincoln: University of Nebraska Press.

Freeman, Michael (1995). "Human rights: Asia and the West." In Tang, James T. H. (Ed.) *Human rights and international relations in the Asia-Pacific region.* London: Pinter.

Fung, Richard (1995). "The trouble with 'Asians'" in Dorenkamp, Monica & Henke, Richard (Eds.). *Negotiating lesbian and gay studies.* New York: Routledge.

Fuss, D. (1989) *Essentially speaking.* London: Routledge.

Heinze, Eric (1995). *Sexual orientation: A human right.* Dordrecht: Martinus Nijhoff Publishers.

Hendricks, Aart, Tielman, Rob, & van der Veen, Evert (Eds.) (1993). *The third pink book.* New York: Prometheus Books.

Humana, Charles (1992). *World human rights guide.* New York: Oxford University Press.

Inada, Kenneth K. (1990). "A Buddhist response to the nature of human rights." In Welch, Charles E. & Leary, Virginia A. (Eds.). *Asian perspectives on human rights.* Boulder: Westview Press.

Jagose, Annamarie (1996). *Queer theory.* Melbourne: Melbourne University Press.

Johnson, Barbara (1993). "Introduction" in Johnson, Barbara (Ed.). *Freedom and interpretation.* New York: Basic Books.

Joseph, Sarah (1994). "Gay rights under the ICCPR: Commentary on Toonen v Australia." *University of Tasmania Law Review* 13(2): 392-411.

Hooker, Virginia & Dick, Howard (1993). "Introduction." *Culture and society in New Order Indonesia.* Kuala Lumpur: Oxford University Press.

La Violette, Nocole & Whitworth, Sandra (no date). "No safe haven: Sexuality as a universal human right and gay and lesbian activism in international politics." *Millenium: Journal of International Studies* 23(3).

Lubis, Todung Mulya (1993). *In search of human rights: Legal-political dilemmas of Indonesia's new order, 1966-1990.* Jakarta: PT Bramedia Pustaka Utama.

Milner, Anthony (Ed.) (1993). *Perceiving "human rights."* Australia-Asian perceptions working paper number 2. University of New South Wales: The Asia-Australia Institute.

Morgan, Wayne (1995). "Queer law: Identity, culture, diversity and law" *Australasian gay and lesbian law journal* 5: 1-41.

Morris, Miranda (1995). *Pink Triangle.* Kensington: University of New South Wales Press.

Murray, Alison (1995). "Where are the Indonesian lesbians?" *Inside Indonesia* March.

Oetomo, Dede (1996). "Warias of the mean streets." *OG* April.

Oetomo, Dede & Emond, Bruce (1991). "Homoseksualitas di Indonesia." *Prisma* 7.

Oetomo, Dede & Emond, Bruce (1992). "Discreetly gay in Indonesia" *OG* 10 Spring.

Offord, Baden (1994). *Human rights in Australian foreign policy with specific reference to the Dili and Tiananmen Square massacres.* Honours thesis. Lismore: Southern Cross University.

Pongsudhirak, Thitinan (1995). "Examining future role of E. Asia." *The Jakarta Post* 28 February.

Pranowo, M. Bambang (1990). "Which Islam and which Pancasila? Islam and the state in Indonesia: A comment." In Budiman, Arief (Ed.). *State and civil society in Indonesia.* Clayton: Centre for Southeast Asian Studies, Monash University.

Princen, H. J. C. (1992). "Protecting human rights Indonesian style." *Inside Indonesia* December.

Said, Edward (1978). *Orientalism.* London: Penguin.

Schwarz, Adam (1994). *A nation in waiting: Indonesia in the 1990s.* Sydney: Allen & Unwin.

Sedgwick, Eve Kosofsky (1990). *Espistemology of the closet* London: Penguin.

Selvanera, George (1994). "Gays in private: The problems with the privacy analysis in furthering human rights" *Adelaide Law Review* 16: 331-340.

Siagian, Sabam (1994). "Indonesia's foreign policy and its relations with Australia" *The Sydney Papers* Winter.

Stein, Edward (1990). *Forms of desire: sexual orientation and the social constructionist controversy* New York: Garland Publishing.

Tomlinson, John (1991). *Cultural imperialism: A critical introduction.* London: Pinter.

Turner, Bryan S. (1994). "Human rights: From local cultures to global systems." In

Kingsbury, D. & Barton, G. (Eds.). *Difference and tolerance: Human rights issues in Southeast Asia.* Geelong: Deakin University Press.

Wintemute, Robert (1995). *Sexual orientation and human rights.* Oxford: Clarendon Press.

Yudhi, Wahdi S. (1996). Letter to the author from Wahdi S. Yudhi, Assistant to the Education and Cultural Attache, Embassy of the Republic of Indonesia in Canberra. 9 December 1996.

Variations on a Common Theme?
Gay and Lesbian Identity
and Community in Asia

Gerard Sullivan

INTRODUCTION

A number of the articles in this volume are informed by post-structuralist ideas and emphasize flexible, shifting, and almost individualistic categories.[1] This contrasts with a more established mode of inquiry that attempts to identify patterns of behavior and social regularities. In his book, *Queer Theory/Sociology,* Steven Seidman (1996) makes a plea for the integration of the two perspectives, and while this volume may not achieve that ambitious goal, both are represented.[2] This article considers some of the categories of homosexuality that have been identified in the cross-cultural literature, as well as the largely structural explanations for the rise of gay identity and community.

PATTERNS OF HOMOSEXUALITY

Following Adam (1985, 1985a, 1987), Murray (1992) refers to four types of homosexual expression; the first three of which occur in (but are not be limited to) pre-industrial societies and the last of which only appears in industrialized societies:

[Haworth co-indexing entry note]: "Variations on a Common Theme? Gay and Lesbian Identity and Community in Asia." Sullivan, Gerard. Co-published simultaneously in *Journal of Homosexuality* (Harrington Park Press, an imprint of The Haworth Press, Inc.) Vol. 40, No. 3/4, 2001, pp. 253-269; and: *Gay and Lesbian Asia: Culture, Identity, Community* (ed: Gerard Sullivan, and Peter A. Jackson) Harrington Park Press, an imprint of The Haworth Press, Inc., 2001, pp. 253-269. Single or multiple copies of this article are available for a fee from The Haworth Document Delivery Service [1-800-342-9678, 9:00 a.m. - 5:00 p.m. (EST). E-mail address: getinfo@haworthpressinc.com].

253

- age-structured homosexuality, which often involves exclusive homosexuality during adolescence but heterosexuality or bisexuality in adulthood;
- profession defined homosexuality such as shamans, dancing boys, or sex workers;
- transgender homosexuality, which involves cross-dressing and typically assimilates same-sex sexuality into kinship codes by redesignating the gender of one partner; and
- egalitarian homosexuality, whereby gay identity and community have become somewhat disconnected from heterosexual institutions and are establishing independent cultural patterns.

Several of the authors in this volume (e.g., Heng, Chao, Tan, Murray, Baba) refer to the second and, especially, the third type of homosexuality. The Malayo-Polynesian world, in particular, has long-recognized transgendered homosexuality and provided it with a position within kinship and other institutions. Authors in this volume also identify variants of the fourth type of homosexuality,[3] which is a more recent development and which bears much in common with western gay and lesbian identity and community (e.g., Baba, Seo, Wan). Some authors suggest that the four types are not mutually exclusive, either at an individual or societal level (e.g., Berry, Khan). What is also apparent, in some cases where the above-mentioned types of homosexuality exist in the same context, is that there is an element of disharmony between the various communities, such as the transgendered and gay-identified groups (e.g., Garcia, 1996, or Tan, in this volume). The question arises as to why we are seeing the emergence of nominally egalitarian homosexuality throughout many parts of Asia, and the extent to which this represents a cultural change which may gradually supplant the other described categories.

Altman (1995, 1996) refers to an international gay identity which appears in a great variety of cultural contexts, and he suggests that globalization plays a vital role in this recent development. Altman (1982, 1996) suggests that social, cultural, political, and economic factors, and international mass media, are all involved in the formation of this transnational gay identity and community which occurs in various societies, but he is not specific about the culture of this community (and any variations which may occur), or the mechanisms by which it develops. Globalization involves both economic interdependence and cultural transfers, mostly (though not exclusively) from the West (and primarily the United States) to other parts of the world. While the homogenization of culture is often lamented and the extent to which it penetrates indigenous cultures is questioned (e.g., by Chou, and Khan, in this volume), there is little doubt that, economically at least, globalization is well advanced and increasing.

Altman (1996) notes that in many developing countries, lifestyle and economy are being reshaped to fit the needs of Western capitalism. Tradition, the modern, and the postmodern sit side-by-side, or sometimes mingle and fuse. He suggests that there has been "an apparent globalization of postmodern gay identities" (Altman, 1996: 77). Those who participate in this lifestyle are usually young, affluent, English-speaking, and educated either in the West or in the liberal tradition (Sullivan & Leong, 1995). Gay commercial space has appeared (in the form of entertainment venues, coffee shops, bars, or stores that predominantly attract a gay clientele), and, in some cases, a gay and lesbian press and political groups have developed (Adam et al., 1999). How can we account for these developments?

DEFINITION OF LESBIAN AND GAY IDENTITY AND COMMUNITY

Before attempting to answer this question, it will be helpful to define what I am referring to in this article when I use the terms lesbian and gay identity and community. Until recently, the assumption was often made that homosexuality occurred in all societies. While this may be so in regard to homosexual acts, Michel Foucault (1978) and many others (e.g., Vance, 1995) have mounted a convincing argument that people who identify themselves as homosexual, i.e., gay men and lesbians, have only existed for the past century and a half or so. While Foucault's analysis may be said to be Eurocentric, and age-structured- , profession-defined- , or transgendered homosexual identity may have had a much longer established place in some non-western societies, I know of no cases in which egalitarian-type homosexuality existed before the modern era.

Many of the articles in this volume explain that the words "gay" and "lesbian" do not have a universal meaning. They have been adopted in many languages to describe a very diverse range of homosexual expression. For the purposes of this article, I would like to use the words more specifically to refer to a type of "egalitarian" homosexuality in which people identify or "perceive themselves–and increasingly present themselves to others–as having a consciousness and a politics which is related to their [homo]sexuality" (Altman, 1995: 126; see also Sullivan & Leong, 1995). Lesbian and gay community may be said to exist where people seek the company of, and interact with, others on the basis of shared lesbian and gay identity, or where "there is a specific gay social institution system–from a specific nonverbal communication system to gay publications–which enable homosexuals to communicate with other gays, supporting gay community consciousness" (Toth, 1994, quoted by Altman, 1995: 127). Altman (1996: 83) suggests that "modern homosexualities are characterized by . . . an emphasis on emotional as much as on sexual relationships, and the development of public homosexual worlds."

THE EMERGENCE OF GAY AND LESBIAN IDENTITY AND COMMUNITY

Altman (1996: 87) writes that "In a sense, globalization is capitalist imperialism writ large, and many of its features continue and perpetuate the erosion of custom, of existing kinship and villages/communities." This suggests that there may be some features of the social organization typical of capitalist societies which facilitate or allow the development of gay and lesbian identity and community. There is a literature which traces this connection for western societies, and I would like now to review it and raise the question of its applicability to contemporary Asian societies. However, before undertaking this, it is important to be mindful of Rosalind Morris's criticism of the model of "linear genealogy–that derives from the West's specific experience of modernity" (1994: 39). Nevertheless, I think the literature is useful to identify specific factors that may be applicable in consideration of specific cases, as Peter Jackson (in this volume) suggests must be done in order to advance knowledge in the field of cross-cultural sexuality.

Several social changes have been identified as having been necessary in order to allow the development of modern, Western homosexual identity. These are often described under the general rubric of capitalism, but essential features for our purposes are the transition to wage labor and the resultant economic independence, urbanization, and socialization associated with bureaucratic forms of organization and competitive capitalism.

Industrialization and Economic Independence

D'Emilio (1983 [1992, 1993, 1999, 1999a]) suggested that it is the development of capitalism, and, in particular, free labor, which has allowed people to call themselves gay, to participate in a community of like-minded women and men, and to become politically organized. Adam (1985: 659) argued that gay identity and community exist only in "advanced capitalist societies and the major metropolises in the semi-peripheries of the modern world system" (such as large cities in Asia and elsewhere). Of primary importance in this process is the expansion of the wage labor sector of the economy, because it has allowed mobility (see Steakley, 1975) and decreases the importance of kinship in obtaining a livelihood. As capitalism expands, it takes over new areas of production (e.g., food preparation or entertainment) and spreads geographically. As this occurs, urbanization increases as more and more people sell their labor to obtain a livelihood. Greenberg and Bystryn (1984) note that in the West, the legislative sanctions against homosexuality declined with the rise of capitalism and that enforcement decreased. This was consistent with the *laissez-faire* or libertarian philosophies associated with the competitive phase of capitalism in which private citizens could do as they would as long as no-one else was injured.[4] With an increasing proportion of adults gaining economic independence, people had more freedom to pursue unconventional lifestyles. Homosexual relations were able to escape the strictures of the dominant, heterosexual kinship system, and exclusive homosexuality, now possible for both partners, became an alternative path to conventional family forms (Adam, 1985 [1996, 1998]).

Urbanization

Greenberg and Bystryn (1984 [1996]) and Greenberg (1988) argue that industrialization encouraged urbanization, which brought opportunities for individuals to expand their circle of acquaintance under circumstances of less informal social control than existed in villages and towns. This enhanced opportunities for sexual expression and allowed homoerotically-inclined people to discover each other and form large-scale social networks, not only because of existing social relationships but also because of their homosexual interests (Adam, 1985).

Changing Family Structure and Ideology

The above-mentioned processes had an enormous effect on the structure, function, and ideology of the family, which was no longer the unit of production or consumption. Where welfare states developed, eventually all adults could expect financial independence. With higher standards of living, the value of children for economic survival has declined. For these reasons, together with technological advances in contraception, the link between sex and procreation has weakened. Though the nurturing of children is still an important role of western families, a more accurate defining feature is that they are a reflection of affective relationships. Other effects of the expansion of capitalism in the West were: that men's work was removed from the household; until recently, women were largely excluded from paid work and encouraged to specialize in domestic work; and an ideology of the family developed in which sex, love, monogamy and procreation were intertwined. While extra-marital sexual expression may not be a particular threat to families tied together primarily by economic relationships, it is more so to those held together primarily by emotional ties. In spite of its facilitating capacities, capitalist relations of production may also produce homophobia and heterosexism as a "pro-family" ideology is promulgated which supports an essentially privatized system of reproduction and child-rearing (D'Emilio, 1983; Greenberg and Bystryn, 1984; Greenberg, 1988; Adam, 1985).[5]

Bureaucratization, Socialization, and the Rise of Homophobia

Bureaucratic forms of social organization are one of the most striking forms of modernity. Greenberg and Bystryn (1984) and Greenberg (1988) assert that bureaucratization fostered competition among men in particular, by encouraging an ethos of self-restraint which was antagonistic to sexual expression. This occurred because entrepreneurs had to focus on profits and, therefore, be competitive, aggressive, and unswayed by affective ties to competitors or employees. To achieve this, middle-class parents raised their boys to be self-assertive and competitive, and discouraged emotional expressiveness, dependence, or nurturance. Accordingly, emotionally intimate or sexual relations between men were discouraged. In addition, the accumulation of resources necessary for capitalist expansion meant that the petty-bourgeoisie developed a culture of frugality and self-discipline which limited consumption (Weber, 1974). This was manifested in the sexual domain by campaigns for sperm conservation, and against masturbation, prostitution, premarital sex, and homosexuality–all forms of "unproductive" sex in which pleasure was important.[6]

In contrast to kinship-structured societies where family ties are preeminent, or feudal societies in which vertical ties of personal loyalty assume great importance, to a greater degree in bureaucratically organized societies, rule enforcement is carried out by well resourced, salaried staff who are supposed to perform their duties according to universalistic criteria, rather than in a particularistic way and regardless of personal commitment to the rules. (The military, which is a total and largely sex-segregated institution, is especially concerned about perceived threats to these values and in some societies has prosecuted or separated members who indicate same-sex sexual or affective ties because of possible involvement with other service personnel, which, it is argued, would threaten loyalty to the chain of command.) Bureaucracies reward people who exhibit the traits of being "methodical, rational, prudent, disciplined, unemotional" and who conform to expectations. Homosexuality represents a threat to successful masculine values. Having a dependent wife and children made workers reliable. The state enhanced its socialization and regulatory role through the expansion of bureaucracies–schools trained the young; prisons punished serious law breakers; hospitals shaped the behavior of the sick, the mad, and the immoral; compulsory military service was common; and factories controlled workers (Greenberg & Bystryn, 1996: 96; Greenberg, 1988; Adam, 1985; Foucault, 1979).

Greenberg and Bystryn (1984) and Greenberg (1988) argue that until relatively recently, bureaucracies were primarily male domains and the sort of socialization they provide often spills over into personal life, therefore affecting men much more so than women. They explain homophobia as being particularly prevalent in men "[b]ecause the formation of the bureaucratic personality in men entails (among other things) the suppression of affective emotional responses toward other males . . . [and thus the creation of] anxiety in the presence of expressions of emotional intimacy or sexual contact between men–or even at the thought of intimacy" (Greenberg & Bystryn, 1996: 97). They suggest that the affluence of the 1960s in first-world countries allowed this fiercely competitive and ascetic socialization, especially of boys, to be relaxed and, hence, the rise of notions of sexuality for pleasure, as opposed to being limited to procreation.

Medicalization

In support of the needs of industry and the economy, and with encouragement by the medical profession, sodomy statutes were introduced or extended in many western (and colonial) jurisdictions, beginning in the late nineteenth century. While this legislation was not restricted to homosexual behavior, enforcement tended to be so targeted. Purity campaigns proscribing non-reproductive sexual expression were conducted (Weeks, 1981; Pearce & Roberts, 1981) with support from the medical establishment. The medicalization of the issue placed emphasis on desire rather than behavior and with this, the concept of a homosexual person was developed, in contrast to emphasis on homosexual acts (Foucault, 1978; Adam; 1985; Greenberg & Bystryn, 1984; Greenberg, 1988). Elsewhere, this discourse may not be prevalent, particularly where the medical establishment is weak or competes with other health providers, such as spiritual healers. Nevertheless, cultures are seldom insulated from outside influences, and the dominance of western medical thought and practice ensures that these ideas in some form, are widespread.

Repression

In many locations, the development of a visible "egalitarian" gay community has been met with oppression by the state, one effect of which has been to publicize the existence of the gay community and stimulate organizing and community development (Sullivan, 1987; Sullivan & Leong, 1995; Adam et al., 1999; Heng and Wan in this volume).

APPLICABILITY

While most of the material presented in this article on the emergence of gay and lesbian "egalitarian" identity and community was written with reference to the West (and to a considerable extent, North America), with the emergence of globalized lesbian and gay identity and community, it is interesting to consider the extent to which some combination of factors like repression and others listed above, provide necessary or sufficient conditions for the emergence of gay and lesbian identity and community in non-western societies. It is beyond the scope of this chapter to make in-depth studies of this nature for particular societies, but it is hoped that historians and social scientists studying lesbian and gay communities in Asia will find these ideas indicative and useful for their inquiries.

Disaggregation

Clearly, the emergence of gay people has not been an undifferentiated process. For example, gay men have been more visible than lesbians; in most societies, the middle class appears to be disproportinately represented in the gay community; and in the West, immigrant groups with strong family ties have been less visible than white lesbians and gay men (Kinsey et al., 1948, 1953; Jackson & Sullivan, 1999). John D'Emilio (1983) argues that these observations are consistent with the degree of economic independence of the various groups.

Lesbian Identity and Community

Adam (1985) explains the slower development of lesbian community compared to that of gay men with the observation that in Europe, legislation restricted women from accepting wage labor so that women were returned to the domestic sphere and became economically dependent on men. Although "romantic friendships" between women developed during this period, these were subordinate to the kinship system–not an alternative to marriage and not the basis for a personal or cultural identity. Patriarchal hegemony[7] could ignore these relationships, which offered no threat. Lesbian relationships presuppose a degree of free choice unavailable to most women who are financially dependent on men (Ferguson, 1981; Faderman, 1981). Murray and Chao (in this volume) show that in Indonesia and Taiwan, respectively, lesbian identity and community exist, but it is sometimes unclear to what extent it is of the egalitarian type, nor how economically independent these women are.

Cross-Cultural Applications

It follows from Greenberg and Bystryn's (1984) thesis that homo-sexually-identified people and communities will be less prevalent in non-capitalist societies and that in less bureaucratized, more family-oriented societies, there should be a relatively tolerant attitude regarding homosexuality. They cite several historical examples to support their case, including China, and suggest that it is no accident that communist states and organizations have criticized homosexuality as bourgeois [western] decadence arising from capitalism.[8]

In pre-industrial societies, there are examples of homosexual relations occurring in households and local communities and emerging from existing social relationships, such as that between master and servant or neighbors and friends. (It might be argued that recent variants of these relationships are described by Khan, 1995; Kala (no date) or are represented in the Filipino movie, *Midnight Dancers*.) Adam (1985) argues that distinctively gay communities originate only when homosexually oriented men come into contact because of their homosexual interests, rather than as a result of situations such as those described at the beginning of this paragraph.

Globalization

Dennis Altman (1996: 87) adds a couple more factors into the cocktail of cultural change, suggesting that "what was once accomplished by . . . [imperialist] conquest is now achieved via shopping malls and cable television." I am not sure, however, that these are primary factors. The existence of consumer culture presupposes a high degree of urbanization and affluence, and there is some doubt as to the effect of television on culture without structural change. (For example, witness the failure of media campaigns for birth control in a number of less industrialized countries.) I suggest that factors like economic independence *and* interaction with other gay men or lesbians (possibly including tourists or via the Internet) are much more important in the process of cultural change.[9] Interaction provides knowledge of other possibilities and an understanding of their suitability for oneself. In many countries, a relatively high degree of affluence and/or education (possibly including competence in a non-native language) is often required for the probability to be very high at all of interaction occurring with "egalitarian" lesbians or gay men.[10]

CONCLUSION

To summarize, Barry Adam suggests that the following structural conditions "make the lesbian and gay worlds possible and, indeed, largely define the lesbian/gay manifestation of same-sex bonding apart from other social constructions of homosexuality" (1985: 658):

- Homosexual relations have been able to escape the strictures of the dominant, heterosexual kinship system;
- Exclusive homosexuality, now possible for both partners, has become an alternative path to conventional family forms;
- Same-sex bonds have developed new forms without being structured around particular age or gender categories;
- People have come to discover each other and form large-scale social networks not only because of existing social relationships but also because of their homosexual interests; and
- Homosexuality has come to be a social formation unto itself characterized by self-awareness and group identity. (Adam, 1995: 7)

This is not to say that economic independence, urbanization, discourses of difference or identity, and perhaps even political repression are not important factors in allowing these changes to occur.

There is a tension between political-economic and anthropological/post-structuralist explanations of changing forms of homosexuality, the former tending towards universalism and the latter toward cultural specifics.[11] Even with their limitations, identity categories are often important in political movements such as gay activism to extend civil and human rights (Hall, 1996; Offord & Cantrell, in this volume).

The task of identifying factors which preceded the emergence of gay and lesbian identity and community in the West has not been undertaken in order to predict the future of homosexual expression and reaction to it in any particular society. However, I think it likely that the analysis is useful in sensitizing us to factors which could be examined in particular societies and which help to explain changes in the expression of homosexuality.[12] In addition, there are likely to be specific circumstances in many of them which affect cultural forms and practices. Some of these may be multinational in nature. For example, it has been argued that the process of mobilization associated with war was important in the United States in bringing homosexually-oriented people together. Similarly, the decline of the Cold War has been said to have led to a general relaxation of political repression in some Southeast Asian countries, which has been conducive to the expression of non-conventional lifestyles and rights movements (Jackson, personal communication). Other sorts of upheavals, such as a catastrophic natural disaster or war, or increased repression could also stimulate identity formation or political movements. For example, AIDS may have resulted in less repression of homosexuals in some authoritarian states because of the need for education to prevent the spread of the disease. For this reason, some governments which harass gay men have provided a level of tolerance of organizations who do health promotion work among homosexuals, provided that these organizations keep a low profile. Nevertheless, one effect appears to have been community development (e.g., Leong, 1995).

A structural condition, which has not been considered here but should be taken into account in explaining homosexual expression in many parts of Asia, is the existence of dual economies in which many people work in traditional occupations, have very low incomes, and are reliant on other family members for survival, while others participate in the modern economy. In these countries, it is often the case that institutionalized transgender homosexuality and emerging "egalitarian" lesbian and gay identities and communities exist side by side, and tensions may develop between the two as they compete for social space.

Repression of homosexuality and kinship ties are two factors that may be of great importance in changing forms of homosexuality. If it is not extreme, repression may encourage a liberation response. Alternatively, lack of repression may result in the absence of an essential factor for political action and hence community development (Tan, 1995; Adam et al., 1999). It may also be the case that economic independence cannot be sufficiently guaranteed for many in countries without strong social welfare programs or their equivalent (such as compulsory savings schemes as in Singapore), and accordingly, kinship patterns such as "compulsory" marriage and procreation remain in place militating against the emergence of "egalitarian" forms of homosexuality.

Much work remains in uncovering the history of homosexuality and understanding predisposing factors that allow particular forms to emerge. To a considerable extent, this enterprise will need to be culture specific and requires identification of major forms of homosexual expression (bearing in mind that they may not be static), and then examining their history and social context, in much the same way as many of the authors cited here have done for the emergence of gay and lesbian identity and communities in the West.

NOTES

1. I am grateful to the following people who are among those who contributed to my thinking about the issues discussed in this article. Some of them may not agree with some (or many) of the ideas expressed, for which I alone am responsible: Ricardo Abad, Eufracio Abaya, Alex Au, Chris Berry, Julius Dasmariñas, Neil Garcia, S. Gunasekaran, Surojit Gupta, Peter Jackson, Romeo Lee, Oliver Patiño, Alphy Plakkoottam, Joseph Plakkoottam, Emma Porio, Danton Remoto, John Silva, Jerome Ty.

2. Many readers may recall debates between students in the humanities and those in the social sciences in which the former expressed scepticism about generalizations made by social scientists. The argument goes that conclusions reached in the sociological literature are often contradicted by specifics in individual cases, which, in the eye of critics, undermines the enterprise of sociology. More recently, those in cultural studies have taken a similar view, complaining that generalizations often do not represent the experience of social minorities. Sociologists respond to these challenges by pointing to patterns of social behavior (e.g., ethnicity or gender and inequality) which clearly identify powerful factors which shape people's experience and life chances. Much sociological research is undertaken with the aims of explaining social developments and determining where interventions are likely to be effective in creating social change, in particular to assist minorities. These discussions reflect the tension between idiographic and nomothetic explanations of human behavior, which have been debated in the social sciences for many years (Audi, 1995; Babbie, 1998; Alasuutari, 1995).

3. It has become commonplace in recent years to refer to "homosexualities," lesbian or gay "identities," and gay or lesbian "communities," even when referring to a specific society. When consciously done, I infer the reason for this to be recognition of the plurality that exists in these categories. In reference to "egalitarian homosexuality" in this essay, I have largely chosen to use "homosexuality," "identity," and "community" as collective nouns, except when referring to (possibly) distinct groups. I recognize that it is rare, if ever, that social groupings do not contain diversity; however, this does not make it impossible to identify analytically meaningful categories in which the members share some characteristics or goals. This process usually requires reference to a higher level of abstraction. Scholars often argue about

the validity of aggregation in order to create analytical categories. For example, some argue that the experience of lesbians and gay men are quite distinct and that they form separate communities. Others suggest that globalization of gay culture is superficial only and that the way homosexuals think of themselves, and their political situations, varies in a fundamental way from society to society. I take a middle path on this issue. I recognize that in many cases, significant differences apply, but that there are often common elements to lesbian and gay experience, identity, and community across societies. Increased communication between groups has facilitated a degree of homogenization.

4. Murray (1996) and others have made the point that capitalism is not a uniform phenomenon and that aspects of its manifestation vary from society to society according to political context, cultural factors, and so on. In some societies, legislative sanctions against homosexuality have not altered in spite of the expansion of wage labor and urbanization. In others, no legal prohibitions of homosexuality existed. For many societies, cultural attitudes toward homosexuality have not been well documented, particularly from a historical point of view, nor have the effects of social changes such as the expansion of wage labor and urbanization been investigated.

5. The key elements thus far associated with the emergence of "egalitarian" lesbian and gay identity and community appear to be economic security independent of family ties, and association with people who have common interests, which is facilitated by urbanization. While these conditions are usually associated with industrialization, theoretically at least, they could occur independently. Industrialization by itself does not guarantee that most adults will obtain economic independence, nor even those engaged in wage labor. Unemployment, or the threat thereof, or low wage rates may not allow independence without the assurance of support from a welfare state. By no means do all capitalist societies develop strong public sector welfare programs (e.g., Heng and Seo, in this volume).

6. The western orientation of Greenberg's ideas is apparent, especially in regard to sexual morés perhaps, though he tests his thesis in some non-western societies.

7. Clearly, like capitalism, patriarchal hegemony is not a uniform and unvarying phenomenon across time and place. Nevertheless, it may well have some common defining features which make it a useful analytical tool.

8. To the extent that social organization (including the emergence of lesbian and gay "egalitarian" identity and community) is associated with capitalism or other forms of economics, and has a longer history in the West, perhaps it is not surprising to hear Asian leaders refer to gay rights and lesbian and gay lifestyles as Western imports (e.g., Offord & Cantrell, and Murray, in this volume).

9. Altman (1996) also identifies these factors but he does not give them primacy.

10. Even where interaction does occur, without economic independence of the partners, the feasibility of "egalitarian" type lesbian or gay identity and community is unlikely to be assessed as a realistic option.

11. Altman (1996: 87, 90) suggests that advocates of either position may be suspected of being either imperialistic or nationalistic, respectively (or, it might be argued as superficiality or myopia). The post-modern critique of categories being essentializing, static, reifying, and exclusive prisons should be borne in mind, but at the

same time the two-way interaction between structure, discourse, and agency needs to be recognized.

12. I do not wish to suggest an overly deterministic model of lesbian and gay identity and community formation. Clearly, social contexts within which homosexuality occurs are complex–usually too much so to establish causality or make reliable predictions. In spite of this, I do not eschew identification of predisposing conditions which make some outcomes more likely than others.

REFERENCES

Adam, Barry D. (1985 [1996] [1998]). "Structural Foundations of the Gay World." *Comparative Studies in Society and History.* 27: 658-71. Reprinted in Seidman, Steven (Ed.). *Queer Theory/Sociology.* Cambridge, Massachusetts: Blackwell, 1996; Reprinted in Nardi, Peter M. & Schneider, Beth E. (1998) (Eds.). *Social Perspectives in Lesbian and Gay Studies: A Reader.* New York: Routledge.

Adam, Barry D. (1985a). "Age, Structure and Sexuality: Reflections on the Anthropological Evidence on Homosexual Relations." *Journal of Homosexuality* 11(3-4): 19-34.

Adam, Barry D. (1987 [1995]). *The Rise of a Gay and Lesbian Movement.* New York: Twayne. Revised edition published in 1995.

Adam, Barry D., Duyvendak, Jan Willem, & Krouwel, Andre (Eds.) (1999). *The Global Emergence of Gay and Lesbian Politics: National Imprints of a Worldwide Movement.* Philadelphia: Temple University Press.

Altman, Dennis (1982). *The Homosexualization of America, The Americanization of Homosexuality.* New York: St Martin's Press.

Altman, Dennis (1995). "The New World of 'Gay Asia'." In Perera, Suvendrini (Ed.). *Asian and Pacific Inscriptions: Identities, Ethnicities, Nationalities.* Bundoora, Victoria, Australia: Meridian

Altman, Dennis (1996). "Rupture or Continuity? The internationalization of gay identities" *Social Text.* 14(3): 77-94 Fall.

Alasuutari, Pertti (1995). *Researching Culture: Qualitative Method and Cultural Studies.* London: Sage.

Audi, Robert (1995). *The Cambridge Dictionary of Philosophy.* Cambridge: Cambridge University Press.

Babbie, Earl R. (1998). *The Practice of Social Research* 8th edition. Belmont, California: Wadsworth.

Bérubé, Allan (1990). *Coming Out Under Fire: The History of Gay Men and Women in World War II.* New York: Macmillan.

Bleys, Rudi C. (1996). *The Geography of Perversion: Male-to-male Sexual Behaviour outside the West and the Ethnographic Imagination, 1750-1918.* London: Cassell.

D'Emilio, John (1983 [1992] [1993] [1999] [1999a]) "Capitalism and Gay Identity." in Snitow, Ann, Stansell, Christine, & Thompson, Sharon (Eds.). *Powers of Desire: The Politics of Sexuality.* New York: Monthly Review Press. Reprinted in D'Emilio, John (1992). *Making Trouble: Essays on Gay History, Politics and the University.* New York: Routledge; reprinted in Abelove, Henry, Barale, Michele

Aina, & Halperin, David M. (1993) (Eds.). *The Lesbian and Gay Studies Reader.* New York: Routledge; reprinted in Parker, Richard & Aggleton, Peter (1999) (Eds.). *Culture, Society and Sexuality: A Reader.* London: University College, London Press; reprinted in Gross, Larry & Woods, James D. (1999a) (Eds.). *The Columbia Reader on Lesbians and Gay Men in Media, Society and Politics.* New York: Columbia University Press.

D'Emilio, John (1983a). *Sexual Politics, Sexual Communities: The Making of a Homosexual Minority in the United States, 1940-1970.* Chicago: University of Chicago Press.

Faderman, Lillian (1981). *Surpassing the Love of Men* New York: Morrow.

Ferguson, Ann (1981). "Patriarchy, sexual identity and the sexual revolution." *Signs* 7(1).

Foucault, Michel (1978). *The History of Sexuality: An Introduction.* New York: Vintage.

Foucault, Michel (1979). *Discipline and Punish: The Birth of the Prison.* New York: Vintage.

Garcia, J. Neil C. (1996). *Philippine Gay Culture: The Last 30 Years: Binabae to Bakla, Silahis to MSM.* Quezon City: University of the Philippines Press.

Greenberg, David F. & Bystryn, Marcia H. (1984 [1996]). "Capitalism, Bureaucracy, and Male Homosexuality." *Contemporary Crimes: Crime, Law and Social Policy* 8: 33-56. Reprinted in Seidman, Steven (1996) (Ed.). *Queer Theory/Sociology.* Cambridge, Massachusetts: Blackwell.

Greenberg, David F. (1988). *The Construction of Homosexuality.* Chicago: University of Chicago Press.

Hall, Stuart (1996). "Introduction: Who Needs Identity?" In Hall, Stuart & du Gay, Paul (Eds.). *Questions of Cultural Identity.* London: Sage.

Kala, Arvind (no date). *Invisible Minority: The Unknown World of the Indian Homosexual.* New Delhi: Dynamic Books.

Katz, Jonathan Ned (1976). *Gay American History.* New York: Crowell.

Khan, Badruddin (1997). *Sex. Longing and Not Belonging: A Gay Muslim's Quest for Love and Meaning.* Oakland, CA: Floating Lotus Press.

Kinsey, Alfred C., Pomeroy, Wardell, B. & Martin, Clyde E. (1948). *Sexual behaviour in the human male.* Philadelphia: Saunders.

Kinsey, Alfred C., Pomeroy, Wardell B., & Martin, Clyde E. (1953). *Sexual behaviour in the human female.* Philadelphia: Saunders.

Jackson, Peter A. & Sullivan, Gerard (1999). *Multicultural Queer: Australian Narratives.* New York: The HaworthPress, Inc.

Leong, Wai Teng (1995). "Walking the Tightrope: The role of *Action for AIDS* in the provision of social services in Singapore." In Sullivan, Gerard & Leong, Laurence Wai Teng (Eds.). *Gays and Lesbians in Asia and the Pacific: Social and Human Services.* New York: The Haworth Press, Inc.

Midnight Dancers. Filipino movie.

Morris, Rosalind C. (1994). "Three Sexes and Four Sexualities: Redressing the discourses on Gender and Sexuality in Contemporary Thailand." *Positions* 2(1): 15-43.

Murray, Stephen O. (1992). "Introduction: Homosexuality in Cross-Cultural Perspective." In Murray, Stephen O. *Oceanic Homosexualities.* New York: Garland.

Murray, Stephen O. (1996). *American Gay.* Chicago: University of Chicago Press.

Seidman, Steven (1996). "Introduction," in Seidman, Steven (Ed.). *Queer Theory/ Sociology* Cambridge, MA: Blackwell.

Sullivan, Gerard (1987). *A Study of Political Campaigns of Discrimination Against Gay People in the United States, 1950–1978.* PhD dissertation. Ann Arbor, MI: University Microfilms International No. 8729425.

Sullivan, Gerard & Leong, Laurence Wai Teng (1995) (Eds.). *Gays and Lesbians in Asia and the Pacific: Social and Human Services.* New York: The Haworth Press, Inc.

Steakley, James (1975). *The Homosexual Emancipation Movement in Germany.* New York: Arno.

Weber, Max (1974). *The Protestant Ethic and the Spirit of Capitalism.* London: Unwin University Books.

About the Contributors

Ismail BABA received his PhD from Barry University School of Social Work, Miami, USA. He is a professor at the Social Work Program, School of Social Sciences, Universiti Sains Malaysia (USM). His main research interests include psychosocial issues related to HIV/AIDS, social work education, and health and services in Malaysia. Dr. Baba is on the board of the Malaysian AIDS Council and is a founder and a former chairperson of the Community AIDS Service Penang (CASP). He is vice-president of the Malaysian Association of Social Workers.

Chris BERRY received his PhD from UCLA and teaches film studies at the University of California, Berkeley. He has published extensively on Asian queer cinema and queer culture, and he is the author of *A Bit On the Side: East-West Topographies of Desire* (Sydney: EMPress, 1994), as well as the co-editor of *The Filmmaker and the Prostitute: Dennis O'Rourke's The Good Woman of Bangkok* (Sydney: Power Institute Press, 1997) together with Annette Hamilton and Laleen Jayamanne.

Leon CANTRELL obtained his BA and MA from the University of Sydney and his PhD from the University of Nebraska. He is dean of arts and social sciences at the University of Western Sydney. His research interests include Australia/Asia relations, multiculturalism, and higher education governance. He is an adviser to both the NSW and Commonwealth governments in Australia.

Y. Antonia CHAO holds a PhD in anthropology from Cornell University and teaches cultural anthropology in the Department of Sociology at Tunghai University (Taiwan). Her previous research dealt with the linkages between state power and the construction of Taiwan's lesbian community. An essay, entitled "Performing Like a Po and Acting as a

271

Big Sister: Reculturating into the Indigenous Lesbian Circle in Taiwan," has recently appeared in *Sex, Sexuality, and the Anthropologist,* published by the University of Illinois Press. At present, Dr. Chao is working on the relationship between representation, diaspora, and the nation-state during Taiwan's White Terror period.

CHOU Wah Shan, PhD, taught at Hong Kong Polytechnic University (1988-1991) and The University of Hong Kong (1994-1998). He has published 20 Chinese books, eight of them on *tongzhi* issues, and has a recent book on the topic published by The Haworth Press. He works in the gender training program of the United Nations Development Programme (UNDP) in Beijing.

Russell HENG Hiang Khng completed his PhD in the Research School of Pacific and Asian Studies, Australian National University. This paper is based on his involvement with *People Like Us,* the obstructed gay movement in Singapore.

Shivananda KHAN is founder and executive director of The Naz Foundation, which is based in the UK, but also conducts projects in South Asia. The agency works exclusively among males who have sex with males (MSM) in the region, and provides technical support, training, and funds for sexual health services for MSM. Since 1996, The Naz Foundation has helped develop six such agencies in South Asia.

Alison J. MURRAY received her PhD from the Australian National University, and subsequently published *No money no honey: A study of street traders and prostitutes in Jakarta* (Oxford University Press, 1991). Her main research interests are urban social geography, subcultures, sex work, sexuality and the body, Indonesia, and other Southeast Asian societies. Dr. Murray is currently employed as a lecturer in Indonesian at The University of Sydney.

Baden OFFORD completed his PhD at Southern Cross University in Australia on the topic of "Interrogating the (Homo)sexual Activist and Human Rights in Indonesia, Singapore and Australia." He lectures in history and cultural studies at Southern Cross University. Dr. Offord's research interests include queer theory/activism, Australia/Asia relations, human rights, and identity studies.

SEO Dong-Jin's research interests include sexuality and cultural studies. He lectures in the School of Film and Multimedia at Korean National University of Arts. He is executive director of the Seoul Queer Film and Video Festival, the first of which was held in 1998. He is author of *Who's Afraid of Sexual Politics?* and *Rock: Rebels of Youth,* as well as *Modernity and Homosexuality* and *The Cultual History of the Revolution* (all in Korean). He is active in promoting the rights of sexual minorities in Korea.

Michael L. TAN is a medical anthropologist. He is a professor at the University of the Philippines and executive director of a non-government organization, Health Action Information Network.

WAN Yanhai holds a Bachelor of Medicine from the School of Public Health, Shanghai Medical University, and has taught in the Department of Health and Anthropology at the Beijing Modern Management College. He organized *Men's World,* a group for gay men and health promotion, and is a co-founder of the *Chinese Society for the Study of Sexual Minorities.*

Index

Action For AIDS (AFA), 84-85
AIDS
    education efforts in China, 56-61
    and homosexuality in China, 54-55
    response to, in Singapore, 84-85
AIDS organizations, 237-238
Altman, Dennis, 1,211-212,237
Anxiety of Inexpression, The (Hong
        Kong/USA film), 226-228
Appadyraum, Arjun, 14
Asia
    diversity in, 5
    g/l/t identities in, 3
    human rights in, 238-239
    marginalization in, 5-6,10-12
    new gender/sex categories in, 1
    sexual/gender minorities in, 2
    understanding gay/lesbian, 5-8
Asian Lesbian Network (ALN),
        173-174
Australia
    concept of homosexuality in,
        235-236
    homosexual rights and, 245-246
Azhary, H., 240

Baba, Ismail, 143-163
Bakla ideology, 120-123
Bali, 172
Bangkok, g/l/t cultures in, 3. *See also*
        Thailand
Berry, Chris, 211-231,237
Bhabha, Homi, 212-213
Broken Branches (South Korean film),
        214,218,219-220
Burden of identity, definition of,
        236,243
Bureaucratization, 258-259

Butch-femme
    in Jakarta, 177
    meanings of, in Indonesia, 169-170

Cantrell, Leon, 233-252
Capitalism, 257,258
Chan, Joseph, 237
Chandra Kirana, 243
Chang Chinsôk, 72
Chao, Y. Antonia, 185-209
Chen Bingzhong, 57,59,60
Cheng Hao, 31
Chen Yiyun, 57
Cheung, Leslie, 43
China. *See also* Taiwan; *Tongzhi*
    coming out in, 32-35,61-62
    concept of self in, 217
    gay representation in films in, 214
    history of sexuality in, 29-32
    homophobia in, 30-31
    importance of family in, 34
    individuality in, 32
    legal issues of homosexuality in,
        52-56
    topic of homosexuality in, 49-52
    traditional same-sex terms, 29-30
Chou Wah-Shan, 27-46
Chu Wei-cheng, 45
Come Together (Korean student
        organization), 71-79
Coming home, experiences of *tongzhi*
        of, 35,36-40
Coming out
    in China, 32-35,61-62
    in films, 224-225
    for g/l in Malaysia, 153-155
    Taiwanese strategies for, 42-46
Community, lesbian/gay
    definition of, 256
    differing growths of, 261

The Pursuit of Sodomy: Male Homosexuality in Renaissance and Enlightenment Europe, edited by Kent Gerard, PhD, and Gert Hekma, PhD (Vol. 16, No. 1/2, 1989). *"Presenting a wealth of information in a compact form, this book should be welcomed by anyone with an interest in this period in European history or in the precursors to modern concepts of homosexuality." (The Canadian Journal of Human Sexuality)*

Psychopathology and Psychotherapy in Homosexuality, edited by Michael W. Ross, PhD (Vol. 15, No. 1/2, 1988). *"One of the more objective, scientific collections of articles concerning the mental health of gays and lesbians. . . . Extraordinarily thoughtful. . . . New thoughts about treatments. Vital viewpoints." (The Book Reader)*

Psychotherapy with Homosexual Men and Women: Integrated Identity Approaches for Clinical Practice, edited by Eli Coleman, PhD (Vol. 14, No. 1/2, 1987). *"An invaluable tool. . . . This is an extremely useful book for the clinician seeking better ways to understand gay and lesbian patients." (Hospital and Community Psychiatry)*

Interdisciplinary Research on Homosexuality in The Netherlands, edited by A. X. van Naerssen, PhD (Vol. 13, No. 2/3, 1987). *"Valuable not just for its insightful analysis of the evolution of gay rights in The Netherlands, but also for the lessons that can be extracted by our own society from the Dutch tradition of tolerance for homosexuals." (The San Francisco Chronicle)*

Historical, Literary, and Erotic Aspects of Lesbianism, edited by Monica Kehoe, PhD (Vol. 12, No. 3/4, 1986). *"Fascinating . . . Even though this entire volume is serious scholarship penned by degreed writers, most of it is vital, accessible, and thoroughly readable even to the casual student of lesbian history." (Lambda Rising)*

Anthropology and Homosexual Behavior, edited by Evelyn Blackwood, PhD (cand.) (Vol. 11, No. 3/4, 1986). *"A fascinating account of homosexuality during various historical periods and in non-Western cultures." (SIECUS Report)*

Bisexualities: Theory and Research, edited by Fritz Klein, MD, and Timothy J. Wolf, PhD (Vol. 11, No. 1/2, 1985). *"The editors have brought together a formidable array of new data challenging old stereotypes about a very important human phenomenon . . . A milestone in furthering our knowledge about sexual orientation." (David P. McWhirter, Co-author, The Male Couple)*

Homophobia: An Overview, edited by John P. De Cecco, PhD (Vol. 10, No. 1/2, 1984). *"Breaks ground in helping to make the study of homophobia a science." (Contemporary Psychiatry)*

Bisexual and Homosexual Identities: Critical Clinical Issues, edited by John P. De Cecco, PhD (Vol. 9, No. 4, 1985). *Leading experts provide valuable insights into sexual identity within a clinical context–broadly defined to include depth psychology, diagnostic classification, therapy, and psychomedical research on the hormonal basis of homosexuality.*

Bisexual and Homosexual Identities: Critical Theoretical Issues, edited by John P. De Cecco, PhD, and Michael G. Shively, MA (Vol. 9, No. 2/3, 1984). *"A valuable book . . . The careful scholarship, analytic rigor, and lucid exposition of virtually all of these essays make them thought-provoking and worth more than one reading." (Sex Roles, A Journal of Research)*

Homosexuality and Social Sex Roles, edited by Michael W. Ross, PhD (Vol. 9, No. 1, 1983). *"For a comprehensive review of the literature in this domain, exposure to some interesting methodological models, and a glance at 'older' theories undergoing contemporary scrutiny, I recommend this book." (Journal of Sex Education & Therapy)*

Literary Visions of Homosexuality, edited by Stuart Kellogg, PhD (Vol. 8, No. 3/4, 1985). *"An important book. Gay sensibility has never been given such a boost." (The Advocate)*

Alcoholism and Homosexuality, edited by Thomas O. Ziebold, PhD, and John E. Mongeon (Vol. 7, No. 4, 1985). *"A landmark in the fields of both alcoholism and homosexuality . . . a very lush work of high caliber." (The Journal of Sex Research)*

Homosexuality and Psychotherapy: A Practitioner's Handbook of Affirmative Models, edited by John C. Gonsiorek, PhD (Vol. 7, No. 2/3, 1985). *"A book that seeks to create affirmative psychotherapeutic models. . . . To say this book is needed by all doing therapy with gay or lesbian clients is an understatement." (The Advocate)*

Nature and Causes of Homosexuality: A Philosophic and Scientific Inquiry, edited by Noretta Koertge, PhD (Vol. 6, No. 4, 1982). *"An interesting, thought-provoking book, well worth reading as a corrective to much of the research literature on homosexuality." (Australian Journal of Sex, Marriage & Family)*

Historical Perspectives on Homosexuality, edited by Salvatore J. Licata, PhD, and Robert P. Petersen, PhD (cand.) (Vol. 6, No. 1/2, 1986). *"Scholarly and excellent. Its authority is impeccable, and its treatment of this neglected area exemplary." (Choice)*

Homosexuality and the Law, edited by Donald C. Knutson, PhD (Vol. 5, No. 1/2, 1979). *A comprehensive analysis of current legal issues and court decisions relevant to male and female homosexuality.*

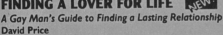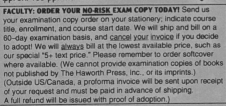

MORE FORTHCOMING AND NEW BOOKS FROM HAWORTH GAY & LESBIAN STUDIES

FROM HATE CRIMES TO HUMAN RIGHTS

A Tribute to Matthew Shepard
**Edited by Mary E. Swigonski, PhD, LCSW,
Robin S. Mama, PhD, and Kelly Ward, LCSW**
This volume takes an unsparing look at the interconnections of prejudice and hate crimes in the lives of LGBT individuals, in such diverse areas as international law, the child welfare system, minority cultures, and LGBT relationships.
(A monograph published simultaneously as the Journal of Gay & Lesbian Social Services, Vol. 13, Nos. 1/2.)
$59.95 hard. ISBN: 1-56023-256-0.
$24.95 soft. ISBN: 1-56023-257-9.
Available Spring 2001. Approx. 240 pp. with Index.

TRANSGENDER AND HIV

Risks, Prevention, and Care
Edited by Walter O. Bockting, PhD, and Sheila Kirk, MD
This unique book reports on the first generation of prevention interventions targeting this community, discusses guidelines for providing sex reassignment services to HIV-positive transsexuals, and encourages collaboration between communities at risk, researchers, and people in the helping professions.
$49.95 hard. ISBN: 0-7890-1267-7.
$24.95 soft. ISBN: 0-7890-1268-5.
Available Spring 2001. Approx. 200 pp. with Index.

SISSYPHOBIA

Gay Men and Effeminate Behavior
Tim Bergling
Here is a revealing look into male effeminacy: why some gay men are swishy, why other gay men are more masculine, and why effeminate men arouse anger, disgust, and disdain in both gay and straight men.
$29.95 hard. ISBN: 1-56023-989-1.
$14.95 soft. ISBN: 1-56023-990-5.
Available Spring 2001. Approx. 153 pp. with Index.

BEING GAY AND LESBIAN IN A CATHOLIC HIGH SCHOOL

Beyond the Uniform
Michael Maher, PhD
This powerful and moving book presents personal testimonies and an original study of Catholic students' attitudes toward gays and lesbians, as well as reprinting the actual teachings of the Church on homosexuals and homosexuality.
$49.95 hard. ISBN: 1-56023-182-3.
$17.95 soft. ISBN: 1-56023-183-1.
Available Spring 2001. Approx. 181 pp. with Index.

GAY AND LESBIAN ASIA

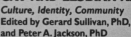

Culture, Identity, Community
Edited by Gerard Sullivan, PhD, and Peter A. Jackson, PhD
This book presents some of the most original, powerful current thought available on cultural, political, sexual, and gender issues for queers in Asian cultures.
$49.95 hard. ISBN: 1-56023-145-9.
$24.95 soft. ISBN: 1-56023-146-7.
(A monograph published simultaneously as the Journal of Homosexuality, Vol. 40, Nos. 3/4)
Available Spring 2001. Approx. 280 pp. with Index.

HIS HANDS, HIS TOOLS, HIS SEX, HIS DRESS

Lesbian Writers on Their Fathers
Edited by Catherine Reid, PhD, and Holly K. Iglesias
Examines the complicated and critical relationship between lesbians and their fathers and the way it permeates and shapes their lives.
$44.95 hard. ISBN: 1-56023-210-2.
$19.95 soft. ISBN: 1-56023-211-0.
2001. Available now. 204 pp.

THE BEAR BOOK II

Further Readings in the History and Evolution of a Gay Male Subculture
Edited by Les Wright, PhD
A continuation of **The Bear Book**, published in 1997, this study of typically big, hairy, and bearded gay men explores bears on a societal and personal level, giving a wide voice to bears of all ages, nationalities, and cultures.
$49.95 hard. ISBN: 0-7890-0636-7.
$24.95 soft. ISBN: 1-56023-165-3.
2001. Available now. 482 pp. with Index.

ADDICTIONS IN THE GAY AND LESBIAN COMMUNITY

Edited by Jeffrey R. Guss, MD, and Jack Drescher, MD Editor-in-Chief,
Journal of Gay and Lesbian Psychotherapy
Offers both personal experiences of addiction and recovery and insightful original research into the sources and treatment of addictions among gays and lesbians.
(A monograph published simultaneously as the Journal of Gay & Lesbian Psychotherapy, Vol. 3, Nos. 3/4.)
$69.95 hard. ISBN: 0-7890-1037-2.
$24.95 soft. ISBN: 0-7890-1038-0.
2000. 191 pp. with Index.

AVAILABLE FROM YOUR LOCAL BOOKSTORE

If unavailable at your local bookstore, contact: Harrington Park Press,
10 Alice Street, Binghamton, New York 13904–1580 USA
Phone: 1-800-429-6784 (outside US/Canada + 607-722-5857)
Fax: 1-800-895-0582 (outside US/Canada + 607-771-0012)
E-Mail: getinfo@haworthpressinc.com • Web: http://www.haworthpress.com

 04/01 BIC01